The DESTINY of the RIGHTEOUS in the PSALMS

The DESTINY of the RIGHTEOUS in the PSALMS

JEROME F. D. CREACH

CHALICE PRESS
ST. LOUIS, MISSOURI

Copyright © 2008 by Jerome F. D. Creach

All rights reserved. For permission to reuse content, please contact Copyright Clearance Center, 222 Rosewood Drive, Danvers, MA 01923, (978) 750-8400, www.copyright.com.

Bible quotations, unless otherwise noted, are from the *New Revised Standard Version Bible,* copyright 1989, Division of Christian Education of the National Council of the Churches of Christ in the United States of America. In some instances language has been changed to make it more gender inclusive. Used by permission. All rights reserved.

Scripture quotations marked (NIV) are taken from the HOLY BIBLE, NEW INTERNATIONAL VERSION®. NIV®. Copyright © 1973, 1978, 1984 by International Bible Society. Used by permission of Zondervan Publishing House. All rights reserved.

Scripture marked NASB is taken from the *NEW AMERICAN STANDARD BIBLE* ®, © Copyright The Lockman Foundation 1960, 1962, 1963, 1968, 1971, 1972, 1973, 1975, 1977, 1995. Used by permission.

Biblical quotations marked (JPS) are taken from *The TANAKH, the new JPS translation according to the traditional Hebrew text,* copyright © 1985 by the Jewish Publication Society. All rights reserved. Used by permission.

Cover image: Digital Stock
Cover and interior design: Elizabeth Wright

Visit Chalice Press on the World Wide Web at
www.chalicepress.com

10 9 8 7 6 5 4 3 2 1   08 09 10 11 12

Library of Congress Cataloging-in-Publication Data

Creach, Jerome F. D. (Jerome Frederick Davis), 1962-
  The destiny of the righteous in the Psalms /
by Jerome F.D. Creach.
     p. cm.
  ISBN 978-0-8272-0634-2
  1. Bible. O.T. Psalms—Criticism, interpretation, etc. 2. Righteousness—Biblical teaching. I. Title.

BS1430.52.C73 2008
223'.206—dc22

2008012071

Printed in the United States of America

Contents

Acknowledgments   vii

Introduction   1

PART I
Who Are the Righteous in the Psalms?

1. Prayer and the Profile of the Righteous   18
2. Clean Hands and Pure Hearts   30
3. To Be Near God   42

PART II
The Destiny of the Righteous and the Shape of the Psalter

4. The Lord's Anointed and the Suffering of the Righteous   54
5. The Suffering Servants as the Lord's Anointed   70

PART III
The Embodied Hope of the Righteous

6. David: Defender of the Righteous   86
7. David: The Enduring Hope   99
8. Mount Zion   111
9. Zion and the Longing of the Righteous   124
10. Torah   135

Conclusion   150

Notes   155

Acknowledgments

A book as long in the making as this one has accumulated significant debt, not the least of which is due its editor. I would like to thank Trent Butler and the staff at Chalice Press for their patience as I delayed the completion of the volume several times. I am also grateful to Trent for his valuable advice on the content, arrangement, and style of the work. When the book was originally conceived, Jon Berquist was the academic editor, and I would also like to express my thanks to him for his initial interest and helpful guidance of the project.

In the early period of writing, the work was supported by a Young Scholar's Grant from the Catholic Biblical Association of America. I would like to thank the CBA for their funding. My colleagues at Barton College at that time made it possible for me to have time off to concentrate on this work. Department chair Coleman Markham was a particularly supportive colleague.

In the process of writing and rewriting this book, I have benefited from conversations with numerous others whose insights have steered me away from various pitfalls and directed me toward valuable insights. Among them are Dale C. Allison, William P. Brown, Julie Galambush, Erhard S. Gerstenberger, David M. Howard, J. Clinton McCann Jr., Patrick D. Miller Jr., Ron E. Tappy, Marvin E. Tate, Steven S. Tuell, Dennis Tucker, and the late Gerald H. Wilson. I have appreciated the ongoing conversation on the Psalms with scholars in the Society of Biblical Literature's Book of Psalms Section, particularly with members of the Steering Committee. I also gained much from participating in the 2005 meeting of the Tyndale Fellowship–in Nantwich, England–a meeting devoted to a discussion of issues in Psalms interpretation. I am grateful to Philip S. Johnston and David G. Firth for their invitation to be part of that gathering. I wrote portions of the book in the serene environment of the Franciscan Spirit and Life Center, Castle Shannon, Pa. I extend my thanks to the Sisters who care for that wonderful retreat.

As always, my wife, Page, has encouraged and advised me throughout this project. Apart from the moral support I often needed, she also kept the needs of the church in front of me when it would have been easy to forget them.

Finally, I want to say a special word of thanks to James Luther Mays. In many ways this book began in conversations with him during my doctoral work at Union Theological Seminary (now Union-PSCE). In the intervening years I have been honored to have him as a colleague and mentor. The mistakes and cases of failed judgment in this book are mine alone. But I must attribute to his influence whatever helpful contribution the work might make to our understanding of the Psalms.

Introduction

Anyone who reads through the book of Psalms is surely struck by the attention given to the righteous and how life will turn out for them. The Psalter begins with a psalm that sets forth the life of the righteous over against the wicked (Ps. 1:1–3) and then declares what the end will be like for the two groups: the wicked will be swept away while the righteous are kept in God's care (vv. 4–6). In the psalms that follow, the concern for the destiny of the righteous does not diminish. In fact, the vocabulary related to the righteous and their plight appears so frequently that it draws constant attention to the subject. The term "righteous" (*ṣaddîq*; plural *ṣaddîqîm*) itself occurs fifty-two times in the Psalms. Only Proverbs uses the term more often (sixty-six times). The related word "upright" (*yāšār*) appears more often in the Psalms than any other book (twenty-five times). Furthermore, the term "wicked" (*rāšāʿ*; plural *rěšāʿîm*), which signifies those who oppress and persecute the righteous, appears eighty-two times in the Psalter, far more frequently than any other book of the Old Testament. The impressive frequency of this terminology alone makes it hard to escape the crucial importance of the righteous to the book. But the Psalms' intense interest in the righteous is even more extensive than this list of vocabulary reveals. Indeed, the prayers in the Psalter that call out to God for help are the prayers of those the Psalms call righteous. When this is recognized, it might well be concluded that the destiny of the righteous is the primary subject of the Psalms.[1] Hence, this book intends to argue that the concern for the destiny of the righteous is a central organizing subject that provides a fruitful entrée into the Psalter as a whole.

The main purpose of focusing on the Psalms' concern for the destiny of the righteous is to illuminate the literary and theological features of the Psalter. That is, this book intends to provide a way to read the Psalms all together rather than as separate pieces. Such a unified reading of the Psalter has been practiced for centuries, but has largely been abandoned in the modern period. As a result of the loss of the Psalms as a book, much of the theological significance of the Psalter to the church has been lost as well. Indeed, although the Psalter has continued to serve as a resource for liturgy, prayer, and devotion, the notion of the Psalms as a unified work of theology has largely been forgotten in the modern period.[2] One intended byproduct of reading the Psalter under the rubric of the destiny of the righteous is to aid in the recovery of the Psalms as a theological resource that may influence what the church believes about God and how the church conducts its ministry.[3]

This subject would seem for the church a natural means by which to read the Psalms as part of Christian scripture since the concern for the righteous is central to the New Testament as well. Indeed, the concern for righteousness and for those called righteous (and wicked) in the Psalms is directly related to some of the main questions of the Christian faith, such as: What is the character of God? (God is righteous; Rom. 3:21–26.) How can humans be reconciled with God? (By faith they are reckoned as righteous; Gal. 3:6–9.) Who is Jesus Christ and what is the meaning of his death? (He is one of the righteous who suffered at the hands of the wicked; Lk. 23:47.) How will humans be judged and what will the end of things be like? (Righteous and wicked will be separated and rewarded according to the compassion they showed to those in need; Mt. 25:31–46.) Moreover, the New Testament speaks of the future hope for the people of God as a hope for the righteous (1 Pet. 4:18).

For many Christians, however, the concern for the destiny of the righteous may seem an outmoded topic that enlightened people have moved beyond. The language of righteousness and talk of the righteous and the wicked is almost completely missing in contemporary religious life. This may be due to the assumption that the use of words such as *righteous* and *wicked* lead inevitably to narrow judgmental attitudes of the sort the Pharisees displayed (Mt. 23:13–28). To be sure, such language can be used for self-congratulation or for the exclusion of others. This book is written with the conviction, however, that avoidance of this language and of the theological ideas associated with it diminishes the church's theology and ethical imperative substantially.

To cite one example, the terms *righteous* and *wicked* in the Psalms have the potential for calling the church in North America to identify with those persons in the world who are economically impoverished and denied basic human dignity, since this language in the Psalter is closely tied to such issues (Ps. 10:17–18). In other words, the church's solidarity with the poor and oppressed of the world is at stake in the use or avoidance of this language. Such solidarity with the poor is grounded, most importantly, in an understanding of Jesus Christ, who appears in the New Testament as one of the righteous who called out to God in need (Mt. 27:46; Mk. 15:34). Before saying more about the impact of this language on the church, however, it is necessary to explore further what is meant by the term "righteous" in the Psalms.

Who Are the Righteous?

Many Christians mistakenly believe the term "righteous" in the Psalms and in the Old Testament reveals an understanding of human goodness and salvation that the New Testament rejects. Therefore, it may be helpful to begin by addressing some common misunderstandings of this word and what it signifies. One common misconception is that since the term "righteous" essentially means "to have a just cause" or "to be free of guilt" (Deut. 25:1), the word refers to moral purity. Such a designation of persons may seem to contradict Paul's declaration in Romans 3:10, "There is no one who is righteous, not even one." The problem is compounded by the fact that the first appearance of the righteous in the Psalms describes them as those whose "delight is in the law of the LORD, / and on his law they meditate day and night" (Ps. 1:2). Such a description of the righteous may seem to go against another of Paul's famous arguments, that "a person is justified by faith apart from works prescribed by the law" (Rom. 3:28).

A closer look at the word *righteous* in the Psalms and in Paul's letters, however, reveals that these two parts of the canon actually have similar ideas about what it means to be righteous. Although the Psalter recognizes that a person may be free of guilt in a particular situation (Ps. 17:1, "Hear a just [*sedeq*; 'right'] cause, O Lord"), it states emphatically that absolute "rightness" is impossible for humans. Psalm 143:2 puts it best: "no one living is righteous before you." Paul makes his argument about justification by faith in Romans 3 (and against justification by the law) mainly by quoting and making references to the Psalms. In fact, he largely follows the argument of Psalm 143.[4] In other words, Paul does not contradict the Psalter's assessment of some persons as righteous; rather, he develops his ideas by using the Psalms as his main authority!

The term "righteous" in the Psalms and in the Old Testament refers to a person who fulfills obligations (thus who acts rightly) in relationships, not to one who is morally superior to others. For example, when Judah declares concerning his daughter-in-law Tamar, "She is more righteous than I" (Gen. 38:26; my translation; NRSV renders "in the right" rather than "righteous"), he refers to Tamar's efforts to have a son for her dead husband in fulfillment of the expectation of levirate marriage (Deut. 25:5–10). Judah made this judgment despite Tamar's posing as a temple prostitute and deceiving him, both of which would be considered morally wrong in the abstract (Gen. 38:12–19). But in terms of what was expected in her relationship to her dead husband, Tamar goes to great lengths to fulfill her obligations.

The righteous in the Psalms are those who have a right relationship with God and whose relationships with other people are governed by God's expectations for human community. The main sign of their fidelity in that relationship is that they recognize God is in control of the world, that "the Lord reigns." Therefore, the righteous are called God's "servants" (*'ebed*; plural *'ăbādîm*; Ps. 90:13, 16).[5] They place themselves under divine authority and look to God as the source of life and blessing. Hence, the Psalms often express this aspect of the relationship by saying the righteous person "seeks refuge" in God rather than in other sources of security (Ps. 2:12; 37:40). The righteous also do not rest in their own goodness; they readily confess their sins before God and seek God's mercy in response to their sinfulness (see the identification of the righteous at the end of Ps. 32, after confession of sin).

The righteous in the Psalms are also portrayed as those who respond to God in praise and joy and who call on God for help. Prayer and worship are the activities of the righteous because such activities grow out of an awareness of God as the source of all that is good. In other words, the righteous in the Psalms are very much the same as those Paul calls righteous, those who live by faith (Rom. 1:17).

This understanding of the righteous in submission to God's sovereignty makes the idea that they meditate on "the law" more understandable. The word "law" does not imply that they adhere to a legalistic understanding of morality. On the contrary, "law" here translates the word *tôrâ* which means "instruction" (see further chapter 10). To say that the righteous meditate on torah is to say the righteous constantly seek to understand what God is doing in the world and to align themselves with it. As people who constantly meditate on this "instruction," the righteous are those who do not go their own way. They live in accordance with Proverbs 3:5: "Trust in the LORD with all you heart, / and do not rely on your own insight." Indeed, the righteous find insight, instruction, in torah.

The righteous in the Psalms are recognized by certain moral characteristics; but their right actions result from a relationship with God, not from a state of moral perfection. Indeed, the Psalms identify righteousness mainly as an aspect of God's character in which humans may participate. (Hebrew has two terms for righteousness, one masculine, *ṣedeq,* and one feminine, *ṣĕdāqâ,* both of which are used for divine righteousness). For example, Psalm 4 calls "O God of my righteousness" (v. 1, NASB [2 in Masoretic Text (MT)]), and Psalm 5 petitions God to "lead me, O LORD, in your righteousness" (v. 8 [9]).

Divine righteousness represents the harmonious order with which God made the world, including God's intentions for human society.[6] Hence the words, "justice" (*mišpat*) and "well-being" (*šālôm)* are closely related to righteousness as what God intends for God's people. The righteous grant others the well-being God intends for them precisely because they recognize God's righteousness as the order by which life should be lived.[7] Therefore, the Psalter's understanding of righteousness again is similar to that of Paul, who insists that humans can only be made righteous through the grace of God, the only one perfectly righteous, the one who showed his righteousness in Jesus Christ (Rom. 3:21–26). Although the identification of the righteous in the Psalms includes a moral dimension, the right actions of the righteous are mainly actions resulting from an orientation toward the righteousness of God.[8]

The emphasis on the righteous as those who participate in God's desire to create a community of justice and equity raises another very important feature of the term "righteous" in the Psalms: the righteous are not just those who grant God-given rights to others; the designation also applies to those who have had their rights taken away.[9] Therefore, the righteous are often described as helpless and afflicted. They are called "poor" (*'ānî*) twenty-three times in the Psalter; they are also "powerless" and "oppressed" (*dal,* five times; cf. Ex. 23:3) and "needy" (*'ebyôn,* twenty-three times; cf. Am.

4:1). God has compassion on such persons because they are victims. God works to bring them salvation, to restore šālôm. To be sure, their victim status alone does not render them righteous. The Psalms indicate that such persons recognize their spiritual "poverty."[10] In other words, the experience of being a victim has produced in the righteous an attitude of dependence on God and on God's reign.

What has been said thus far indicates that the righteous in the Psalms are cast as figures worthy of admiration and sympathy. They are powerless to overcome the wicked and so call out to God for deliverance. Four additional considerations are needed to address the negative impressions of this language:

1. *Regardless of how deserving of compassion the righteous may be, the label "righteous" may seem essentially self-righteous.* However, "righteous" is never a self-designation in the Psalms. The psalmist never says, "I am righteous." Rather, the label is always given to others. When it appears in the Psalter it represents a divine perspective.[11]

2. *The identification of some as wicked may seem judgmental.* Yet the label "wicked" is reserved for those who oppose the order God intended for the world and for the human community. "Wicked" refers not just to personal enemies (see chapter 1) but to the forces that are against God, forces that have a structural or cosmic significance. The righteous in the Psalms are constantly set over against the wicked, and God's righteousness is set over against wickedness. Wickedness amounts to opposition to God's intentions to create šālôm.

3. *This language may seem vengeful when it is used to call on God to punish the wicked.* Such language, however, is the logical consequence of the previous point. If the wicked represent evil on a large scale, then the psalms that call God to judge the wicked are essentially asking for what Christians request when they pray, "thy kingdom come." Indeed, these psalms are spoken in recognition of both the overwhelming power of wickedness and the powerlessness of the righteous to act against it. As the righteous appeal to God for help, they also give up their own inclinations to seek revenge and act violently in response to the wicked. With this in view, even the most difficult examples of the so-called psalms of vengeance (notably Ps. 137) can be understood in a positive light (see further chapter 1).

4. *Finally, the Psalms' emphasis on the righteous prospering (Ps. 1:3) and the wicked perishing (Ps. 1:6) is sometimes perceived as part of a retribution theology that focuses on material reward for obedience to God.* However, the Psalms emphasize that the righteous' greatest "reward" is to be in God's presence. This is summed up in the psalmist's declaration, "One thing I asked of the LORD, / that will I seek after: / to live in the house of the LORD / all the days of my life" (Ps. 27:4). The righteous claim that the Lord is their "portion" or inheritance; thus, God is all they need (Ps. 73:26).

The Individual and Communal Identity of the Righteous in the Psalms

The individual righteous who speak through the Psalms are anonymous. The Psalms clearly identify the righteous as victims of the wicked and as loyal and dependent subjects of the Lord, but the prayers of the righteous and the descriptions of them provide no information that reveals precisely who they are or when they lived. For people of faith who have for centuries looked to the Psalms as model prayers, the anonymity of the righteous has allowed the Psalms to become their prayers as well. Apart from their superscriptions, the Psalms are not tied to any particular period in Israel's history. As Patrick Miller puts it, the Psalms are "by their content not time bound."[12] This makes the prayers of the righteous available to be used as model prayers for all who identify with them.

Still, to interpret the Psalms properly, one must acknowledge at least two dimensions of the identity of the righteous. One involves the righteous as Israel. The other relates the righteous to David.

The Righteous as Israel

During the exilic and postexilic periods of Israel's history, worshipers used and reused psalms. In so doing they came to understand Israel as the righteous who suffer at the hand of the wicked. The wicked, conversely, became a trope for the nations at whose hands Israel suffered. The growth toward this type of corporate identity is evident in psalms that feature an individual's voice but that are applied to the whole people through liturgical additions.[13] For example, in Psalm 130 an individual speaks throughout the first six verses: "I cry to you" (v. 1); "I wait for the LORD" (v. 5); "my soul waits for the Lord" (v. 6). But the last two verses turn attention to Israel: "O Israel, hope in the LORD!" (v. 7). The shift is even more pronounced in the psalm that follows. Psalm 131 contains some of the most personal language of any psalm, so much so that some scholars believe they can identify the gender of the psalmist as female.[14] And yet the psalm ends as does Psalm 130, with a call for Israel to "hope in the LORD" (v. 3). The individual who perhaps once spoke only for herself now speaks for Israel in worship. In Psalm 129 the individual voice at the beginning ("Often have they attacked me from my youth," v. 1a) is broken by the liturgical direction, "let Israel now say" (v. 1b). It is clear from these examples that Israel, the community gathered for worship, saw itself represented by those righteous individuals in its midst and that "the righteous" came to be understood as Israel, the worshiping community.

As this communal identity of the righteous developed, the wicked came under the rubric of "the enemy," those nations who brought about Israel's political and military demise. Psalm 73 may reflect such communal identity of the righteous and their plight. The psalm begins: "Surely God is good to *Israel,* / to those who are pure in heart" (NIV, emphasis added). Although the remainder of the psalm seems to record an individual's dismay at the prosperity of the wicked, the first verse nevertheless identifies the "pure in heart" as Israel.

Some scholars have thought this quite odd and have determined that the term *yiśrā'ēl* (Israel) is actually the result of a scribal error whereby a term meaning "upright" (*yāšar*) was combined with the first two letters in the word for God (*'ēl*, which itself is a word meaning "God"). Thus, the opening of the psalm should read, "Truly God is good to the upright, to those who are pure in heart" (NRSV). In this way of thinking the speaker of the psalm identifies himself as one of the upright and laments that his current circumstances do not reflect God's goodness to those so designated. Logical though this argument may be, no textual evidence supports it. No Hebrew manuscript or any of the earliest translations contained such a reading. The "pure in heart" are identified as Israel and, therefore, the speaker of the psalm seems to represent the nation.

If indeed Psalm 73 represents Israel's complaint over the prosperity of the wicked, it would seem to follow that the wicked described there were understood as those nations that participated in Israel's downfall. Psalm 73 makes no direct indication of that association. It is interesting, however, that the characterization of the wicked in verses 4–14 is similar to the portrayal of Babylon in some prophetic texts that likely date to, and wrestle with, the Babylonian exile. Isaiah 47:8–11 comes from that portion of the book of Isaiah commonly called Second Isaiah that has the same exilic setting as the Psalter and that has many structural and theological affinities as well. According to Second Isaiah, the Babylonians deny God's sovereignty by proclaiming to themselves ("in your heart"), "I am, and there is no one besides me" (Isa. 47:8) and by saying concerning their wickedness, "No one sees me" (v. 10). This is precisely the problem with the wicked in Psalm 73. They are "at ease" (v. 12) in their certainty that God does not recognize their sinfulness (v. 11, "And they say, 'How can God know? / Is there knowledge in the Most High?'").

Although Israel in exile seems to be identified as the righteous in many psalms (and is perhaps the overarching identity in the final form of the Psalter), the corporate identity of the righteous in some psalms is clearly more narrowly the faithful *within* Israel. Conversely, the wicked in such psalms are the reprobate within the people of God. For example, Psalm 50:16–18 shows the righteous as those within the community who worship God in spirit and in truth, not just in ritual performance. They are distinguished from participants in the cult who are "friends with a thief" and "keep company with adulterers" (v. 18).[15]

When those within Israel do not act in accordance with God's intentions, they become like the nations (such as Babylon) that oppose the Lord and the Lord's anointed (Ps. 2:1–3) by undercutting the divine purpose that comes through Israel. When the nations oppress God's people, they become like the wicked within Israel who "lurk that they may seize the poor" (Ps. 10:9).

David and the Righteous

The Psalter identifies the righteous with Israel. It then focuses that corporate identity in a profound way by identifying David as the righteous who suffers. David appears in twelve psalms that present events in his life as the contexts in which he prayed the words of those psalms (Pss. 3, 7, 18, 51, 52, 54, 56, 57, 59, 60, 62, 142).[16] In almost every case David is presented as one who suffers, who pleads to God for mercy, and who expresses confidence that God will deliver him. David's name also appears in the simple ascription, *lĕdāwid* ("of David") in sixty-one other psalm titles. Although these references probably did not signify authorship originally, they came to be read in light of the longer headings. As James L. Mays says concerning David's appearance in these psalms, David's name here and elsewhere "does not so much claim the psalms as the voice of a king as it identifies him, in the psalms that are claimed for David, with the lowly."[17] In other words, David in the Psalms represents the righteous who suffer at the hands of the wicked.

The identity of David as one of the righteous does not negate his role as king; rather it makes use of that role to portray Israel's suffering. The wicked are enemies of the people of God by virtue of the fact that they are his enemies, those who plot against the Lord's anointed (Ps. 2:1). David's appearance as king also has another important dimension. Namely, as king he is the defender of the righteous as well as one of the righteous who suffers.

An important aspect of this relationship between the king and the righteous is that David (and his son Solomon in Ps. 72 and 127) is the only king identified in the Psalms. David appears in the text of five psalms that identify him as the ruler of Israel (Ps. 18:50; 78:70; 89:3, 20, 35, 49; 132:1, 10, 11–12, 17; 144:10 [see also the reference to the "house of David" in Ps. 122:5]). This is a relatively short list. It is important, however, because the reader learns by these references who the David of the psalms' titles is. In these psalms David is identified as the king, the servant of the Lord, the chosen one, the anointed one, the one with whom God covenanted to establish his dynasty forever. The identification of David in these ways, and the absence of any other figure in the Psalter so identified, encourages an exclusive association of David with the royal labels, even when the psalms do not make such a connection explicit. As Mays astutely observes:

> These few texts furnish the inner textual code for reading other psalms in which David is not mentioned. When these titles appear in psalms which do not name David, they furnish the identification for the speaker or subject of the psalm. The "messiah" or "the king" or God's "servant" are textual directions to think of David.[18]

The nearly exclusive identification of David with kingship in the Psalter gives a cast to the Psalter's view of kingship that must guide conclusions on the Psalter's theology with regard to human rule. In the final form of the book of Psalms, David is *the* king. David is an authoritative voice from the past that instructs and provides hope for Israel in exile and beyond. Because of the exclusive association of the king with David, the Psalter creates the expectation of a new David who will stand with the lowly as their defender. This double identity of David—as one of the righteous who suffers and as their defender—prepares the way for the church to understand the ministry of Jesus. He is the "son of David," the "king of the Jews," but he is also the righteous sufferer who cries out to God for deliverance (Mk. 15:34; Ps. 22:1).[19]

Benefits of This Organizing Rubric
Destiny of the Righteous and the Shape of the Psalter

The way of reading the Psalter proposed here would seem to have at least three significant theological benefits.

First, the organizing theme of the destiny of the righteous provides a plausible way to discern the literary shape of the Psalter, and to understand the Psalms as a book of theology. This way of reading the Psalms, in turn, brings to the surface the theological significance of the whole that is more than the sum of its parts.

Modern scholars have typically rejected the unity of the book of Psalms because they have had trouble identifying anything in the Psalms themselves that hold them together theologically.[20] The loss of the Psalms as a book stems in part from the fact that scholars in the modern era have largely rejected the idea that the Psalms cohere in the life of David, which is the traditional notion of the Psalter's unity. Indeed, scholars have determined that David (the historical figure who ruled Israel in the tenth century B.C.E.) could not have authored all the psalms, if he was responsible for any at all.

At the same time, scholars searching for literary unity in the Psalter—for signs of development and editing—have been struck more by signs of their diversity. To be sure, many scholars recently have looked much more favorably on the idea that the Psalter is the result of purposeful editorial shaping,[21] but even these efforts have not produced a way to read the Psalms comprehensively that has widespread support. While there is some agreement that Psalms 1 and 2 were intended to introduce the whole book and that the book has a fivefold structure, the exact message of the introduction and that structure is far from clear. Compounding the problem, the Psalter seems to have two distinct sections that have different, albeit complementary, theological emphases: Psalms 1–89 (Books 1–3 of the Psalter) are quite concerned with the Davidic king and the nature of his reign, so much so that this portion of the book is sometimes called the "messianic Psalter."[22] Psalms 90–150 (Books 4 and 5) seem to address the situation of exile and the loss of monarchy with an emphasis on the reign of God.[23]

The subject of the destiny of the righteous may offer a way beyond the impasse of reading the Psalter all together. When the righteous are properly identified and their various labels recognized, they appear as perhaps the dominant concern in every segment of the Psalter. For example, the central importance of the subject is obvious in Psalms 1 and 2, which introduce the Psalter. Although these two works are quite different in tone and content, they are united by an interest in the two ways one can choose in life: the way of the righteous and the way of the wicked (see the term *derek*, "way" in Ps. 1:6; 2:12). The final statement in Psalm 2 summarizes the character and destiny of the righteous: "Happy are all who take refuge in him" (v. 2:12d). This line enhances the connection between Psalms 1 and 2 and points forward to the many descriptions of the righteous as those who "take refuge" in the Lord in the rest of the Psalter.[24] As Psalms 1 and 2 invite the reader into the book, they present the character of the righteous as an example to be followed, and the problem of the destiny of the righteous as something to be solved.[25]

As the following discussion will show, this subject appears at every other major juncture of the Psalter as well (see chapters 4 and 5).

The Lord's Anointed as One of the Righteous

Focusing on the concern for the plight of the righteous in the Psalms may also reconnect the reader to the traditional notion that David is central to the book. To do so does not require claiming that David is author of the Psalms in an historical sense. Rather, he is a literary figure who dominates the Psalms and has a particular profile. As noted above, David appears in the Psalms as one of the righteous, as one who suffers at the hands of the wicked and who calls out to God for deliverance (Ps. 3; see chapter 4).

When David is seen as one of the righteous who suffers in the Psalms, another connection to traditional Christian readings of the Psalms becomes apparent. The suffering of the anointed–David–in the Psalms illuminates the New Testament's portrait of Jesus' suffering. The influence of the Psalms on this matter is particularly apparent in Luke and Acts. At Jesus' death in Luke 23:47, the centurion beneath the cross "praised God and said, 'Surely this *was* a righteous man'" (NIV). Here the centurion uses the Greek term (*dikaios*) that is equivalent to the Hebrew word *ṣaddiq*. Later when Jesus explains to his disciples that his suffering, death, and resurrection were foretold "in the law of Moses, the prophets, and the psalms" (Lk. 24:44), it is likely that the suffering of the anointed in the Psalms stands in the background of the reference to the Psalter.

Indeed, in Acts 2, Peter appeals to the suffering of David in the Psalms and to God's vindication of him to explain the suffering and resurrection of Jesus (Acts 2:25–36).[26] In other words, the New Testament authors paint a picture of Jesus as one who suffers like the righteous in the Psalms. Jesus' destiny—his resurrection and continued presence with God—is understood as patterned after the destiny of the righteous in the Psalter, particularly as the righteous are represented by the anointed of the Lord, David. (Note the confidence that God will preserve the righteous in Ps. 16:8, which Peter cites in Acts 2:25.) Precisely because of this connection, the early church saw the book of Psalms as a work of theological gravity; and the Psalms continued for centuries to be read as an "abiding theological witness" to Jesus Christ.[27]

The Righteous and the Reign of God

The organizing rubric proposed here also illuminates the larger concept of the reign of God, which is sometimes noted itself as an organizing subject in the Psalms. Mays, in a seminal essay, "The Center of the Psalms: 'The Lord Reigns' as Root Metaphor," argues that the Hebrew sentence, *Yhwh mālak* ("the Lord reigns") is the central theological claim in the Psalter and serves as its organizing center.[28]

Mays is certainly right that the understanding of God as king and of the world as God's kingdom orders and explains the Psalter's claims about God more than any other theological concept. In the Psalter, however, the concern for the destiny of the righteous provides the theological context for the claim that "the Lord reigns." This is apparent, for example, in Psalm 5, which contains the first occurrence of the label "King" (*melek*) for God in the Psalter. Here the psalmist invokes God's kingship as part of a plea for deliverance from the wicked. He calls on God with confidence that God's just rule does not permit wickedness to prevail (v. 4 [5]) and that the Lord, as a beneficent monarch, spreads protection over the righteous (vv. 11–12 [12–13]).

"The Lord reigns" occurs most frequently in a portion of the Psalter that was edited to address the problem of the righteous and wicked on a large scale. Book 4 (Ps. 90–106) wrestles with the fact that the righteous people, Israel, have suffered defeat and exile. Book 4 responds to that circumstance with the continued affirmation that "the Lord reigns" (Ps. 93:1; 96:10; 97:1; 99:1; NRSV translates the sentence in each case, "the LORD is king").[29] In other words, the affirmation that "the Lord reigns" is offered in the midst of circumstances that would seem to indicate otherwise, circumstances centered on the situation of the righteous vis-à-vis the wicked.

God's kingship represents the basis of hope for the righteous, whose future at present is far from certain. By beginning with the concern for the destiny of the righteous, the Psalter places the portrait of God as king in its larger theological context and sheds light on the theological significance of the claim that the Lord reigns (see further chapter 5).

The notion of the reign of God includes at least three sub-topics that are also illuminated by placing the idea of God's sovereignty in the larger context of the Psalter's concern for the destiny of the righteous. Each of these three subjects represents tangible signs of God's reign. They are the "embodied hope" of the righteous and will be treated under this label in the following discussion (see chapters 6–10).

1. David, the Lord's anointed, is a central figure in the Psalms, as already noted. One of the righteous, he is also the monarch who represents the Heavenly King on earth. In this role the anointed is not just one of the righteous but the defender of the righteous as well. His main charge is to ensure justice for the "poor." (See Ps. 72 and 101.)

2. Mount Zion, on which the earthly king is enthroned and from which God's reign is shown to the world, is the place the righteous experience God's presence and protection. Zion is thus the place the righteous long to be (Ps. 42–43). It is "home" for them (Ps. 15 and 24).

3. Finally, torah is the "polity of the reign of God" and, as such, is the ultimate hope for the righteous. As Psalm 1:3 makes clear, the righteous are made secure, "like trees / planted by streams of water," as a result of meditating on torah.

The Language of Righteousness in the Psalms and the Ministry of the Church

Having considered these theological benefits of reading the Psalter under the rubric of the destiny of the righteous, it may be helpful to consider briefly how attention to this subject might enhance the ministry of the church. Four points seem important to keep in mind before moving to the treatment of the Psalms themselves.

First, the Psalter's focus on the righteous as discussed below may aid the church in establishing (or reestablishing) a constructive understanding of divine judgment. Although unpopular with many Christians today, the idea of God's judgment, if properly nuanced, is absolutely essential for the Christian faith. The Psalter's concern for the righteous provides an important perspective on the matter. As already noted, righteousness is a key part of God's character, and indicates God's desire to restore the created order and to bring to fruition what was begun in the original good design. This vision of what God intends to do in the world includes judgment of those elements that would thwart justice and promote chaos. Hence, the language of righteousness and judgment is the language of hope for a future in which God's kingdom is evident.

An important aspect of this language is the recognition of human sinfulness that is essential to Christian prayer and worship. As Karl Barth said, humankind is constantly under the grace of God's "yes," while at the same time under the judgment of God's "no."[30] As the following discussion will point out, denial of the divine "no" is characteristic of the wicked. They deny that God judges their sinfulness. As a result of that denial, they act as though God does not care how they live. Such denial, in turn, leads to violence against the righteous (Ps. 73:8–11).

Second, as the language of "righteous and wicked" in the Psalms highlights God's justice and God's judgment, it may also promote dialogue with people of other faiths who are also concerned with issues of justice. Careful attention to this language will not allow Christians to focus narrowly on the identification of those within their circle as righteous, or on those outside their circle as wicked. If Matthew 25:31–46 provides any guidance for thinking about the identity of the righteous in the world today, the identification of the righteous remains open to any who humbly stand before God, rely on God's grace, and participate in God's righteousness. In that passage, the "nations" appear before Christ at the final judgment. They are separated into two groups, the righteous and the wicked, thus identified by whether or not they have shown compassion to those in need. It is significant that those called righteous have not followed Jesus or participated in his ministry. They are surprised to learn they are identified as righteous.

Their compassion toward the helpless of the world, however, is counted as a response to Jesus nonetheless.[31] As Douglas Hare puts it, "The good deeds performed by pagans are not treated as atoning for their sins, nor as evidence that they imitate God, but as indicating *a relationship with Jesus!*"[32] So, in an age when the church desperately needs to build bridges to people of other faiths, the language of righteousness may actually be one avenue to do so.

Third, the portrait of the righteous and their destiny in the Psalms may give the church words to address the consumer-driven society that shapes its members. As noted above, Psalm 27:4 testifies that the righteous desire only "one thing," to be in God's presence. That is exactly what the righteous seek and expect to receive from God. Although the righteous expect God to address the injustice in the world that promotes the wicked and allows the wicked to prosper, their destiny right now is simply "to be near God" (Ps. 73:28).

Finally, the Psalter's concern for the destiny of the righteous provides an important resource for the church's theological reflection on the plight of the poor and oppressed. Too often Christian reflection and spirituality operates on an unreal and overly optimistic view of the world. The Psalms, however, constantly place before the church the picture of the righteous as powerless and persecuted and of God as their defender. This perspective is particularly apparent in the so-called "psalms of vengeance," psalms the church largely ignores today even as it avoids the language of "righteous and wicked" (see further chapter 1).[33] A recovery of such psalms in the church's prayer, liturgy, and proclamation can inform Christian theology and ethics in important ways.

Specifically, the concern for the righteous in the Psalms suggests for the church a particular understanding of human suffering. The portrayal of the suffering of the righteous in the Psalms suggests that God abhors such suffering and stands with the powerless as their defender and against those who cause their suffering.

Walter Brueggemann says it well: "The Psalm writers will not tolerate a faith in which human well-being is not honored."[34] In other words, the Psalter will not promote the view of the poor and oppressed as scapegoats. Nor does it let us understand their suffering as something that may be tolerated.[35] Instead, the Psalms address human suffering with complaint and petition and with pleas for God to put the wicked in their place. They also present God as one who stands with such persons and fights for them against the wicked.

The Psalms recognize and name the wicked as oppressors, call on God as liberator, and expect a real change to occur in the world. Careful attention to the Psalter's concern for the destiny of the righteous may contribute to the recovery of these psalms and the theological and political outcomes they voice. This does not mean, of course, that the concern for the destiny of the righteous may be reduced to issues of economic injustice. A proper understanding of the righteous in the Psalms will urge all people of faith to recognize their spiritual need and to seek the presence of God to meet that need. But as the Psalms do that work on the soul of the believer, they also encourage solidarity with the literal poor of the world. Those who suffer become the illustration of what it means to be "poor and needy," in need of God's work to restore šālôm.

The Psalter's perspective on such matters also forces the church to come to grips with the "preference for the poor" in the gospel.[36] This perspective is particularly important for Christians in North America who are part of economic and social systems that are by nature oppressive to many in the world. The Psalms' harsh judgment on the wicked should give pause to all people of privilege and create in them a recurring self-examination. Indeed, as José Miranda observes, the Psalms' descriptions of the righteous and wicked are often tied closely to economic issues; the righteous may be spiritually "poor" (*dal* or *ʿānî*), but they are often also literally poor as well. The wicked take advantage of them for the wicked's material gain. (See especially Ps. 9–10.) Miranda thus characterizes the book of Psalms: "It can surely be said that the Psalter presents a struggle of the just against the unjust."[37]

With that in mind, the Psalms offer an important resource for the church to approach God in repentance for its own complicity with wickedness and in supplication for those who suffer. Indeed, since the righteous in the Psalms are those who are victims of the wicked, a reading of the Psalter that focuses on the destiny of the righteous urges Christians to evaluate whether they are standing with the oppressive forces of the world (thus with the wicked) or with the God who would free the oppressed.

The Plan of This Book

The discussion that follows will explore the destiny of the righteous in three parts. Part I (chapters 1–3) looks more closely at what has already been introduced here, the character and destiny of the righteous. The reader will be presented with basic features of the Psalms' portrait of the righteous that will reappear in subsequent sections. Chapter 1 examines the righteous' relationship to God by means of their prayers. It will consider first the basic notion that the prayers of the righteous depict them as those who are aware of their helplessness and dependence on God. Then the chapter will look more closely at two particular kinds of prayers: prayers of confession and the so-called "psalms of vengeance." It will be shown that the former reveal the righteous' dependence on God for forgiveness of sins and the latter show them in dependence on God for protection from the wicked. A key characteristic of the righteous will be highlighted—namely, their vulnerability to the wicked and their reliance on God.

Chapter 2 considers the activity of the righteous that results from their relationship with God. It will introduce praise as the primary "activity" of the righteous out of which all right action grows. The final chapter in Part I (chapter 3) takes up the subject of the reward due the righteous, their destiny. It will show that the main feature of the righteous' destiny is simply "to be near God." That is, although the Psalms speak at times of material reward for the righteous, the main outcome of their right relationship with God is the relationship itself. Three features of the righteous emerge from these chapters in Part I that will be important for sections that follow: the righteous' suffering at the hands of the wicked; their faith in God to deliver them; and their unending desire to be in God's presence.

Part II (chapters 4–5) will consider how the concern for the destiny of the righteous is seen in the shape of the Psalter. Chapter 4 will examine Psalms 1–89 (Books 1–3 of the Psalter) and will give particular attention to the role of David, the Lord's anointed as the suffering one. The discussion will show that this section of the Psalter moves to a point of supreme despair, as Psalm 89 laments over the anointed's suffering. But it will also be noted that this conclusion to Book 3 of the Psalter already contains signs of hope for the future. The promises to David are even here beginning to be transferred to God's servants, the chosen people, and the ground is laid for David to be a future hope for the righteous.

Chapter 5 will then treat Psalms 90–150. Attention will be paid to how these psalms address the issues raised in Psalm 89, especially how these psalms reaffirm that the Lord has not abandoned his servants, the righteous. Indeed, the claim that "the Lord reigns" recurs in Psalms 90–150 in order to assure the righteous that God has neither forsaken them nor ceded control of the world to the wicked. Moreover, although the emphasis on divine rule encourages the righteous to put confidence in God, the Heavenly King, these psalms show that there remains an expectation for a David of the future who will reveal the rule and justice of God again on earth.

Part III zeroes in on three important topics in the Psalms that represent the "embodied hope" of the righteous. Chapters 6 and 7 address the way the Davidic king served as defender of the righteous and the hope for God's establishment of justice. One of the main concerns of these chapters will be how the king was understood as a protector of the righteous after the Babylonian exile brought an end to monarchy in Israel. These chapters will show that David is the symbol for the suffering people, the righteous, and is cast as a future hope, one who will reappear in the future to defend God's servants.

Chapters 8 and 9 explore the Psalms' portrayal of Zion, and particularly the righteous' longing to be on Zion and in its temple. The reason for such longing is that Zion is presented as the place God's reign is experienced and known and therefore the place where the righteous are most at home. Finally, chapter 10 will consider the role of torah, God's "instruction," in the life of the righteous. It will be shown that (1) torah appears in Psalms 1; 19; and 119 as a source of protection for the righteous; (2) torah is an expression of God's refuge; and (3) by meditation on torah, the righteous find true security. As these features of torah are explored, however, it will also be shown that torah is presented in the Psalms as the ultimate expression of protection for the righteous; indeed, torah serves as a substitute and replacement for Zion and is intended to provide direction for the activity of the king.

Throughout these ten chapters, it will be pointed out that the Psalter's presentation of the righteous serves as a foundation for the New Testament's understanding of the life and ministry of Jesus. Indeed, Jesus is the righteous one who suffers. In this way he is similar to David, who suffered at the hands of the wicked. However, for the church Jesus also is the "embodied hope" of the righteous. He is the "new David" who is able to defend the righteous. He is the sign of God's presence, the locus of God's nearness to humans, as Zion had once been. Jesus is also the Divine Word that makes known God's intentions to the world, as did torah.

This presentation of Jesus does not make obsolete what the Psalter says about the righteous and their reliance on David, Zion, and torah. On the contrary, the Psalms create the form and foundation of this faith of the church. Hence, as this book explores the concern for the righteous in the Psalms, it also begins to explore the foundations of much of the church's theology as well. It is hoped that this study of the Psalms will serve as a reminder that the founder of the Christian faith was one who sought God's presence (Ps. 22:1) and cried out to God when in trouble. He was one of the righteous.

PART I

Who Are the Righteous in the Psalms?

1

Prayer and the Profile of the Righteous

"Surely this was a righteous man" (Lk. 23:47, NIV). Luke's account of Jesus' death includes this surprising statement from the Gentile centurion beneath the cross. What prompted the soldier's assessment of Jesus, no one knows. One possible explanation is that Jesus immediately before death called out to God in prayer using the words of Psalm 31:5, "Father, into your hand I commit my spirit." Whatever the reason for the centurion's words, Jesus, at the moment of his death, does appear as one of the righteous, praying in the midst of suffering, just as the ones in the Psalms.

The prayers in the Psalter originated as parts of ceremonies by which Israel ministered to those in life-threatening circumstances.[1] But now in the canon of scripture these prayers have a common theological setting in the Psalter: they are the words of those the Psalter identifies as ṣaddiq, "righteous," setting them apart from those called "wicked."[2] These prayers of the righteous provide a window into the Psalter's understanding of the righteous and their relationship with God.[3] They allow the reader to gain a purchase on what it means to be righteous, how the ṣaddiq speaks out of his or her need to God and how such a person imagines God to be and to act.

Perhaps the reason prayer is so central to the life of the righteous is that prayer functions for them as an avenue into God's presence. As the introduction indicated, and as chapter 3 will explore further, being near God is what the righteous seek more than anything else. James L. Mays puts the relationship between prayer and the presence of God this way: "To 'call on the name of God' is to place oneself in his presence. The prayer describes the self, presents the self to God in all its weakness and need. It lets the self be in the real Presence."[4]

As chapter 3 will show, being in the presence of God is the destiny of the righteous. By examining how and under what circumstances the righteous pray, this chapter begins to address in an implicit way that most-certain feature of the future of the righteous. It also illustrates the essential point that the faith and destiny of the righteous cannot be separated. The righteous do not live rightly to be rewarded in the future. The way they live *is* their future, because they live in and for the presence of God. Prayer is a key to being in God's presence.

The discussion below begins with the most general feature of prayer—namely, its assumption of need on the part of the one who prays and the accompanying assumption of God's ability and willingness to hear and to act. The chapter moves then to psalms that express two specific types of need: the need for God's forgiveness and the need for God's protection from enemies.

Prayer and Dependence

The act of prayer identifies the righteous because it indicates their dependence on God. In prayer the righteous recognize that they are "poor and needy." One of the Desert Fathers, Isaac the Syrian, related prayer and the righteous' humility this way: "When they know they are in need of Divine help, they make many prayers. And by as much as they multiply them, their hearts are humbled, for there is no one who will not be humbled when making supplication and entreaty."[5]

Indeed, prayer distinguishes the righteous, who know they need God's salvation, from the wicked, who think they are self-sufficient.

My Heart Is Not Lifted Up: Psalm 131

The prayer in Psalm 131 is one of the most powerful expressions of dependence on God in the Psalter. This, the shortest prayer in the Psalms, captures the humility that is at the heart of the righteous' relationship with God.[6] The psalm consists of two sections. Verses 1–2 express complete trust in God. Verse 3 then urges this dependence on God on all Israel.

The first section of Psalm 131 expresses a childlike faith that captures well what it means to depend on God:

> O LORD, my heart is not lifted up,
> my eyes are not raised too high;
> I do not occupy myself with things
> > too great and too marvelous for me.
> But I have calmed and quieted my soul,
> > like a weaned child with its mother;
> > my soul is like the weaned child that is with me. (vv. 1–2)

This portion of the psalm begins with three negative statements that swear off arrogance and self-assertion in relation to God. References to the "heart lifted up" and "eyes raised" are used in other parts of the Old Testament to describe the way of the wicked. For example, Proverbs uses these same expressions to warn against a way that is destructive, that God opposes (Prov. 6:17; 18:12). Narrative and prophetic traditions in the Old Testament characterize those with "heart raised" and "eyes lifted" as presumptive towards God (2 Chr. 32:25). Ezekiel 28 goes so far as to suggest one who lives in this way is pretending to be God (vv. 2, 5, 17).[7] The one who speaks Psalm 131 knows well that only God is God and that God's protective presence is needed more than anything else in life.

Verse 1 also confesses limited knowledge and understanding of God's control of the world, and thus further expresses helplessness before the Creator: "I do not occupy myself with things / too great and too marvelous for me." "Things too great and too marvelous" probably refers to the deeds of Yahweh, since these words have that meaning in nearly every other occurrence in the Old Testament (Deut. 10:21; Jer. 33:3; Job 5:9). At least two important figures in the Old Testament speak in a similar way of "things too marvelous for me." One is the sage who spoke the words of Proverb 30:18–19:

> Three things are too wonderful for me;
>   four I do not understand:
> the way of an eagle in the sky,
>   the way of a snake on a rock,
> the way of a ship on the high seas,
>   and the way of a man with a girl.

This "intellectual" who is otherwise so adept at analyzing and explaining the order of the world confesses that his mind is limited. Some things are simply beyond human comprehension. The confession puts the sage in right relationship to God, the only one who holds all understanding (Prov. 1:7; 3:5–8). So also the person who speaks Psalm 131 speaks with the same message.

The other Old Testament voice in concert with the speaker of Psalm 131 is Job. In his final speech Job confesses that his charge against God was uttered in ignorance[8]: "Therefore I have uttered what I did not understand, / things too wonderful for me, which I did not know" (Job 42:3).

Job has struggled with and protested his circumstances. At the end of struggle and complaint, however, Job trusts in God. So also the speaker of Psalm 131 is not occupied "with things / too great and too marvelous for me." As verse 2 attests, the limitations of the dependent child become for the psalmist a way of existing before God. The one who prays in Psalm 131 has become like a child in relationship with the Lord (Mt. 18:1–5; Mk. 9:33–37; Lk. 9:46–48).

The declaration of helplessness in verses 1–2 has a peculiar feature that may help illuminate further the character of the righteous. As many interpreters have noticed, the speaker of these words seems to be a woman who used her own place in life to illustrate the proper relationship with God.[9] Indeed, the final portion of verse 2, "the weaned child that is *with me*" (emphasis added), seems to identify the speaker as female, a mother. Although this identity is not necessary to understand the prayer, it gives a particular cast to what is said to God and illuminates at least one type of person the Psalter may have in mind when it uses the term "righteous."

The woman who prayed Psalm 131 undoubtedly knew submission and humility in relation to men in her world. Therefore, "I have calmed and quieted my soul" (v. 2) may imply a resignation forced by her circumstances.[10] It may also be the case that the woman's reflection on the "too great and too marvelous things" meant that serious thinking on such things was restricted to males in her world. That being said, two points are important in order to understand the speaker of Psalm 131 as a model of righteousness. First, given the stance of God toward the plight of the righteous in the Psalms, this passage should not be read as an approval of heirarchy. On the contrary, the Psalms rail against the notion that the "poor and needy" should be kept in their place. Second, by the presence of her prayer in the Psalter—and now as scripture—the woman's words stand alongside those of Job and the speaker of Proverbs 30:18–19 as an authoritative word to Israel. As Miller says, the experience of the woman has become "the vehicle for discerning, not the way that human beings relate to each other and live together, but the way that life is to be set before God."[11] The woman now teaches Israel the way of the righteous. Her way of relating to God is urged upon the community: "O Israel, hope in the LORD / from this time on and forevermore" (v. 3).[12]

In the LORD I Take Refuge: Psalm 11

Psalm 11 is not a prayer. Nevertheless, it provides instruction in how to approach God and presents the benefits of prayer. This psalm highlights the righteous' dependence on God with one of the most important theological terms in the Psalter: "refuge."[13] "Refuge" and related terms represent the most common expressions of the righteous' dependence on God.[14] The psalmist calls God refuge (*maḥsê*; 14:6), fortress (*māʿōz*; 28:8; *miśgab*; 9:9 [10]), or rock (*selaʾ* ; 31:3 [4]). The psalmist in Psalm 11:1 professes to "take refuge" in the Lord (using forms of the verb *ḥāsâ*; 2:12; 5:11; [12]). This language draws upon images of taking shelter (Isa. 28:17) or shade (Jon. 4:6), finding a place to hide (Isa. 32:2), or finding a defensible position from which enemies are no longer a threat (Ps. 142:5–6).

In speaking of God as a refuge, the psalmist imagines God as a fortress or as a tower of defense. The righteous' declarations of seeking refuge in God are metaphorical expressions of dependence on God. Therefore, this language is closely related to words that communicate the notion of having confidence in and reliance on God. One closely related expression is "trust"

(Hebrew root *bāṭaḥ*). While the language of refuge draws from images of escape and hiding, "trust" communicates an inner sense of security in God (Ps. 28:7). Another expression related to refuge is "wait"/"hope in" (roots *qāwâ* and *yāḥal*). In other words, the person who declares in Psalm 11:1, "In the LORD I take refuge," is acting according to the instruction given at the end of Psalm 131: "O Israel, hope in the LORD" (v. 3).

The language of refuge is often connected to the problem of the destiny of the righteous in the face of the threats of the wicked. The righteous ask God to be delivered from the enemy (Ps. 143:9), not to be "put to shame" (Ps. 31:1[2]), to know God's mercy (Ps 57:1 [2]) because they have sought shelter in God or under God's "wings" (Ps. 61:4[5]). The speaker of Psalm 11 professes to have placed himself or herself in God's care in this way.

Psalm 11 has two distinctive parts, though the two are closely related to each other. Verses 1–3 form the testimony of one who knows the proper way to find safety from the threats of the wicked. Security is found in trusting God, not in hiding from the wicked or relying on one's own skills of self-preservation. Verses 4–7 provide assurance that the way suggested in verses 1–3 is ultimately the right way for the righteous; their destiny is guaranteed by the watchful care of God.

After the psalm's opening declaration, "In the LORD I take refuge" (v. 1a) verses 1b–3 make clear that the psalmist's declaration of taking refuge in God represents a choice of the Lord over other potential sources of safety from the wicked. The psalmist asks,

> How can you say to me,
>   "Flee like a bird to the mountains;
> for look, the wicked bend the bow,
>   they have fitted their arrow to the string,
>   to shoot in the dark at the upright in heart.
> If the foundations are destroyed,
>   what can the righteous do?"

Here "fleeing to the mountains" represents the psalmist's seeking protection by means of his own resources. The hills and rocky crags in the Palestinian wilderness were prime places to set up defenses against an enemy or to hide out in times of attack.[15]

The option of fleeing to the mountains might seem prudent and practical. But the psalmist says trust in God is the only truly wise reaction to the threats of the wicked. That response to the advice to "flee to the mountains" may seem naïve. Is prayer and dependence on God the only valid response to the attack of an enemy? Perhaps for some isolated and time-bound circumstances the answer to this question is no. But the remainder of Psalm 11 indicates that there is a larger reality concerning the wicked that can only be addressed by the protective power of God. Verse 4 notes that God's view of the righteous and the wicked are not limited as the human view is. Rather, "The LORD is in his holy temple," that is, he is enthroned in heaven (v. 4aα). With this bird's eye view God looks down on all humankind (v. 4aβ-b). The implication is that the problem of the wicked is bigger than merely the threats of personal enemies. For that reason it cannot be dealt with by normal human response. Martin Luther addressed this point beautifully in his famous hymn, "A Mighty Fortress Is Our God," a hymn written with the language of God as refuge in mind (particularly as it appears in Ps. 46). In the second verse Luther captures the choice that is inherent in the language when he writes, "Did we in our own strength confide, our striving would be losing." The righteous have identified and claimed Yahweh as their hiding place above their own strength and wisdom and above all other sources of protection and security.

Psalm 11 ends with three verses that insist God does not look down as a disinterested party or as a dispassionate observer. "The LORD tests the righteous and the wicked, / and his soul hates the lover of violence" (v. 5). Verse 6 declares that God will destroy the wicked ("on the wicked he will rain coals of fire and sulfur"). The psalm concludes with an explanation for God's action against the wicked that is directly tied to God's character: "For the LORD is righteous; / he loves righteous deeds" (v. 7a). Therefore, verses 4–7a make two important points concerning the destiny of the righteous:

1. the problem of the wicked is too big to be dealt with by human action;
2. in the end the wicked and wickedness cannot prevail!

God, by God's very nature, is against the wicked and for the righteous. The psalm ends, therefore, with the appropriate promise of God's presence with the righteous, "The upright shall behold his face" (v. 7b).[16]

Prayer and Confession

In some psalms the righteous' dependence on God takes the form of confession of sins. The righteous recognize their sinfulness and depend on God's grace and forgiveness. While the righteous may argue for their innocence before accusers (Ps. 17:1), they readily acknowledge their brokenness before God (Ps. 143:2). Moreover, the righteous have a particular understanding of God. They believe God judges unrighteousness, but they are confident in God's willingness to forgive. In contrast, the wicked act as though God does not notice their evil deeds and continue to live as though their destiny did not depend upon God's grace.

Early Christian interpreters isolated seven "penitential" psalms they believed gave voice to confession particularly well (Ps. 6; 32; 38; 51; 102; 130; 143). These psalms, which formed the basis of the church's institution of penitence, illustrate the righteous' humility with regard to their sins. Psalm 51 is perhaps the best-known example. As indicated in the psalm's superscription, the psalm is presented as the prayer of David "when the prophet Nathan came to him, after he had gone in to Bathsheba." The association with the Bathsheba episode was probably prompted by several key expressions in Psalm 51 that also occur in 2 Samuel 11–12: "Against you, you alone, have I sinned" (Ps. 51:4a [6]) is very similar to David's confession to Nathan, "I have sinned against the Lord" (2 Sam. 12:13); "and done what is evil in your sight" (Ps. 51:4b [6]) is similar to the final words of 2 Samuel 11, "But the thing that David had done displeased the Lord," in both cases the Hebrew reading literally "in your/the Lord's eyes."

Although Psalm 51 is set in the context of David's sin with Bathsheba, the psalmist speaks of his sinfulness as something that encompasses his entire being. The psalm opens with a plea for God's mercy in light of the psalmist's failings before God. Three terms express this broken state: "transgressions," "iniquity," and "sin." The psalmist's confession of his sinful nature becomes clearer as the psalm unfolds. "My sin is ever before me" (v. 3b [5b]) could refer to awareness of a particular sinful act, but the following two verses suggest otherwise. In verse 4 (6) the psalmist recognizes God's justice in passing judgment on sin. The verbs here are imperfect, which in this context suggests either future action or typical, ongoing action. NRSV is probably right to translate them as the latter. God's judgment is always upon the psalmist in a sense because of his sinful state. The metaphor in verse 5 makes this clear: "Indeed, I was born guilty, / a sinner when my mother conceived me."

Augustine captures the weight of this metaphorical expression when he says that the sin spoken of here is the first human rebellion: "What is it that he saith himself to have been in iniquity conceived, except that iniquity is drawn from Adam?"[17] Although it would be anachronistic to suggest the psalmist had an Augustinian view of original sin, the psalmist does recognize sin's all-encompassing character in his life.

The confessional psalms emphasize repentance and the grace of God to forgive and restore to life. Modern scholars typically have discussed the penitential psalms as prayers offered in ceremonies of healing.[18] The association of penitence with such ceremonies makes sense in that these psalms often mention, or hint that sickness resulted from or at least accompanied sin and guilt (Ps. 6:2; 38:3-8; 51:8). The psalmist's awareness of sinfulness is manifest in descriptions of bodily affliction that arises from it. In the penitential psalms sickness and the awareness of sin are interrelated. Frequently in these penitential psalms and other psalms closely related in style and content, the psalmist describes physical pain that is connected with guilt. Psalm 51:8 (10) pleads, "Let the bones that you have crushed rejoice." Psalm 38:3 exclaims, "There is no soundness in my flesh / because of your indignation; / there is no health in my bones / because of my sin."

The psalmist may have thought of sin and sickness being linked, that God's wrath against particular sins was expressed as sickness. What is important about the bodily experience of sinfulness here, however, is that it is distinctive to the experience of the righteous, but conspicuously absent from the consciousness of the wicked. Or put another way, the righteous are so keenly aware of their sin that they are pained by it, while the wicked live in denial of sin and its consequences and experience no physical ill effects (Ps. 73:4). The contrast of the righteous and the wicked on the matter of bodily pain is striking. Ever cognizant of their unworthiness, the righteous are in agony over their sin. Psalm 102:9–10 displays well the stance of the righteous:

> For I eat ashes like bread,
>   and mingle tears with my drink,
> because of your indignation and anger;
>   for you have lifted me up and thrown me aside.

The righteous realize they are in "the depths," as Psalm 130:1 puts it. The wicked, however, are those who are "at ease" (Ps. 73:12), who live in denial of their sinful state. Concerning the impact of guilt upon the body, Psalm 73 tellingly links the soundness of the bodies of the wicked (v. 4) to their pride and arrogance (v. 6). Confession of sin is a fundamental expression of the larger mark of righteousness, namely, to stand before God as a helpless creature, seeking God as refuge and eschewing all other sources of security. As McCann says, the righteous' "happiness derives ultimately from God's forgiveness (see Ps 32:1–2) and the gift of God's faithful love (see Ps 32:10–11)."[19] In sum, the righteous are those who are fully aware of their need for God's grace, God's protection, and God's guidance. That awareness, it is fair to say, constitutes the "way" of the righteous (Ps. 1:6) and sets them apart from the wicked.

Another aspect of confession central to the life of the righteous is the awareness of the presence of God, the key issue regarding their destiny. In Psalm 51:11 (13) the psalmist pleads, "Do not cast me from your presence, / and do not take your holy spirit from me." Sinfulness has created a distance from God that leaves the righteous person disoriented. At the same time, however, the psalmist asks God to "hide your face from my sins" (v. 9 [11]), for the face of God turned toward iniquity is too much. Turning the divine countenance away from the psalmist's sin is a sign of grace.[20] But the wicked neither desire the divine presence nor fear the divine countenance.

Prayer and Vengeance: The Righteous and Their Enemies

If the prayers in the Psalter give a glimpse into the character of the righteous, as this chapter has suggested thus far, one other type of prayer must be considered, namely, those psalms in which the righteous call for God to bring vengeance on their enemies. On the surface these psalms may seem far from the character of the righteous. They do not seem to fit as the prayers of those who are humble in spirit. The examples that follow illustrate the problem.

Psalm 58 calls on God to "break the teeth in their mouths; / tear out the fangs of the young lions" (v. 6 [7]), and concludes with a picture of the righteous satisfied when vengeance is done ("they will bathe their feet in the blood of the wicked," v. 10 [11]).

Psalm 139 is often quoted for its expression of God's intimate knowledge of the believer ("I praise you, for I am fearfully and wonderfully made," v. 14), but the psalm moves to a crescendo of imprecation with words such as, "O that you would kill the wicked, O God" (v. 19).

Undoubtedly the most difficult of these psalms is Psalm 137 which laments the fall of Jerusalem and the Babylonian captivity. It ends with a troubling beatitude for those who would punish Jerusalem's attackers: "Happy shall they be who take your little ones / and dash them against the rock" (v. 9).

These psalms are often treated in the church as sub-Christian because they seem to countermand Jesus' command to love, bless, and pray for enemies (Mt. 5:43–48; Lk. 9:51–56; cf. Rom. 12:14–21). Yet no other type of psalm may be more essential for understanding who the righteous are and how they stand before God. Understood in the context of the suffering of the righteous, these vindictive psalms exemplify the honesty before God that is central to the Christian faith as well. These psalms express raw emotions and fiercely enunciate the desire for retribution. The final line in Psalm 137 is the most difficult example of such a desire. Nevertheless, when understood in the context of the righteous' suffering at the hands of the wicked, these psalms are seen more clearly as indicators of how the righteous relate to God. Several points are necessary to clarify the nature of these psalms.

First, these psalms are set "in the presence of...enemies" (Ps. 23:5). That setting gives them much in common with all the prayers that call out to God for help. The portrayal of enemies as ravenous beasts illustrates how vulnerable the righteous are to the enemies' attacks. For example, Psalm 58 describes the enemies as having "the venom of a serpent" (v. 4) and as "young lions" (v. 6), very much like the description in Psalm 22:12: "Many bulls encircle me, / strong bulls of Bashan surround me; / they open wide their mouths at me, / like a ravening and roaring lion" (see also Ps. 22:16).

The gospels of Matthew and Mark report that Jesus on the cross prayed the first line of Psalm 22. Although they do not say that he characterized those who crucified him with this animal imagery, much evidence suggests that the content of the whole psalm is meant to form the background of the crucifixion scene. In the first place, the gospel writers may suggest by Jesus' quote of Psalm 22:1 that he prayed the entire psalm since first lines of such psalms served as their titles in the ancient world.[21] Even if such complete quotation is not the intention, Psalm 22 clearly served as a kind of outline for the passion account in these two gospels. The mocking of Jesus by those who pass by (Mk. 15:25–32; Mt. 27:38–44) reflects the mocking of the righteous sufferer in Psalm 22:6-8 (7-9). (Note the shaking of the heads in both texts.)[22]

All four Gospels link Jesus on the cross to Psalm 22:18 when the soldiers cast lots for his clothes (Mt. 27:35; Mk. 15:24; Lk. 23:34b; Jn. 19:24). This makes it clear that the early church understood Jesus as the prime example of a righteous one who suffered at the hands of the wicked. That understanding of Jesus' suffering, in turn, could suggest that the New Testament authors embraced the characterization of enemies like those found in the imprecatory psalms.

A second point is that the enemies in these psalms and the wrongs the enemies perpetrate are not personal or petty. Rather, they represent wickedness on a grand, perhaps even cosmic scale. Erich Zenger thus comments on the portion of Psalm 139 that seems so offensive ("O that you would kill the wicked, O God," v. 19): "Behind verses 17–22 is not an acute threat from enemies, but the very structural violence of 'the wicked' (a collective term) who, as 'the bloodthirsty,' corrupt society and even employ religion for their purposes."[23]

Psalm 58 is a good example of a psalm that identifies the actions of the wicked with this "structural" evil. In this psalm the attendants around God's throne who are supposed to ensure justice are instead siding with the wicked. Psalm 58 begins, "Do you indeed decree what is right, you gods? / Do you judge people fairly?" (v. 1) The word translated "gods" (ʾēlem) is the subject of debate. The form in Masoretic Text means "silent," which makes little sense in the context of this psalm. The early Greek and Latin translators dealt with the word in a variety of ways that just illustrates further the difficulty.[24] Many modern scholars understand the original word to be ʾēlîm, meaning "gods," as NRSV renders. Understood this way, the term refers to the divine beings who were part of God's heavenly court and whom God assigned to ensure the well-being of particular territories. The idea appears in Psalm 82, which describes Yahweh taking his place as head of a heavenly council and calling these minor gods to task for their failure to establish justice (cf. Deut 32:8-9).

If this is what Psalm 58 intends, then the problem of the wicked is indeed significant. The gods who are charged with establishing justice and watching out for the righteous have decided instead for the wicked. The wicked, in turn, are the earthly expression of this heavenly injustice. They stand for the "principalities and powers" that plague this world (Eph. 6:12). The church has traditionally used Psalm 58 and the other imprecatory psalms to speak against sin, death, and the devil.[25] When the psalmist speaks of hating the wicked, he or she is speaking much as Paul spoke against those who oppose the way of God: "Let anyone be accursed who has no love for the Lord" (1 Cor. 16:22).

Third, these psalms also show that the righteous as they stand before the wicked recognize their dependence on God for protection and deliverance and call on God alone for help. In other words, the righteous respond to such circumstances by "seeking refuge" in God, not in their own resources. This was observed earlier in the discussion of Psalm 11. The psalmist's perspective acknowledges that God alone can ultimately deal with the wicked.

This final point has extremely important implications for understanding the meaning of the imprecatory psalms as part of the profile of the righteous. Those who pray such psalms are not perpetrators of violence. If the righteous trusted in their own abilities in their response to the wicked, they might well try to set the wicked right themselves. Instead, they trust in God alone to bring justice to the world. By doing so, the righteous avert human violence because they do not take "vengeance" upon themselves. It is left to God.

As Zenger says concerning the final words of Psalm 137, "[This] is not the song of people who have power to effect a violent change in their situation, nor is it the battle cry of terrorists."[26] Rather, it is the desperate cry of the powerless who are oppressed by the most powerful forces of the world. Zenger further suggests appropriately that Psalm 137:9's reference to Babylon's "little ones" be read as a symbolic reference to members of the royal house that has brought terror on the world.[27] Indeed, the psalm as a whole is a plea for this reign of terror to end and for the kingdom of God to appear in the world.

This understanding of the wicked in the imprecatory psalms leads to one final point: these psalms are ultimately pleas for God's justice and for God's final judgment on a world in which the poor are despoiled and the powerless trodden under the feet of the powerful. That means on the one hand that these psalms are not prayers that invite gloating over the fall of the wicked. The conclusion to Psalm 58 makes this point clear: "People will say, 'Surely there is a reward for the righteous; / surely there is a God who judges on earth'" (v. 11). The double use of "surely" ($'ak$) makes the point emphatic. In the end there is no celebration over the fall of the wicked per se.[28]

On the other hand, the righteous have faith in a God who will ultimately not tolerate the abuse of the righteous. Persecution is not viewed as something that brings God's favor, but as something God is working on bringing to an end. As Renee Girard says, these psalms "subvert the whole mythology of persecution."[29] This faith in God who desires and works for the end of the righteous' suffering in turn allows Christians to read the imprecatory psalms alongside Jesus' command to love their enemies, not in opposition to it. To love enemies and pray for those who persecute the righteous is possible because of the belief that God alone has prerogative to mete out justice; conversely, to pray for God to avenge the wrongs perpetrated by the wicked is to believe that there is a larger system of justice that, if the righteous trust in it, gives them space to love their enemies. The psalms of vengeance express one pole of this theological tension.[30]

Conclusion

This chapter has focused on the primary feature of the character of the righteous: dependence on God. Indeed, it has shown that the righteous are distinguished from the wicked mainly by their confession of helplessness; they are "poor and needy," "oppressed," and therefore they "seek refuge" in the Lord. The righteous express their dependence on God in at least two specific ways that have been explored here. Namely, they recognize their sinfulness and pray for divine forgiveness; and they plead for deliverance from enemies. In both of these ways the righteous show they understand the most fundamental aspect of relationship with God: God is creator and those who approach God are creatures.

The next chapter will show that for both the righteous and the wicked particular actions arise from their character. The righteous act in concert with God's will for the šālôm of the community. The wicked, unaware of God's will, look out for themselves, which inevitably means they act violently toward the righteous.

2

Clean Hands and Pure Hearts

The Activity of the Righteous

"For I have kept the ways of the Lord." (Ps. 18:21)

The righteous are characterized by their dependence on God in all aspects of life, as chapter 1 showed. The next chapter will show that this openness to God and reliance on God is expressed by an overwhelming desire to be in God's presence; to be near God is the destiny the righteous hope for (Ps. 73:28). In other words, the righteous are those who live by faith and who are guided and motivated by a relationship with God.

Nevertheless, the identity of the righteous contains a moral dimension. To be in right relationship with God leads naturally to right action toward others. Moreover, the Psalms make an unequivocal connection between the behavior of the righteous and their destiny.[1] Those who follow the way of the righteous, who live according to divine standards, "shall never be moved" (Ps. 15:5).

One word of caution is needed. Modern people typically separate faith and action as though they belong to different spheres of reality. According to this way of thinking, faith involves belief and operates on a mental and emotional level, while action involves activity and is essentially physical in nature. The Psalms suggest that faith includes action and, conversely, action reflects one's faith. So, although the last chapter dealt with certain types of prayers the righteous make to God, the prayers should not be placed too far from the actions of the righteous. For that reason this discussion of the activity of the righteous begins in what may seem an unlikely place: praise.

Praise is not just a way of speaking about God or to God; it is also a way of living in light of one's relationship with God. Praise is the most basic "activity" of the righteous, the action from which all else emerges.

Praise as the Activity of Righteousness

According to one creed of the Reformed tradition, praise is the "chief and highest end of humanity."[2] Appropriately, then, the Psalter speaks of praise as the activity of the righteous, for the righteous are those who understand their "chief end," their proper place before God. As Psalm 33:1 declares, "Praise befits the upright." That means, however, that praise is much more than warm words of approval given to God.[3] Indeed, praise is service to God.[4] It is the sum of all that the righteous do. To understand what praise is for the righteous requires a comprehensive understanding of praise.

Walter Brueggemann offers three key observations about praise that may contribute to a proper understanding of praise as it relates to the righteous in the Psalms:

1. Praise is an act that involves "world making,"–that is, to praise God is to envision the world in a way that may not seem obvious to everyone.[5] The righteous are called "happy" or "fortunate" even though they suffer at present. In a similar way, to praise God is to view the world for what it will become, not for what it is right now. In other words, the world is viewed with a future orientation. This is the nature of praise.
2. Praise acknowledges that God rules the world, or, as the Psalms express it, "The Lord reigns."[6] This claim, of course, is the basis for hope in the future noted in point 1. But that is not all. To acknowledge that the Lord reigns also requires the one who makes such a claim to align with God's vision for the world. Praise is intimately connected to ethics. Real praise cannot but produce action that is consistent with the reign of God.
3. Finally, praise occurs within the "matrix" of pain.[7] Suffering and hardship are the context in which praise is offered. This final point may explain why the Hebrew title of the book of Psalms is *tĕhillîm*, "praises," even though the Psalter contains many more complaints than hymns. It may also explain why Psalm 33 declares that "praise befits the upright" and why praise is not an activity of the wicked.

Praise can only be offered by those who recognize that they are in need–they are "poor" (*'anî*)–and that their good fortune, whether experienced now or merely hoped for, is (or will be) the result of God's grace.

Praise is most plainly presented as the activity of the righteous at the end of Psalm 32 (vv. 10–11) and at the beginning of Psalm 33 (vv. 1–3).

Psalm 32 is one of the so-called penitential psalms discussed in the last chapter. The psalm alternates between proclamation of the benefits of the Lord's gracious forgiveness (vv. 1–2, 10), instruction in the ways of penitence and faith (vv. 8–9, 11), and testimony by one who has approached God in confession of sin and now knows the Lord's mercy (vv. 3–7). The psalm ends with two verses that give assurance (v. 10: "steadfast love surrounds those who trust in the LORD") and call the righteous to praise God (v. 11). The praise offered appears in the matrix of pain, as Brueggemann says.

Praise involves the whole person. Three imperatives in the concluding verses of Psalm 32 make this clear. "Be glad" (*śimḥû*) may be understood as a call to feel joy internally. "Rejoice" (*gîlû*) suggests that such gladness is voiced or expressed through motion and is often associated with rituals that involve shrieking ecstatically or dancing in ecstasy.[8] If that word does not make the physical nature of praise clear, the next one–"shout" (*harnînû*)–does.[9] This sequence of terms may be a poetic way of urging the righteous to praise God from the most-inward expressions, thoughts, and emotions ("be glad") to the most-outward declarations ("shout").[10] Whatever the exact intention behind each of these terms, in the end praise is something that is enacted–spoken or performed–not just felt internally. The physical character of praise in worship, in turn, provides the beginning point for actions outside worship that are also considered praise.

Psalm 33 begins the same way Psalm 32 ended, with a call for the righteous to praise God: "Rejoice (*rannĕnû*) in the LORD, O you righteous. / Praise befits the upright" (v. 1).

This beginning of Psalm 33 that is so much like the end of Psalm 32 is probably the reason they appear side-by-side in the Psalter. Furthermore, since Psalm 33 does not have a title, it is likely that this psalm is meant to be read as a continuation of Psalm 32. In other words, what is said of praise in Psalm 32 is continued and advanced in Psalm 33. Psalm 33:2–3 goes even farther than Psalm 32:11 in describing praise as an activity. These verses imply that praise is not something that can be done by rote; rather, it requires skill, effort, and imagination.

Verse 2 includes two statements about praising God with musical instruments: "Praise the LORD with the lyre; / make melody to him with the harp of ten strings." Then verse 3 continues this call to praise with two statements that indicate praise is an activity forever being renewed and refreshed by the relationship with God. The first statement, "Sing to him a new song" does not mean that a song is to be sung that has never been sung before. Rather, as Robert Davidson says, "It calls on the congregation to express in their singing the sense of being gripped anew by the majesty and wonder of the God they worship."[11] The praise prescribed for the righteous involves a fresh appreciation for and expression of God's goodness and might.

The statement that follows implies the same awareness of God's present action for the righteous. The expression "play skillfully" (*hêṭîbû nagēn*) might better be translated "do the playing well" as Hans Joiachim-Kraus suggests.[12] The playing of stringed instruments is to be accompanied by shouts (bitrûʿâ). The praise of the righteous is something consciously created. The righteous "work at" praise and develop an ability in it.

Verses 4–5 (and the rest of the psalm) are sometimes understood as the reason praise should be offered. This section is perhaps better understood, however, as the content of the praise that verses 1–3 call forth. The word often translated "for" (Hebrew *kî*) is better rendered "indeed," or perhaps understood as the equivalent of Hebrew quotation marks. Regardless of how this word is treated, the content of praise in these verses gives a marvelous view of God and the world as the righteous envision them:

> For the word of the Lord is upright,
> and all his work is done in faithfulness.
> He loves righteousness and justice;
> the earth is full of the steadfast love of the Lord.

Verse 4 has a structure in Hebrew that enhances its message. It begins and ends with words that describe the reliability of God: "upright" (*yāšār*) and "faithfulness" (*ʾĕmûnâ*). At the center of the verse are two phrases that express what about God is upright and faithful. Namely, the "word of the Lord" and "all his work" can be counted on. It is hard to imagine a broader or bolder statement of God's character. All God says (in scripture; through prophets, priests, and sages) and all God does is evidence of God's consistent benevolence.

The next verse continues this portrait of God, but it includes the world as well. The Lord loves righteousness (*sedāqâ*) and justice (*mišpaṭ*). This statement is perhaps not surprising since other texts declare that "righteousness and justice are the foundation of his throne" (Ps. 97:3b). But the words that follow show that the righteous see the world in a way that may seem counter to reality. They declare that "the earth is full of the steadfast love (*hesed*) of the LORD." The Hebrew of verse 5b actually favors an active verb in the translation that may make the point more emphatic: "the steadfast love of the Lord fills the earth." In other words, God's *hesed* rules the world! This claim, of course, is a way of saying that "the Lord reigns." The Lord and the Lord's vision for the world are ultimately in charge and will prevail.

Who May Abide in Your Tent? Psalms 15 and 24

When understood comprehensively, then, praise can only be uttered by the righteous, by those who acknowledge that the Lord reigns. Understood in this way, praise cannot be limited to what is traditionally considered "worship." Rather, praise is the sum of the righteous' activity as well. To come before God in praise means to live as though God rules the world. Two psalms connect such praise directly with specific behavior, thus making the link between the two unmistakable.

Psalms 15 and 24 zero in on the actions of the righteous and make clear that action is inextricably bound to praise. These two psalms specifically link right action with being among worshipers who praise God. This makes clear again that praise is action and right action is praise.

Psalm 24 begins with a statement much like Psalm 33:5 ("the steadfast love of the Lord fills the earth," [author's translation]): "The earth is the LORD's and all that is in it" (v. 1). God is in control of the world. The following question about who may ascend the "holy hill" is really a question of who acknowledges this fact.

Psalms 15 and 24 both address the issue of right living because it is related to the righteousness and holiness of God. The question is, "Who shall ascend the hill of the LORD?" (Ps. 24:3a; and the similar question in Ps. 15:1b, "Who may dwell on your holy hill?").[13]

The question really has to do with who is able to praise God. The answer that follows in both psalms describes certain behavior. Close examination shows the characteristics of those permitted to enter the holy place are not so much requirements to participate in worship as they are characteristics of those who do worship "in spirit and in truth."

The necessary holiness of those allowed to ascend the holy mountain is cast in comprehensive terms that will not allow a narrow legalistic understanding of human righteousness. Psalm 24:4 answers the question of who is worthy to be in God's presence with two sweeping statements. The righteous have "clean hands and pure hearts" (v. 4a). "Hand" and "heart" refer, respectively, to exterior acts and inner motivation.[14] The verse suggests that compliance with the letter of the law must be accompanied by proper attention to the spirit of the law as well. In the pairing of these two aspects of righteousness the psalm is similar to a portion of the teachings of Jesus in the Sermon on the Mount (Mt. 5:21–48). The righteous have "clean hands" because they have "pure hearts" (Ps. 24:4).

Psalm 24:4b fills out the profile of righteous activity. Verse 4b gives a comprehensive cast to the righteous obedience, obedience ultimately grounded in relationship with God. This portion of the verse makes two statements about the righteous: they do not "lift up their souls to what is false" and they do not "swear deceitfully." Swearing deceitfully refers to faithfulness in dealing with one's neighbor. The same language of "deceit" appears in Hosea 12:8 and Micah 6:11 to refer to false weights that dishonest merchants used to cheat their customers. "Swear deceitfully" implies taking advantage of a neighbor by dishonest means. The language is thus sweeping, referring to the overall obligation to act rightly–to be fair and just–toward others. "Lift up their souls to what is false" is more oblique.

Nevertheless, it seems to point to comprehensive right action toward God. The same terms translated "lift up" (*nāsā'*) and "false" (*šāw'*) appear in the third commandment: "You shall not swear falsely by the name of the Lord your God" (Ex. 20:7, JPS). The word "false" in some other texts refers to idols (Ps. 31:7; Jer. 18:5). Therefore, this portion of Psalm 24:4 could intend to say that the righteous do not "lift up their souls" (that is, bow down in worship) to other gods. Regardless of the exact intention, it seems clear that the description of the righteous as those who do not "lift up their souls to what is false" is of one who is faithful in all ways to God.[15]

Even if the psalmist in Psalm 24:4 is not drawing on the Ten Commandments in a specific way, Psalm 24 has general parallels to the commandments. As with the Decalogue, this psalm presents right relationships in two categories: one must be right with God and with one's neighbor. Also similar to the Ten Commandments, Psalm 24 portrays the right actions of the righteous as actions that arise from a "pure heart." Indeed, just as the commandments conclude with a requirement of the heart ("you shall not covet;" Ex. 20:17; Deut. 5:21), so Psalm 24:4 introduces the requirements for righteousness as a matter of internal purity.[16]

In other words, Psalm 24 and the Decalogue suggest that ethics begins with dependence on God, not on adherence to a legal code. The order of these two dimensions of righteousness is essential for understanding the activity of the righteous. Their right action is always based on and grows out of relationship. Righteousness can never be obtained in the abstract. The characterization of the righteous in relationships to God and neighbor also shows that the righteous are those who are not focused primarily on themselves and their own desires. Rather, they are open to God and God's reign on the one hand, and to the needs of others, to the well-being of the community, on the other hand. This openness to instruction (from God) and need (that they see in others) separates them from the wicked, who are most concerned about their own possessions and power.

Psalm 15 presents a more extensive description of the activity of the righteous, but the description in this psalm, as in Psalm 24, "is a picture, not a prescription."[17] The specific points of conduct illustrate the righteous' overall orientation to God that produces right actions toward neighbor. Also as in Psalm 24, Psalm 15 presents the activity of the righteous in terms of outward acts coupled with inward motivation.

Psalm 15:8 introduces those able to "dwell on your holy hill" (v. 1b) as those who "walk blamelessly," "do what is right," and "speak the truth from their heart." The first two statements describe exterior acts in general terms. The word "blamelessly" translates a Hebrew term that is sometimes rendered "with integrity." The term is the one that describes the character of Job, for example (Job 1:1; cf. Prov. 2:7). "Blamelessly" refers to a type of life that is consistent and complete, in every way in line with God's intentions. The second statement, "do what is right" is similar to the first and qualifies it further. The righteous person maintains the order of the world God established by means of actions that uphold that order.[18] The final description in verse 2, however, makes clear that the right actions the psalmist has in mind do not amount to rote adherence to a legal standard. Rather, they grow out of the meditations of the heart.[19] In other words, the person Psalm 15 describes is similar the person portrayed in the first psalm, one whose "delight is in the law of the LORD" and who will "meditate" on the law day and night (Ps. 1:2). Obedience follows devotion and submission to God's direction.

The specific behaviors of the righteous that are listed in Psalm 15, though illustrative and not comprehensive, nevertheless give insight into the orientation of the Psalms toward right action. The acts that are named all have in common a concern for the well-being of the community on various levels. For example, concerning the near neighbor, perhaps those in one's own extended family with whom a person has close contact, the righteous person does not slander or participate in such destructive activity (v. 3). The point of the verse is not that slander would be acceptable against a distant relative; rather, it is meant to speak against the type of injustice that would typically be committed against someone in one's own family circle.

Concerning the wider community, the righteous person despises the wicked, but will "honor those who fear the LORD" (v. 4a). The term translated "wicked" is not the common term, $rāšā\,^c$; rather, it is a word that could be rendered, "one who is rejected or despised" ($nim\,^{\!\!\!,}ās$). In Psalm 15:4 the term appears in contrast with "those who fear the LORD." What the verse is saying, therefore, is that the righteous person is one who honors those who are honorable and does not honor those who do not deserve honor. The righteous person stands outside the influence of the wicked, those who act in ways that bring divine rejection, but stands with and under the influence of those who submit to God's rule. This verse is similar to Psalm 1:1, which says the righteous person does "not follow the advice of the wicked, or take the path that sinners tread, or sit in the seat of scoffers."[20]

The final description of righteous activity in Psalm 15 (v. 5) is the most specific, but it has broad implications for the community. In Hebrew the first word in the verse is the general term for capital ($kesep;$ "silver"). That is appropriate since both parts of the verse focus on the proper use of money. The righteous "do not lend money at interest" and "do not take a bribe against the innocent." The first description may seem quite strange to people who regularly receive offers to borrow money, all at interest, and who likely have more than one outstanding loan at any given time to maintain a "First World" lifestyle. But the world that gave rise to this sketch of the righteous was agrarian; money was rare, as was the necessity of borrowing money. Those who sought to borrow were typically in desperate circumstances and could be easily abused. For that reason those who loaned money were to think of themselves as giving assistance (Ex. 22:24; Lev. 25:36; Deut.

23:20). Those who loaned at interest, by contrast, were what today would be termed loan sharks. To enrich themselves, they took advantage of the misfortune of those seeking a loan, sometimes sending the unfortunate borrower into slavery to pay the debt.

Seen in this light, this first description of the righteous' economic practices is similar in severity to the second: they "do not take a bribe against the innocent." This final description is general, and the implications of taking a bribe are not spelled out. Deuteronomy 27:25 uses similar language, however, to link taking a bribe with shedding "innocent blood." This passage may have in mind a judge who takes money in exchange for a guilty verdict on one who killed another by accident, thus permitting a kinsman (an "avenger of blood") to seek revenge (see Deut. 19:10).[21] Whatever the description in Psalm 15:5 has in mind specifically, it seems from these other references that it is likely a matter of life and death. The one who takes the bribe has no concern for community health, but only for his own economic advancement. The righteous are not so. They are in accord with the righteousness of God, which ensures the health and well-being of the whole society. As a result of such righteous activity, Psalm 15 declares, they "shall never be moved" (v. 5b).

The Activity of the Righteous and the Shelter of Yahweh's Wings

This chapter thus far has treated the activity of the righteous as something that grows out of their faith in God. Chapter 1 examined the various ways the righteous express that faith, noting especially that the righteous declare they "seek refuge" in the Lord. Before going further, it seems helpful to show how these two ideas are interrelated. Namely, the activity of the righteous shows they align themselves with God's desire to create community well-being, and their activity is part of God's creative, justice-establishing efforts. The essential connection between the two may be observed in Ruth 2:12, which includes the language of refuge to describe Ruth's attempts to secure life for her and her mother-in-law. The verse comes after Ruth entered the field of Boaz to pick up grain his reapers left behind (2:1–7). This practice of gleaning was a form of charity extended to destitute people such as Naomi and Ruth (Lev. 19:9–10; Deut. 24:19). In the story, the two women are literally "poor." The laws about gleaning were in place to protect them (Lev. 19:9–10): "When you reap the harvest of your land, you shall not reap to the very edges of your field, or gather the gleanings of your harvest. You…shall leave them for the poor and the alien."

When Boaz meets Ruth in the field, he is aware of her great efforts to provide for Naomi and how she placed herself on the mercy of Israelite society. He responds to her by saying, "May the Lord reward you for your deeds, and may you have a full reward from the Lord, the God of Israel, under whose wings you have come for refuge!" (Ruth 2:12). The word translated "come for refuge" (*laḥăsôt*) is a form of the same verb (*ḥāsâ*) that appears frequently in the Psalms to express the righteous' desire to find protection in God.

The implication of Boaz' words, therefore, is that Ruth's future remains in the Lord's hands. But that future—thus, the Lord's refuge—in this case depends on Boaz and people like him who cooperate with the divine efforts to leave grain in his field for Ruth to collect. But there is more. The word rendered "wings" (of the Lord) is a form of the same word (*kānāp*) that occurs later in Ruth 3:9 when Ruth lies down beside Boaz and asks him to spread his "cloak" over her. Boaz does as Ruth asks, of course, thus providing "refuge" for Ruth and Naomi from their desperate economic circumstances.

The story of Ruth illustrates an important point about the activity of the righteous. Though it does not exhaust God's provision of refuge, it is an important element of it. The righteous live in symbiotic relationship with the protecting presence of God. As the last chapter showed, the righteous seek refuge in the Lord; they trust in God alone as their protector and guide. However, in relationship with the One who provides that refuge, the righteous also help to make it real for themselves and for others. The activity of the righteous is an essential part of the righteous' faith. Their righteousness is not about trying to achieve moral purity as much as it an attempt to make God's justice a reality where they live.

Profile of the Wicked

Having examined some of the features of the lifestyle of the righteous, it seems appropriate to conclude with some observations on the character of the wicked. While the righteous act in ways that support the health of the community, the wicked do the opposite. They look out for themselves at the expense of the community. Their activity goes directly against the righteous and the way they live.

As observed already, the righteous may be delineated as those who praise God, with praise being understood comprehensively as something that encompasses all of life. Conversely, the wicked are those who do not praise God. Praise emerges from a perceived need, but the wicked have an overwhelming sense of self-sufficiency. Instead of praising God, "they flatter themselves," as Psalm 36:2 puts it. This self-flattery inevitably leads to violent and destructive action. Theologian Michael Welker gives a helpful perspective on the connection between self-praise and sinfulness. He links the roots of sin to God's statement in Genesis 3:22 that the first humans had "become like one of us, knowing good and evil." Though knowledge of good and evil has at times been cast as a desirable sign of enlightenment, Welker rightly sees that the author of Genesis has another point in mind—namely, that becoming like God is delusional. He writes, "They fancy themselves free, superior, secure, powerful, indeed equal to God. They think they have their life fully in hand and under control."[22]

This is precisely what the Psalms say about the wicked. Their sense of self-sufficiency is not just delusional. It is destructive to human life. Indeed, it is the source of evil the wicked perpetrate upon the righteous.[23]

This characterization of nonpraise indicates that the wicked live as though the Lord is not in charge of the world. They do not seek God's presence, and thus they do not praise God either. The result of such nonpraise is oppression and violence.

Psalm 52 provides a good example of such a person who exhibits self-sufficiency that leads to wickedness. This psalm begins with a description of one who boasts of evil deeds. The person is called a "mighty one" (*haggibbôr*) by NRSV, but the Hebrew word has the sarcastic connotation of "big shot" (v. 1 [2]).[24] The person being described thinks too much of himself. Accordingly, the psalmist describes him as one who "would not take / refuge in God, / but trusted in abundant riches, / and sought refuge in wealth" (v. 7 [8]). The description of the wicked not seeking refuge in God and not trusting in the Lord is the polar opposite of the righteous, who are characterized by their dependence on God.

The main concern of the Psalms is that this stance toward God leads to the wicked's oppression of the righteous. Psalm 52:7 (9) hints at how the two are related. The translation, "sought refuge in wealth" (consonants bhwno) given above is from the Syriac version of this psalm. The primary Hebrew manuscript (MT) has a word, very close in appearance, that means "destruction" (consonants bhwto). The Hebrew text may be the result of scribal error, as the NRSV translators conclude. Nevertheless, the ideas behind the two readings are closer than they seem at first glance. Not trusting in God (v. 7a), in the psalmist's view, naturally leads to violence. In other words, trust in riches might well be related to the performance of destructive acts.

As the Psalter depicts the wicked's violence that emerges from their sense of self-sufficiency, it depicts their wicked actions as the polar opposite of the community-building acts of the righteous in Psalms 15 and 24. First, whereas the righteous "do not slander with their tongue" (Ps. 15:3), the wicked are said to threaten the righteous with their speech. The wicked have "lying lips" (Ps. 31:18); "they make their tongue sharp as a snake's, / and under their lips is the venom of vipers" (Ps. 140:3); they are always "plotting destruction" with a tongue "like a sharp razor" (Ps. 52:2).

The exact nature or goal of the injurious speech is not always certain. In some cases it seems clear that "lying lips" of the wicked break the ninth commandment, "You shall not bear false witness against your neighbor" (Ex. 20:16; Deut. 5:20; 19:15–21). Psalm 109 seems to reflect such a setting. As the psalm opens, the righteous person gives testimony to the plots of the wicked against him: "For wicked and deceitful mouths are opened against me, / speaking against me with lying tongues" (v. 2). Scholars debate whether verses 6–19 are the words of the psalmist's accusers (note that the words are spoken against "him," a singular reference) or the curse of the psalmist against those who oppose him (note the Hebrew does not have "they say" at the beginning of verse 6, as some translations render).[25] If the former is correct, the psalmist in these verses recalls how the wicked plotted against him, saying, "Appoint a wicked man against him; / let an accuser stand on his right. / When he is tried, let him be found guilty" (vv. 6–7a).

The wicked also use the market as an instrument of evil. Psalm 15:5 includes in its outline of requirements for entry into the house of God not lending money at interest (Deut. 23:19–20). Acting faithfully in matters of lending and trade is an essential feature of righteousness, a reflection of one's dependence on God. In ancient Israel's tribal culture the family gave access to the economy. Therefore, the economically deprived are identified not only as "poor and needy" (Ps. 37:14), but also, and especially, as widow, orphan, and stranger. These terms describe those who had lost their place, or never had a place, in the basic patriarchal unit, the "household of the father" (*bêt ʾāb*).[26] Such individuals existed on the edge of life and were to have extended to them compassion and generosity (Deut. 24:17–22). In opposition to this divine mandate, however, the Psalms declare that the wicked "kill the widow and the stranger, / they murder the orphan" (Ps. 94:6; cf. 109:16). That is, they take advantage of the most vulnerable members of society for their own advancement.

Psalm 10 deals almost entirely with this aspect of the wicked. "Greedy for gain" (v. 3), the wicked "stealthily watch for the helpless; / they lurk in secret like a lion in its covert; / they lurk that they may seize the poor" (vv. 8b–9a). Later the psalm identifies the "helpless" specifically as the widow and orphan as it calls God to rescue those oppressed by the wicked (vv. 14, 18). The wicked oppose the very foundational tenets of Israel's system of justice and compassion. Their behavior is "anti-social" on the largest scale possible in that they attempt to undercut that which makes for a healthy society to prosper themselves.

All the actions of the wicked described thus far could be classified as violence. But the wicked are said to participate in violence in the more narrow sense of physical assault. The psalmist describes the wicked as those who seek to do physical harm to those who depend upon God. The Psalter gives three prominent nuances to this image. Some references are clearly drawn from the *hunt,* either by humans of animals (Ps. 57:6; 140:5) or animals with their prey (Ps. 59:14–15). Others are derived from situations of *ambush* set by robbers. Still other images come from the *battlefield.* Regardless of which image appears, each of these depicts the wicked as those on the prowl, as those who stalk the righteous to kill them. In other words, they are depicted as against life itself.

Conclusion

This chapter has suggested that the actions of the righteous as compared with those of the wicked stem from their praise of God. The righteous praise

God because they recognize that God rules the world and that they stand in need of God's help. The wicked, by contrast, do not praise God; instead, they act as though they are self-sufficient and autonomous. This difference in how the two groups stand before God, in turn, shapes the way they treat others. The righteous, aware of God's sovereignty, align themselves with God's efforts to bring šālôm. Hence, they are oriented toward the needs of the community. The wicked, however, are only concerned with their own well-being. Since they are oriented only toward themselves, they inevitably take advantage of others. Hence, the way the righteous and wicked live is tied to their acceptance or denial of the claim that "the Lord reigns."

3

To Be Near God

The Destiny of the Righteous

"It is good to be near God." (Ps. 73:28)

The last two chapters explored the faith and activity of those called righteous in the Psalms. Chapter 1 showed that the main feature of the righteous' faith is their dependence on God, particularly their reliance on God to protect them from the wicked. Chapter 2 noted that the actions of the righteous toward others are such that promote the well-being of the community in contrast to the actions of the wicked, characterized by self-promotion and selfish ambition.

This chapter turns to the next logical subject concerning the righteous: the nature of their destiny. What future do the righteous expect and hope for? At times people assume that the Psalter's confident declarations of the future of the righteous and the punishment of the wicked amounts to a simple retribution theology—the righteous will be rewarded in tangible ways in exchange for their faithfulness. But the Psalms will not allow such a simplistic view. Indeed, the Psalms themselves testify to the struggle of the righteous to believe they are favored by God in light of the current well-being of the wicked (Ps. 73).

Some of the promises to the righteous were likely reinterpreted, in light of the apocalyptic eschatology in books such as Daniel, as promises for vindication beyond this life.[1] But the destiny of the righteous is not just a future hope. Indeed, the Psalms cast the destiny of the righteous mainly in terms of the righteous' relationship with God in the present, specifically in terms of the righteous' desire to be in God's presence.[2] In a real sense the fulfillment of the righteous' destiny "is not so much a reward as a result of life's connection with the source of life."[3] Indeed, the righteous' faith does not operate as a *quid pro quo*. Just like the righteous' faith and the righteous' activity, the righteous' destiny centers on their relationship with God. This chapter will examine portions of four psalms that illustrate this point. Three of the psalms discussed below show clearly that the primary benefit the righteous enjoy as a result of their faith is "being near God." Even Psalm 37, which refers to a tangible reward (possessing the land) for the righteous speaks of that reward in tandem with the life of faith and dependence on God. That is the destiny of the righteous.

I Shall Dwell in the House of the Lord: Psalm 23

Psalm 23 includes two clear statements about the righteous' future. Both statements are directly related to the idea of the righteous being in God's presence. This subject (of being near God) is most clear in the final verse of the psalm: "I shall dwell in the house of the LORD / my whole life long" (v. 6b). But as the following discussion will show, the idea of being near God is really the subject of the entire psalm.

The first portion of Psalm 23:1 contains perhaps the most famous words in the Bible: "The LORD is my shepherd." Though quite well known, these words communicate a radical declaration of faith that should make everyone who says them uncomfortable. The proclamation of the Lord as shepherd is essentially a claim that God has been chosen over all other sources of guidance and security.[4] The second half of verse 1 then states the outcome of this choice: "I shall not want" (JPS, "I shall not lack a thing"). The implication of Psalm 23:1, therefore, is that because the psalmist chose the Lord, all needs are provided.[5] Verse 1b could be taken to mean that God fulfills all desires (a promise of wealth and material prosperity), or that God provides what is absolutely essential (implying that not much is really needed). Both of these interpretations really miss the point. The verse seems to say, rather, "For the psalmist, God is the only necessity of life."[6] In other words, "I shall not want" is really a declaration about the essential nature of being near God.

Ron E. Tappy offers an interesting interpretation of Psalm 23:1b that helps clarify that Psalm 23:1b is concerned mainly about being in God's presence. Tappy proposes that the best translation of this portion of the verse is, "I shall not be absent (from the Lord)" rather than, "I shall not want."[7] He bases his rendering in part on the fact that the verb *ḥāsar* ("to lack") in Psalm 23:1b does not have an object, and yet, most English translations render *ḥāsar* as though it does.[8] Those who favor the translation, "I shall not want" sometimes compare the occurrence of the verb in Psalm 23:1 to that in Deuteronomy 2:7, in which Moses reminds Israel that though they wandered in the wilderness, they "have not lacked *a thing*" (NASB). (See also Ps. 34:10b, "Those who seek the LORD lack no *good thing*.")

When the verb appears without an object, however, it typically communicates the idea that the verb's subject (in this case, the psalmist, "I") is "lacking" rather than the idea that the subject is in need of something. For example, in Genesis 8:3 and 5, the term refers to the waters of the flood that have receded (the waters are "lacking"). There is still more evidence for Tappy's translation in texts from the closely related Ugaritic language.[9] For example, in one story about the god Baal and his sister Anat, the term refers to Baal being dead, thus "missing among humankind."[10]

With these points in mind, Tappy proposes that Psalm 23:1b intends to declare a desire to be always in the presence of God.[11] This interpretation further makes sense in light of what verses 2–5 say about the psalmist's relationship with God. Given the close association of the verb *hāsar* with death in other writings, Psalm 23:1b probably provides the key to the claim that the Lord "restores my soul" (v. 3a) and also to the confidence that the psalmist has passed through the "darkest valley" (v. 4a).[12] The psalmist's escape from the dangerous valley is due, after all, to the protecting presence of the Lord ("you are with me," v. 4b).[13]

Psalm 23 concludes with another declaration of desire to be in God's presence: "I shall dwell in the house of the [Lord] / my whole life long" (v. 6b). In the house of the Lord the psalmist will have all that is needed for life: "goodness" (*tôb*) and "mercy" (*hesed*). The "house of the LORD" likely refers to the temple in Jerusalem.[14] Because of the great provisions provided in this place, Tappy suggests that "house" is meant to connote "household." The background to "house of the LORD," he argues, is the notion of God as an adopting father. Images of shepherd (vv. 1–4) and host (v. 5) culminate finally in this portrait of the Lord in verse 6. In other words, the psalmist in Psalm 23 is not only shepherded and protected by God; he or she has become part of the family of God as well.

Such familial language and imagery, of course, appears throughout the Bible (Jn. 14:2, 18), but its intended impact is often not recognized by people in industrial societies that emphasize career choices over family and clan identity. In the Old Testament world, however, to be without an extended family was to be without an identity and also without the basic provisions of life. What Tappy is proposing is that Psalm 23 has such a desperate family-less situation in mind. God adopts the one who has no family and provides shelter and protection. As a member of God's household, the psalmist is now due an inheritance as well. The inheritance in turn gives a permanent place in God's presence. (See below the discussion of Ps. 73:26; God is the psalmist's "portion.")[15] The main provision God gives is God's own self, known in this case in the "house of the LORD" (v. 6b).

Good to Be Near God: Psalm 73

Psalm 23 portrays through its rich imagery the destiny of the righteous as being in God's presence. Psalm 73 makes this point explicit in its words.

This psalm expresses the need to find the "good" (Ps. 73:1, 27), just as Psalm 23 spoke with confidence that "goodness" is found in God's presence (the term is the same in both psalms, *tôb*). Psalm 73, also like Psalm 23, speaks of God's presence providing an inheritance, the psalmist's "portion" (v. 26).

Psalm 73 begins with a pronouncement: "Surely God is good to Israel, / to those who are pure in heart" (v. 1, NIV). As noted in the introduction, this opening line is spoken by an individual whose experience with the wicked and their prosperity represents the suffering of Israel. Psalm 73 raises the question of when the righteous will know the good that is promised them. But as the psalmist wrestles with this question, he or she seems to change the thinking about what the good is. Indeed, at the end of the psalm the psalmist concludes that, though there will come a day when God will reverse the present fortunes of righteous and wicked, he or she already knows the good since knowing the good means knowing God (v. 28).

The psalm has three main sections (vv. 1–12, 13–17, 18–28), marked off in each case at the beginning by a Hebrew emphatic particle (ʾak) sometimes translated "truly" (as in vv. 1 and 18). In the first division, the psalmist testifies to being tortured by the realization that the wicked prosper. Verse 3 sums up the problem: "For I was envious of the arrogant; / I saw the prosperity of the wicked."

The word "prosperity" here translates the Hebrew term, *šālôm*. Frequently rendered "peace," this word has a range of meaning that often defies the ability of translators and interpreters to capture its proper nuance in a particular context. What is clear, however, is that the Western conception of peace can easily mislead us into reducing *šālôm* to friendly relations. To be sure, the word can have that connotation (Ps. 28:3; 120:6–7), but even when it does, it carries a richer meaning than simply the absence of war or conflict. Indeed, in most contexts the word has to do with wholeness, fulfillment, and completion.[16] In Psalm 73 *šālôm* seems to point to a comprehensive wholeness that includes physical well-being (v. 4), acclaim in the community (v. 10), and wealth (v. 12). All of these features of the life of the wicked, as that life appears presently, are expected to characterize the life of the righteous. Their destiny is *šālôm*.

Verses 4–12 portray the prosperity of the wicked in as comprehensive a way as possible. Mays appropriately describes this section as a "verbal cartoon" of those who are *not* upright in heart.[17] Their prosperity is manifest in physical (v. 4), economic (v. 12), and social success (v. 10). Their arrogance in turn finds expression in the misuse of their tongues both to threaten the righteous with false accusation and violence (v. 8) and to defy God (v. 11).

The next division of the psalm (vv. 13–17) reflects on the apparent futility of maintaining a pure heart. If the wicked know *šālôm*, what reason is there to "have kept my heart clean / and washed my hands in innocence" (v. 13)? But the psalmist does not give in to such cynicism. Instead, the struggle with the problem continues until the psalmist goes "into the sanctuary of God; / then I perceived their end" (v. 17). The word translated "sanctuary" here is unusual in that it is a plural term (*miqdĕšîm*). Given the accompanying references to being "near God" and "seeking refuge in God" (v. 28) in that place, however, it seems that the location of great insight is the temple in Jerusalem.[18] In the temple, with the righteous who gather for worship, the psalmist sees the end of the wicked; the justice of God comes into view.

Verses 18–28 then present the insight gained in the sanctuary. The wicked will be swept away, the psalmist is assured (vv. 18–20). But the insight gained from this "vision" is not so much that the wicked will be punished, but that the righteous will be kept in God's presence. In the end the psalmist affirms the opening claim of faith. The word "good" occurs in the last verse (v. 28) just as it did in the first. But the "good" the psalmist speaks of in conclusion is "to be near God." This "being near" may have something to do with the psalmist being part of the worshiping community, with being in the sanctuary where the end of the wicked became clear, but not necessarily.[19] The two words translated as "being near" (*qirbâ*) and "God" stand in genitival relationship. In English the ambiguity of the construction might be communicated by the translation, "nearness of God." Such a rendering could be taken to mean that God has drawn near to the psalmist or that the psalmist has drawn near to God. The latter could be accomplished by the psalmist's visit to the temple. There is much to suggest, however, that the former interpretation is best here. Verses 23–24 emphasize God's initiative on the psalmist's behalf. God alone guides and saves.[20] Whatever the connotation of the phrase, it is clear that "being near God" is equivalent to "[making]…GOD my refuge" (v. 28). In other words, the real reward for the faithful is in knowing God as God. Putting trust in the right place, "seeking refuge" in God, provides the experience of goodness and *šālôm* that will never be known by those far from God (v. 27). They indeed will perish. It cannot be otherwise, for to know God as God is to live.

In verse 25 the psalmist speaks of God as destiny and reward in the most radical terms: "Whom have I in heaven but you? / And there is nothing on earth that I desire other than you." Verse 26 speaks in language that recalls the experience of the Levites in land distribution (Num. 18:10; Deut. 10:9; 12:12). They would not receive a parcel of land like the other tribes. Instead, the Lord would be their "portion." With this statement, the psalmist makes clear that the greatest reward or destiny, is the Lord himself.

The Righteous Shall Inherit the Land: Psalm 37

So far this chapter has made the point that the destiny of the righteous in the Psalms is mainly the state of being near God, of depending on God. Psalm 37, however, speaks of the righteous' future numerous times in concrete terms that may seem to contradict this point. It also may seem to run counter to Christian ideas about the benefits of righteousness. In this psalm the possession of the land and the realization of its blessings is the primary point of division between righteous and wicked. Declarations that the righteous shall "live in the land" or "inherit the land" appear four times in Psalm 37 to draw attention to this feature of God's provision for those who submit to divine rule (vv. 3, 11, 22, 29).

The problem for many Christians is that the concrete nature of this promise may seem to exemplify a notion of retribution that the New Testament spiritualizes and perhaps rejects altogether. W. D. Davies argues that the New Testament alters this interest in land by casting the inheritance of the righteous as something boundless and eternal.[21] He notes specifically that Matthew 5:5 ("the meek...will inherit the earth," taken from Ps. 37:11) speaks of "the earth" broadly, not only as the whole inhabited sphere, but also as a glorified earth of the eschaton.[22] Given this evidence, Davies is certainly right that the New Testament moves away from the focus on literal divisions of land as a sign of God's blessings. In contrast, Psalm 37 probably reflects a time in the post-exilic period in Israel when the literal repossession of land and redistribution of land were contentious issues and when land possession was thought to be a sign of God's favor upon the faithful within Israel.

In light of the emphasis on possessing the land in Psalm 37, it is tempting to caricature the view of the destiny of the righteous in the Psalter (and the Old Testament) as purely material, unlike the New Testament which views it as spiritual. A close reading of this psalm, however, shows that land possession as a sign of God's favor is not simply a matter of occupying territory. The psalm does emphasize actual inheritance of property, but the real "reward" comes through a particular experience on the land and a particular stance before God. The righteous and wicked are not so much divided by land possession itself as by the realization of the intended blessings of the land, blessings that only come to "the meek" (Ps. 37:11; cf. Mt. 5:5).[23]

Psalm 37 begins with an admonition to the righteous not to worry about the wicked or to be "envious of the wrongdoers," for they will quickly pass away (vv. 1-2). Verse 3a gives instructions in how to live ("trust in the LORD, and do good"), which verse 3b follows with two imperatives that indicate the benefits for the righteous: "live in the land" and "enjoy security." NRSV connects the two parts of the verse with a causative "so," which gives the impression that the righteous trust in God in order to "live in the land." Such a rendering, however, can lead easily to a focus on the reward of the righteous, something the psalm does not seem to intend.

Psalm 37 is spoken at a time when the wicked are prospering. In that setting, the psalmist looks forward to the time in the future when "the wicked shall be cut off" (v. 9a). The psalm is an attempt to deal with the present reality–the wicked "prosper in their way" (v. 7aβ)–with the belief that "the Lord laughs at the wicked, / for he knows their day is coming" (v. 13, NIV). In other words, the psalm is about a future hope that God will set the expected destiny of the righteous and the wicked in place.

The emphasis in Psalm 37 on the future gives an important cast to the message about the destiny of the righteous. As McCann observes, "To live eschatologically means not only to live *for* the future but also to live *by* the future."[24] In other words, Psalm 37 does not just encourage an expectation, but also urges a particular type of life in light of that expectation. Indeed, the psalm is dominated by imperatives that command the righteous to live by faith: "Do not fret" (v. 1); "trust in the LORD" (v. 3); "take delight in the LORD" (v. 4); "commit your way to the LORD; / trust in him" (v. 5); "be still before the LORD, and wait patiently for him" (v. 7). Trusting God does not so much produce security as it is security itself.

The manner in which the righteous are rewarded for their faith is clarified in part by the word rendered "security" in verse 3. The Hebrew term is *'ĕmûnâ,* a word used most often in the Psalms to speak of God's faithfulness (Ps. 40:11; 88:12; 100:5). If this is the correct understanding of the term here, it implies that those addressed by the Psalm are to "enjoy" the provisions of God that flow from God's faithfulness to his promises. As some interpreters point out, it is possible that in Psalm 37:3 this term refers to faithfulness that is urged upon the righteous; if that is the intended meaning, then the righteous are not being told to "enjoy security," but to "observe faithfulness." This interpretation is possible because the term often translated "enjoy" is the common word for "see" (Hebrew *rā'â*). According to this line of reasoning, therefore, the term is used figuratively in this verse; it refers to "observing" or "maintaining" faithfulness.[25]

Although this interpretation is possible, it seems unlikely. The word in question rarely (perhaps never) carries such a figurative meaning, but it does have the sense of "enjoy" in some texts (1 Sam. 16:19; another term *šāmar,* meaning "observe" typically is used to communicate such an idea). Therefore, it seems best to understand verse 3 as saying that the righteous will know God's faithfulness in his promises concerning the land. The land will be "safe pasture" for those who trust in the Lord (as NIV translates). While the land is the tangible resource from which security comes, God is the one who provides that security; and it is only available to those who place themselves in God's care.

Given the close relationship between trusting in God and experiencing security, it is not surprising that Psalm 37:3 begins with the word *bātaḥ,* "trust," and ends with *'ĕmûna,* "security." The divine origins of security as delineated above may be illuminated further by considering the word rendered "trust" in more detail. The most common use of *bātaḥ* is to denote reliance or dependence on someone or something. Some occurrences of the term, however, communicate an inner certainty, a *feeling* of security that arises from that dependent state. For example, Psalm 27:3 declares, "Though an army encamp against me, / my heart shall not fear; / though war rise up against me, / yet I will be confident (*bōteăḥ*)." In cases like this, the key issue for translation and interpretation is whom or what is trusted. If, as in the example just cited, the Lord is the source of protection, then *bāṭaḥ* is translated "be confident," "rest secure," or the like (Ps. 16:9). If, however, the presumed security rests on some other source, whether it be confidence in one's wisdom or in human military capacity, the term is translated "be at ease" in the sense of naïve overconfidence (Isa. 32:11).

The point is that true security for the righteous is not something that can be attained through the accumulation of material goods, through the acquisition of power, or by possession of the land. Security is God's gift and comes from God's faithfulness. The act of trust itself cannot *produce* security. Although the Psalms urge human faithfulness (in Ps. 37:3 "trust" and "do good") and trust in God is necessary for security, trust is not a receptor that allows the righteous to receive security; trust is, in a sense, the reward itself.

Verse 11 expresses the second promise of blessing that comes from the land. This verse is most famous because it is the source from which Jesus draws when he says, "Blessed are the meek, for they will inherit the earth" (Mt. 5:5; here the Greek term *kosmos* probably has the broad meaning "earth," since Matthew could well have used another expression, "holy land," which was common; Hebrew *'ereṣ* seems to refer more narrowly to the land).

"*Meek*" in Ps 37:11 translates a common word in the Psalms (*'ănāwîm*) that sometimes indicates a social status. This class of individuals is poor in the figurative sense of being completely at the mercy and disposal of God. The promise to them in Psalm 37:11 comes in two parts. The first segment declares, similar to Jesus' saying, that "the meek shall inherit the land" (v. 11a). "Inherit" is the first and primary term that indicates something significant is at stake in the difference between the righteous and the wicked. This word translates the Hebrew *yāraš*, a term that means simultaneously "possess" and "dispossess." The word appears in the Pentateuch in promises that God will "drive out" the Canaanites to give Israel the land (Num. 21:32; Deut. 2:12). This term does not merely carry the sense of "inherit," as of property that passes from parent to child in an ordered and benign way. It also communicates the idea that if someone possesses the land, someone else loses the opportunity to do so. In this case the righteous possess, the wicked do not. But, as in verse 3, the real issue here is not so much possession of the land itself but the realization of promises that go with it.

The second half of verse 11 says the meek "delight themselves in abundant prosperity." "Prosperity" here translates the word *šālôm*. In Psalm 37:11 the term relates to the full realization of the benefits of the land. It may be helpful in understanding the meaning of *šālôm* here to recall that the same word appears in Psalm 73:3 in which the psalmist complains, "I saw the prosperity (šālôm) of the wicked." The context of Psalm 73 suggests the psalmist saw the wicked being fulfilled in every way, with health, physical safety, and abundant economic wealth, which would have included the presence of children and a large extended family. One should imagine the meek delighting themselves in this sense of šālôm in Psalm 37:11.

The notion that šālôm is reserved for the righteous is expressed in a particularly pointed way in verse 37, though the meaning of the verse is disputed. Most modern translations read close to NRSV: "Mark the blameless, and behold the upright, / for there is posterity for the peaceable." The translators take the first part of the verse as an injunction to look at or take account of the "blameless" and "upright." These two descriptive words, *blameless* and *upright*, are synonyms of ṣaddîq, "righteous." Both terms communicate character in terms of honesty and integrity (note, for example, the prominence of the first term, *tam*, in Job 1–2). Although it is possible to argue that the Hebrew text is flawed and that these words should be read as adjectives, thus as marks of character to be maintained (with the verbs being read figuratively as "keep" and "observe"), there is no reason to do so.[26]

Verse 37a makes good sense as translated. That is not the case with the second half of the verse, however. The translation "peaceable" renders two words, the term for "man," followed by šālôm. Although the two terms may stand in relation to each other, meaning something like "person of peace," that usage of the two words would be quite odd here. Other occurrences of these two words in such a relationship typically connote the meaning "friend" (Jer. 20:10; 38:22).[27] Since the "man" in Psalm 37:37b refers to the blameless and upright in Psalm 37:37a, it seems best to understand the words "man" and šālôm as separate in this case. Thus, the end of the verse might be better translated, "the end of [such] a person is šālôm." In other words, this verse seems to affirm that šālôm naturally follows after and eventually meets up with the righteous. Whether this is the intended meaning of Psalm 37:37 or not, it seems appropriate to think of the fate of the righteous as characterized by šālôm, given the broad and positive meaning of that term. The security of the righteous is known through the experience of šālôm and is characterized by all that word implies: wholeness and harmony, peace and prosperity, completion and contentment.

The picture of the destiny of the righteous that Psalm 37 paints deserves further comment if it is not to be misunderstood as an ancient version of present-day health and wealth religion. This chapter has tried to draw the promises of Psalm 37 concerning the land and the prosperity of the righteous close to the promise in Matthew 5:5 that "the meek…will inherit the earth." But some distance remains between them. It seems that Psalm 37 promises the righteous a tangible reward in this life, not a spiritualized reward in the Messianic age.

Two observations on Psalm 37, however, put these promises in proper perspective. First, the psalm is speaking to people who at present are oppressed (vv. 12, 14, 32, 35) by the wicked. The psalmist's concern, therefore, is not with the acquisition of wealth, but with God's justice. In such a context there is no need to apologize for dealing with tangible realities. As one writer says concerning this aspect of Psalm 37, "The problem is that the rich have seized the earth and are not permitting the rest of the population to live."[28] The overarching promise of the psalm is expressed in verse 28: "For the LORD loves justice; / he will not forsake his faithful ones." Acquisition of wealth is a by-product of the Lord's justice, but the real concern is that the oppression of the wicked, and the prosperity *they* now experience will not last. That material reward itself is not the issue is clear from verse 16: "Better is a little that the righteous person has / than the abundance of many wicked."

Second, the righteous are not recognized by their material possessions. Indeed, in the present, such a criterion could very well lead to the wrong identity. The righteous are recognized by their dependence on God. It is appropriate that Psalm 37 ends with this point: "The LORD helps them and rescues them; / he rescues them from the wicked, and saves them, / because they take refuge in him (v. 40).

To bring together these two points: the righteous are identified by their dependence on God. They find security in *the promise* of prosperity, which ultimately gives evidence of God's reign and God's justice. But the promise requires hope. Promise and trust are bound together and cannot be separated in the life of the righteous. The present reward of the righteous is, in a real sense, the ability to live in view of a destiny that is not now realized. Their present "reward" is what marks them as righteous—namely, their trust in the Lord.

"Planted" in God's Presence: Psalm 1:3

The final passage to be considered in the discussion of the nature of the destiny of the righteous in the Psalms is the single verse in Psalm 1 that describes the righteous "like trees / planted by streams of water" (v. 3). These few words evoke a powerful image of the righteous as permanent and prosperous because they are securely fixed in God's presence. The imagery of the trees "planted" implies that the righteous are secure because they have yielded to God's control and are therefore planted near God.

The comparison of a person to a plant to characterize stability was common in the ancient Near East and in the Old Testament.[29] Isaiah 65:22 uses the image to speak of Israel's security: "for like the days of a tree shall the days of my people be, / and my chosen shall long enjoy the work of their hands." The tree in a garden, near a source of water, is a common cipher for security (Jer. 17:8). But the language in Psalm 1:3 has a particular fecundity that suggests the righteous person is planted in God's presence and that that location is key to the righteous' security.

According to most translations, a tree is "planted." The Hebrew term here (*šātûl*), however, more properly means "transplanted." That is, it connotes a plant that begins from its seed in one location and then is moved to a more advantageous plot. Reference to a transplanted tree connects Psalm 1:3 with an important web of associations. Particularly important is the association of trees to ancient Near Eastern kings and the gardens they planted. It was common for these rulers to boast of their skills of planting and transplanting various plants into their gardens. They were not really interested in being perceived as gardeners, however. The gardens were filled with vegetation they acquired on military campaigns. They were victory gardens, symbols of their domination of other lands and peoples.

This is particularly apparent in one relief created by Assyrian king Assurbanipal. The scene depicts the king and his courtiers celebrating in the midst of a well-kept garden. But one of the trees in the garden is adorned with the head of the king of Elam, whom Assurbanipal defeated.[30] Although care must be taken not to make too much of such imagery as it relates to Psalm 1:3, the identify of the righteous in this verse as transplanted into God's presence makes perfect sense. The righteous are "planted" beside a life-giving source. The particular nuance of the verb ("transplanted") implies their submission to God's creative, gardening activity. This image, therefore, suggests something similar to the point of Psalm 73, that the destiny of the righteous is characterized by being near God and being ruled by God.

Conclusion

The Psalms express the conviction that the destiny of the righteous will be marked ultimately by a reward for being faithful to God and being aligned with God's will (Ps. 37). But the destiny of the righteous is known in the present through a faith that draws upon such hope. The most important aspect of the destiny of the righteous is the present state of being near God (Ps. 73:28). In a real sense the desire to be in God's presence, to be instructed and led by God, *is* their destiny. Although the righteous wait for God's justice and for the downfall of the wicked, that future hope is most important for the way it informs life in the present. The righteous have something in the present that the wicked cannot take away–namely, the favor of God and the pleasure of having God's face shine upon them (Ps. 17:15).

The Psalms give a particular understanding of security. Security can ultimately be conceived only as nearness to the source of life. This understanding of the destiny of the righteous also provides a critique of much current thinking about the "benefits" of faith. Faith is often thought to "do" something for the believer. In this way of thinking, faith becomes a means to success and prosperity in the common understanding of these. For the righteous in the Psalms, however, the primary benefit of faith, and perhaps the only benefit on which one may depend, is to "to be near God."

PART II

The Destiny of the Righteous and the Shape of the Psalter

4

The Lord's Anointed and the Suffering of the Righteous

Psalms 1–89

> O LORD, how many are my foes!
>   Many are rising against me;
> many are saying to me,
>   "There is no help for you in God." (Ps. 3:1–2)

What an unexpected statement to open the main body of the Psalter! Is suffering at the hands of enemies the norm for living for the righteous? Does this opening line find reinforcement in the following psalms? Or does the shape of the Psalter point to a different conclusion?

Many scholars today believe the book of Psalms has a distinctive and theologically significant "shape," a literary structure that provides a context in which to read and interpret individual psalms.[1] This belief about the Psalter implies that the book has some discernible movement, that as one begins reading with Psalm 1 and proceeds to Psalm 150 a theological message unfolds that would not be evident from reading individual psalms.[2] Moreover, the book as a whole is meant to be a source of instruction; it is torah.[3] The purpose of this chapter and the next is to look closely at how the concern for the destiny of the righteous is communicated by means of the shape of the book. These two chapters will suggest that though many subjects are important in the shape of the Psalter, all such subjects work together to say something about the subject being explored here: the destiny of the righteous.

This chapter and the next will pay attention to two major features of the shape of the Psalter. First, the Psalter has a framework of key psalms that hold the whole together: Psalms 1 and 2 serve as an introduction, and Psalms 146–150 a conclusion; in-between the introduction and conclusion the Psalter has two main sections–Psalms 3–89 (Books 1–3) and 90–145 (Books 4 and 5)–each with its own editorial features. Since many scholars consider the division between Books 3 and 4 of the Psalter a major break in the book (between Ps. 89 and 90), this chapter will address Psalms 1–89, and the next chapter will examine Psalms 90–150.[4] Particularly important in Books 1–3 are the psalms that appear at the major breaks or "book" divisions. Gerald Wilson has shown that psalms about the king appear precisely here as part of an editorial framework (Ps. 2; 41; 72; and 89). Therefore, this chapter will give attention to the two introductory psalms and to some of the psalms that appear at or near the "seams" of Books 1–3: Psalms 3; 40; 41; 42–43; 73; 74; 88 and 89. Each of these psalms gives a particular perspective on the righteous' struggle with their present state of oppression by the wicked. The chapter will show, however, that throughout Psalms 1–89 the problem of the destiny of the righteous appears as a problem for the Lord's anointed.

After the two introductory psalms, the anointed is identified as David. David is the righteous one who suffers (see especially Ps. 3), and his suffering represents the suffering of the nation, the righteous people (Ps. 89). As the introduction states, the king–David–is intimately connected to the righteous. Within this basic framework of the Psalms, one may clearly see the two emphases on the king that have already been mentioned: he appears as one of the suffering righteous and, thus, serves as an example for how to seek God's sheltering presence. He is also the defender of the righteous, God's instrument to bring justice for the righteous against the wicked.

Second, the Psalter has a general movement, from laments (complaints and petitions to God), which appear in greater numbers at the beginning, to psalms of praise, which occur in greater numbers at the end.[5] This movement is crucially important for understanding what the Psalter is saying about the nature of the righteous and their destiny. Their praise (which, as chapter 2 suggests, includes all aspects of life) is offered in the context of suffering and oppression. Conversely, their suffering and oppression do not have the last word. Indeed, the last word is "the Lord reigns!"

Psalms 1 and 2

Psalms 1 and 2 form a dual introduction to the Psalter.[6] These two psalms identify "two ways that lie before each person: the way of righteousness and the way of wickedness."[7] They both speak of the "way" of the righteous and the wicked also as a direction in life–either for or against the way of God–and as a future that is determined. The way of the righteous will endure; the way of the wicked will not.

These two introductory psalms are set off from the psalms that follow by the fact that they lack a superscription.[8] They are linked to each other by common vocabulary that serves to contrast the righteous and the wicked.[9] For example, while the righteous "meditate" on the torah of the Lord (Ps. 1:2) the wicked meditate on plans to thwart the work of God (Ps. 2:1; usually translated "plot," but from the same term, Hebrew *hāgâ*); the "way" (*derek*) of the righteous is observed and rewarded by the Lord, but the way of the wicked will "perish" (*'ābad;* Ps. 1:6; 2:12). Creating an envelope around Psalms 1 and 2 is the word "happy" (*'ašrê;* 1:1; 2:12). This term characterizes the righteous who enjoy God's favor (and are thus "happy" or "fortunate") and sets them apart from the wicked who know only God's wrath.[10]

Psalm 1:1–2: The Righteous Delight in the Law

So, Psalm 1, along with Psalm 2, sets the righteous over against the wicked in terms of character and destiny. In terms of character, Psalm 1 distinguishes between the two by presenting the righteous as those whose "delight is in the law of the LORD" and on that law "meditate day and night" (v. 2), as opposed to the wicked who are characterized as "sinners" and "scoffers" (v. 1). Christian readers of this psalm may not resonate with the term "law" and may think this term is not something in which anyone should "delight." But as the introduction notes, the word here does not signify an instrument of self-righteousness or a burdensome legal code that restricts life. Rather, the term translates the Hebrew *tôrâ,* which essentially means instruction. The word is used variously in the Old Testament to refer to guidelines for life as broad-ranging as prophetic oracles (Isa. 1:10) to the book of Deuteronomy (Deut. 31:24). Torah includes laws such as those in the law codes of Exodus, Leviticus, and Deuteronomy. Those law codes are torah, however, because they instruct and illuminate a way of life consistent with God's will.[11]

In Psalm 1:2, "law" (torah) is a comprehensive term that refers to any and all sources of insight into the reign of God in the world (see the further discussion in chapter 10). As Mays puts it, torah is the "instrument of his ordering" of the world, the polity of his reign.[12]

To understand better how torah could be a source of delight, it may be helpful to compare Psalm 1:2 with a related passage, Jeremiah 17:7–8. The Jeremiah text declares, "Blessed are those who trust in the LORD, / whose trust is the LORD" (v. 7), for "they shall be like a tree planted by water" (v. 8). According to this passage, therefore, the one who trusts in God has a secure future that is characterized in terms almost identical to the righteous person in Psalm 1.[13] In the description of the righteous person in Psalm 1, however, the psalmist substitutes "trust in the Lord" with "delight…in the law of the LORD." The change does not mean that the psalmist substituted faith for confidence in legal prescriptions and the ability of the righteous person to abide by them. Rather, torah is for the righteous a means by which faith is exercised.[14] Torah is the delight of the righteous because it provides opportunity to reflect on ("meditate," Ps. 1:2) the nature of God's reign, and it gives structure to a life of obedience to God's will.

Psalm 1:3–6: The Righteous Ever in the Presence of God

The first psalm also presents a strikingly different destiny for the righteous and the wicked. Verses 3–4 particularly address the differences between the futures of the two groups. These verses use evocative images to communicate the point. As noted above, Psalm 1:3 portrays the righteous "like trees / planted by streams of water, / which yield their fruit in its season, / and their leaves do not wither" (v. 3a); the wicked, conversely, are "like chaff that the wind drives away" (v. 4b). Both images speak to the destiny of the two groups in terms of their presence or absence before God. The righteous will be near God, planted in God's garden, while the wicked will be far removed from God's presence.

The remainder of the psalm concludes the comparison of the righteous and wicked with language that recalls the first verse and makes the point again that the righteous and the wicked are finally separated by being in or not being in God's presence. The "way" of the wicked in verse 1 (*derek*, translated as "path" in v. 1, is the same word that appears in v. 6) represents a way of life that the righteous do not follow. Verse 6 makes emphatic that the "way" of the wicked will perish, but God watches over the way of the righteous. "Way" refers to both direction in life—to behavior—and to destiny. The way of the wicked leads to destruction; the wicked "perish." The meaning of "judgment" in verse 5 is not certain. The pairing of this word with "in the congregation of the righteous," however, suggests that the destiny of the wicked is to *not* be in God's presence.

The wicked are often characterized as those who think God does not notice them (Ps. 14:1a; 73:11). Psalm 1 concludes with the ironic assertion that at the end God will not pay attention to the wicked; God will not grace them with his presence. This is at least one important part of what it means for them to "perish" (v. 6).[15] There may be other dimensions to the judgment of the wicked, of course, but Psalm 1 emphasizes precisely this point: "the LORD watches over the way of the righteous" (v. 6). The destiny of the two groups is defined in the most basic terms, of being or not being near God.

Psalm 2

Psalm 2 is very different from Psalm 1. By its tone and vocabulary Psalm 1 seems to belong to the instruction of sages.[16] The neat division of humankind into categories of righteous and wicked is characteristic of such literature. Psalm 2, by contrast, takes the reader into the political realm, into the world of kings and international politics. The subject of Psalm 2 is the reception of the Lord's anointed by the nations and his suffering at their hands (vv. 1–3). Psalm 2 characterizes the righteous as those who "take refuge" in God (v. 12). They align themselves with God's reign, particularly as it is expressed through the anointed, the Davidic king (vv. 4–6, 7–12). Readers familiar with the story in 2 Samuel 7 may recognize that Psalm 2 makes claims specific to the Davidic monarchy. The king, who is enthroned on Mount Zion, is the human representative of God's cosmic reign (Ps. 2:5–6). He is the one through whom divine rule is made known.

Despite these important differences, Psalm 2, as with Psalm 1, has an overarching interest in identifying a kind of existence that leads to permanence and prosperity. This is most clear in the way Psalm 2 ends, namely just as Psalm 1 began, with a statement about what makes a person "happy" (Ps. 2:12). The final line of Psalm 2 ("Happy are all who take refuge in him") was likely added to this work in the process of creating the introduction to the Psalter.[17] In fact the final three verses of the second psalm may have been appended for that purpose. Whether or not this particular suggestion is correct, it is striking that both psalms near their conclusions have statements about a path that does not endure, with Psalm 2 using the same words as in Psalm 1, "way" and "perish" (Ps. 1:6; 2:12). In other words, Psalms 1 and 2 both show that a way to security and blessing is through submission to the rule of God.

Psalm 1 expresses this as devotion to torah, to divine instruction. Psalm 2 characterizes it in terms of divine sovereignty known on Mount Zion in the person referred to as the Lord's anointed. But indeed, both psalms emphasize the fact that the one who depends on God finds true security.

The combination of Psalms 1 and 2 at the beginning of the Psalter not only points to the concern for the destiny of the righteous as an entrée into the Psalter; it also gives clues as to the shape of that concern we should expect to find in the psalms that follow. The wicked are characterized in a particular way by the juxtaposition of Psalms 1 and 2. This group in Psalm 1 is identified simply by the label *rĕšāʿîm* ("guilty ones"; see chapter 1). In Psalm 2, however, the wicked are implicitly identified as the recalcitrant kings who oppose the Lord and his anointed (Ps. 2:1–3). That is, they are brought under the rubric of "enemies."[18]

It is significant therefore that the next psalm (Ps. 3) portrays David in prayer for deliverance from his foes. The wicked in the Psalms are embodied by those who oppress God's people and God's king. This identity of the wicked as the nations probably reflects the circumstances during and after the Babylonian exile, in which the faithful in Israel came to be identified with the absent king as representative of God before the nations.[19]

The combination of Psalms 1 and 2 also suggests a particular character for the Lord's anointed. When Psalm 1 portrays the righteous as those who "on his law...meditate day and night," it borrows language the Deuteronomistic History (Deuteronomy-Kings) uses to describe the ideal king. The vocabulary of Psalm 1:2 is taken directly from Joshua 1:7–8, a text in which God commissions Joshua as the leader after Moses. But the charge in that text to observe torah and to keep it, not turning from it to the right or to the left, is the instruction for the future king given earlier in Deuteronomy 17:14–20. Subsequent parts of the Deuteronomistic History identify obedience to torah explicitly with the ideal reign of Israel's monarch (1 Kings 1–2; 2 Kings 13).[20] To be sure, Psalm 1 has not borrowed the language exactly. It does not associate torah with a particular written text, as the Deuteronomistic History does. (See Deut. 17:14–20's references to "this book of torah.") Nevertheless, the combination of torah obedience (Ps. 1) and kingship (Ps. 2) points to elements of piety that should not be sharply separated. By adding Psalm 2 to Psalm 1 as an introduction to the Psalter, therefore, psalm editors seem to identify the righteous (unnamed and unidentified in Ps. 1) with the anointed one who stands at the center of Psalm 2. David models torah piety (Ps. 1:2) and he shows how to "seek refuge" in God when plagued by enemies (Ps. 2:12d).

These two introductory psalms both present and raise questions about the reign of God and about the destiny of the righteous in relation to it. God's reign is a reality to which the righteous cling. It is their hope; they believe God indeed "laughs" at those who oppose God's will (Ps. 2:3). But the reign of God is not fully evident. The righteous suffer at the hands of the wicked; the anointed is besieged by enemies (Ps. 2:1–2). So the righteous live with hope that God's reign will overcome the present suffering. That hope, in turn, shapes the present life in terms of nearness to the tangible signs of God's reign available to the righteous. The righteous delight in torah (Ps. 1:2), which gives evidence of God's reign; they see in the Lord's anointed signs of God's justice (Ps. 2:7–10); and they experience God's reign on Mount Zion (Ps. 2:6).

Book 1 (Psalms 3–41)
Psalm 3: The Righteous' Many Foes

Psalm 3 is extremely important for understanding the righteous in the Psalter and the shape of the Psalter as a whole. This psalm is the first psalm in the Psalter that has a title. Psalms 1 and 2 introduce the book and orient the reader to the nature of the righteous person and the plight of the righteous in relation to the wicked. As untitled psalms, these works are not identified explicitly with a particular author.[21] Psalm 3, however, has a title that presents the speaker of the prayer as David. What is more, every psalm that follows, up to Psalm 41, has "of David" in its heading.[22] The association of these psalms with David gives a Davidic cast to the whole Psalter and presents David as representative of the righteous who cry out to God.

Psalm 3 is set "when he (David) fled from his son Absalom." This historical note points to the story in 2 Samuel 15. Absalom is vying for his father's throne and has forced David out of Jerusalem. This setting and the prayer of Psalm 3 give readers the first glimpse of David in the Psalter.

David is king of Israel. He is the anointed one spoken of in Psalm 2. He is the one through whom God makes his will known on Mount Zion. But the most outstanding feature of the portrait of David in Psalm 3 is not his power or influence. Rather, the picture of David is of one who cries out to God when beset by enemies. David is helpless and confesses as much to God. The enemy of which Psalm 2 speaks is now identified specifically as the enemy of David.

The psalm opens with recognition of being overwhelmed by adversaries ("O LORD, how many are my foes!" v. 1 [2]) and a record of enemy taunts ("There is no help for you in God," v. 2 [3]). The word rendered as "many" appears three times in the first two verses to denote the dire circumstances ("how many are my foes" *[rabbû]*, v. 1a [2a]; "many are rising against me" *[rabbîm]*, v. 1b [2b]; "many are saying" *[rabbîm]*, v. 2 [3]). The consensus of those who oppose the anointed, as it were, is that "there is no help for you in God" (v. 2 [3]). Contrary to his foe's claim, David confesses, "But you, O LORD, are a shield around me" (v. 3 [4]).

David's dependence on God in this troubled circumstance comes through in a particularly strong way. In the face of enemies rising (*qāmîm*) against him (v. 1b [2b]), he calls on God to "rise up" (*qûmâ*) and "deliver" (v. 7a [8a]). Matching the threefold reference to the "many" foes, Psalm 3 uses the word *yĕšû'ātâ* three times (translated variously as "help" in v. 2 [3], "deliver" in v. 7a [8a], and "deliverance" in v. 8 [9]) to confess that God alone can deliver. The three appearances of the term have a sequence that drives home this point. The adversaries taunt that there is no "help" in God (v. 2 [3]); David cries for God to "help" or "deliver" (v. 7a [8a]); then at the close of the psalm he confesses that "deliverance" belongs to God (v. 8 [9]). There is no sense here of self-sufficiency. Only the Lord can rescue and save.

The identification of David as the speaker of Psalm 3 and the particular situation Psalm 3 gives as the occasion for the psalm have at least three implications for the Psalter's concern for the destiny of the righteous. First, the presentation of David at this particular point in the Psalter establishes David as the representative of those who confess to being "poor and needy" (Ps. 40:17 [18]).[23] The identification of David as the speaker of Psalm 3 and the other twelve psalms with similar historical titles makes David a "literary vehicle" that exemplifies a piety of dependence on the Lord.[24]

Second, the circumstance given as the setting for Psalm 3 says the destiny promised the righteous will be worked out in the midst of trouble. Absalom's rebellion against David is the capstone for a host of troubled relationships within the Davidic court. Absalom had earlier killed his brother Amnon for raping his sister Tamar (2 Sam. 13). David's brief exile of Absalom and subsequent attempts at reconciliation (2 Sam. 14) prove to be in vain, as Absalom now drives his father from Jerusalem, being supported by some of David's inner circle (2 Sam. 15:30–31). Personal and political turmoil, betrayal, and bloodshed are the circumstances of David's prayer in Psalm 3. That says at least that the destiny of the righteous is not something realized easily or immediately. As McCann rightly puts it, "'The way of the righteous is not a detour around the trials and troubles of life; it is the trust that God is walking with us. God is present in the depths!"[25]

Third, the identification of David as speaker of Psalm 3 connects the destiny of the righteous with the future of David in his role as the Lord's anointed. David at once represents the righteous who suffer *and* the ruling house established in Jerusalem as a sign of God's universal reign. Israel's corporate identity does not permit a sharp separation of these concerns.

Psalm 2 raised the question of how things will turn out for the Lord's anointed and says that God's reign is reflected in the rule of the anointed one. Psalm 3 gives a concrete setting to this question about the anointed. As Mays says, "The reign of the Lord is at stake in the destiny of David."[26] As will be seen in numerous other places in the Psalter, the destiny of the righteous, of David, and of the people Israel are bound up together.

Psalms 40 and 41

The psalms at the end of Book 1 emphasize the character and destiny of the righteous in ways much like Psalms 1 and 2. Psalm 41, the last psalm in Book 1, begins with the word "happy," the same term that appears at the beginning of Psalm 1 and at the end of Psalm 2. Therefore, all of Book 1 is framed by an interest in the human situation, particularly in what characterizes human happiness.[27]

Psalm 41 has two main parts. Verses 1–3 (2–4) declare God's favor on those who "consider the poor" (v. 1 [2]) and then describe God's protection in terms of healing from illness and protection from enemies (which should probably be linked, the latter perhaps causing the former through magic spells, vv. 2–3 [3–4]). In verses 4–12 [5–13] the psalmist speaks as one whom God should favor and save according to the profile just given. The end of this person, however, is far from certain. At present this person experiences bodily ailments that signal to enemies that death is near (vv. 5 [6], 8 [9]); close friends have become adversarial (v. 9 [10]); the future looks dim. And yet, the psalm ends with assurance that God is pleased with the one who prays, as the prayer says to God in conclusion, "[you] set me in your presence forever" (v. 12 [13]).

Book 1 ends just as the Psalter began, with an expression of faith that God watches over the righteous and insures their destiny, even in the midst of present troubles that fly in the face of such faith. Also, the destiny of the righteous is characterized by the righteous' being in God's presence. Their reward is ultimately to be near the Lord, as chapter 3 observed.

Psalm 41 is also like the psalms at the beginning of the Psalter in that it seems to identify the king as the model of righteousness. Although the person identified here is not called "king" explicitly, that identification makes sense in light of the characterization of the person as one who considers the poor.[28] The character of the king will be cast specifically in terms of his protection of the righteous in Psalms 72 and 101 (see chapter 6). If Psalm 41 indeed has the king in mind, he is presented here in the same manner as was the anointed in Psalm 2: he is the earthly expression of divine justice and protection.

As in Psalm 72, Psalm 41 is concerned for the continuation of the "name" of the monarch (41:5 [6]; 72:17). The endurance of his name is good news for the righteous because his name is more than an epithet; it represents his character and the character of his rule. As Psalms 41 and 72 makes clear, the king is characterized primarily as one who defends the righteous. But Psalm 41 also portrays the king as one who suffers, one to whom the promise is given, "The Lord delivers them in the day of trouble" (41:1 [2]).

The next-to-last psalm in Book 1 is also important for the shape of the Psalter, for it too focuses on the character and destiny of the righteous. This psalm points back to Psalms 1 and 2, just as Psalm 41 did. In Psalm 40:7–8 [8–9] the psalmist testifies to dependence on God through a commitment to torah: "Then I said, 'Here I am; / in the scroll of the book it is written concerning me / that my delight is to do the will of my God; / indeed, your instruction is in my inward parts" (author's translation). The "scroll of the book" here refers to a document in which the names of the righteous are recorded so they can be duly rewarded. The book is like the "book of remembrance" in Malachi 3:16–18: "And a book of remembrance was written before him of those who revered the LORD and thought on his name. They shall be mine, says the Lord of hosts, my special possession." (See also Ex. 32:32–33; Phil. 4:3; Rev. 3:5.)

The concern here is specifically for the future of the righteous. The particular characteristic of the righteous in Psalm 40:7–8 (8–9) that brings favor with God is finding delight in torah. Here the word for "delight" (hps) in relation to torah matches that in Psalm 1:2, which says of the righteous that "their delight is in the law of the LORD." This combination of words occurs only in these two places in the Psalter. Therefore, the fact that Book 1 begins and ends with these emphases points to the importance of this aspect of the life of the righteous and the central place of torah obedience in their destiny.

One distinctive feature of the structure of Psalm 40 draws attention to the fact that the righteous right now are suffering and call out to God whom they trust to deliver them. Scholars typically classify the first portion of the psalm (vv. 1–10 [2–11]) as a song of thanksgiving.[29] Such a psalm would have been offered in response to healing or deliverance from trouble. The remainder of Psalm 40 (vv. 11–17 [12–18]), however, turns to complaint and petition, elements usually associated with lament.

In most psalms classified as "laments of the individual," the psalm moves through complaint and petition and ends with words of assurance that God has answered the prayer (see Ps. 13 for one example). But the move from assurance to complaint and petition is quite unusual. It is perhaps not a coincidence that Psalm 40:13–17 (14–18) appears again near the end of Book 2 of the Psalter as Psalm 70. Psalm 70 was likely borrowed to form the present ending of Psalm 40 (though we cannot be certain about this).[30] Regardless of how the two psalms were composed, however, the repetition of this material creates an amazingly similar ending to Books 1 and 2 and creates an important message about the destiny of the righteous. Psalms 40:13–17 (14–18) and 70 are both preceded and followed by psalms that express hope for deliverance from trouble and from enemies (Ps. 40:1–10 [2–11]; 41; 69:30–36 [31–37]; 71). The material before and after presents the eschatological hope of the righteous—namely, that the present troubles will be swept away in the day of God's judgment, that God's future will bring justice for those currently oppressed.

Psalms 40:13–17 (14–18) and 70 occur at the center of that hope. The central place of this material in the psalms at the close of Books 1 and 2 of the Psalter is a reminder that the human is always in need—of forgiveness, deliverance, salvation—and remains so until the coming of God's kingdom. Indeed, these complaints in the midst of hope and assurance near the end of Books 1 and 2 make the theological point emphatic that "whether individually or corporately, we always pray out of need, at least in the sense that no deliverance is final in this mortal life."[31]

Book 2 (Psalms 42–72): Why Do You Cast Me Off?

Book 2 begins much as Book 1 began, with cries to God for deliverance in the face of enemies who declare the faith of the righteous invalid.[32]

Psalms 42–43 (which is really a single psalm and will be treated as such here), similar to Psalm 3, call to God for help and express confidence in God as the sole deliverer (Ps. 43:2, "You are the God in whom I take refuge"). Also similar to Psalm 3, this psalm at the beginning of Book 2 records a taunt of an enemy, "Where is your God?" (42:10 [11]; cf. 3:2), but the psalmist refuses to give in to the taunt, insisting that God is his "help" (42:11 [12]; the word here is the same as in Ps. 3:2 [3], 8 [9]).

In addition to the way Psalms 42–43 speak about the righteous' enemies in the same manner as Psalm 3, this psalm at the opening of Book 2 also speaks about having a place in the presence of God, just as Book 1 ended. Psalms 42–43 communicate the desire to be among worshipers on Zion, God's "holy hill" (Ps. 43:3). The concern at the opening of Book 2 is just like that in Psalm 41, which pleaded to God, "set me in your presence forever" (v. 12). The specific place God's presence is known (God's "holy hill") in Psalms 42–43 is the same locale where David in Psalm 3 sought

God's protection (v. 4 [5]). Hence, these psalms at the beginning of Book 2 continue the concern for the righteous to be in God's presence that has been observed already.

Book 2 of the Psalter introduces a new and perhaps more intense way of expressing the complaint over the righteous' suffering and the need for God's presence. Beginning in Psalms 42–43, the psalms of Book 2 repeat the complaint that God has rejected or "cast off" the righteous. Psalms 42–43 and 44 both declare trust in God with typical language of the righteous: the psalmist takes refuge in God (43:2) and, in contrast to the wicked, does not trust in the bow (44:6 [7]), but instead "in God…boasted continually" (44:8 [9]). In light of this claim of faith, however, these psalms complain that God has "forgotten" the plight of the righteous (42:9 [10]; 44:24 [25]). What is more, the psalmist here complains that God has "cast me off" (43:2) and "rejected" him (44:9 [10]). The words translated "cast off" in Psalm 43:2 and "rejected" in 44:9 (10) are the same in Hebrew (*zānaḥ*). These are the first occurrences of the term in the Psalter, but they will appear numerous other times in Book 3. Moreover, with one exception, the word is confined to Books 2 and 3. The same is true for the closely related term, *māʾas*, which is translated similarly as "rejected" (Ps. 89:38 [39]).

The complaint of being "cast off" by God is particularly strong because it follows in each case the psalmist's claim of faithfulness:

Psalm 43:2:
> For you are the God in whom I take refuge;
> why have you cast me off? (*zĕnaḥtāni*)

Psalm 44:8–9 (9–10):
> In God we have boasted continually,
> and we will give thanks to your name forever.
> *Yet* you have rejected (*zānaḥtâ*) us and abased us,
> and have not gone out with our armies.

With this complaint Book 2 raises the question of the destiny of the righteous quite pointedly. The problem it raises is primarily a problem of God and God's justice. In light of a continual trust in God, why have the righteous people been "cast off"? Have they been rejected by God, or is there another way to understand the current circumstances? The question—which is a question of theodicy—will intensify in Book 3.

Nevertheless, Book 2 does not end with the complaint of being cast off, nor with the question of what God is doing with the righteous. Instead, it ends just as Book 1 ended, with a hopeful portrayal of the king as the defender of the righteous. Psalm 72 declares that the righteousness of God is expressed through the king on behalf of the righteous. The monarch defends the cause of the poor and works to ensure that the righteous have a secure future (Ps. 72:2, 4, 12–14; cf. 41:1 [2]).

Book 3 (Psalms 73–89): Where Is Your Steadfast Love?

Book 3 of the Psalter continues the concern for the destiny of the righteous that appears in Books 1 and 2 with a pattern of psalms similar to that in Book 2.[33] The first psalm in both cases is spoken by an individual, but it has obvious implications for the community. The psalmist in these psalms cries to God in distress, but in the end expresses trust. Also similar to Book 2, Book 3 has as its second psalm a work in which the community complains that God has cast them off (Ps. 43:2; 44:9 [10]; 74:1 [2]). The complaint of being "cast off" by God raises an issue that will become the focus of Book 3.

Psalm 73

Psalm 73 begins Book 3 with questions that test the central claims about the righteous and their destiny that Psalm 1 presented. This is significant in part because of the location of Psalm 73 in the Psalter. Psalm 73 is at or near the middle of the Book of Psalms (not counting the final five psalms of the Psalter that form a conclusion, it comes at exactly the midpoint in the Psalter). Since ancient scribes often marked the exact middle of a biblical book, it would not be surprising if this work had an important place in the Psalter, which, indeed, it seems to have. Even if this psalm is not the exact midpoint in the Psalter, however, Walter Brueggemann notes, "it is central theologically as well as canonically."[34] Also, and perhaps more importantly, the fact that Psalm 73 is the first psalm of Book 3 deserves attention, since the psalms at the "seams" in Books 1–3 seem to have editorial significance.

Psalm 73 begins with a basic affirmation: "Surely God is good to Israel, to those who are pure in heart" (v. 1, NIV). As already noted, many modern translators have thought the term "Israel" here is a mistake. They have proposed that the correct reading is "to the upright." This would seem to make more sense for the first verse of a psalm that is the reflection of an individual who struggles with the fact that the wicked are prospering. And yet, the identification of Israel in the first verse is part of all the ancient translations.[35] Hence, the identification indicates that the Psalter in present form presents the righteous sufferer as a representative of Israel in its suffering.

After stating the central tenet of faith that opens the psalm (God is good to Israel), the next two verses call it into question: "But as for me, my feet had almost stumbled; / my steps had nearly slipped. / For I was envious of the arrogant; / I saw the prosperity of the wicked" (vv. 2–3).

With these words Psalm 73 raises again the problem of theodicy that Psalms 42–43 and 44 also raised. But here the problem is framed differently. The issue in Psalm 73 is not so much why the righteous are suffering; rather, the question is why the wicked are flourishing. To be sure, there is a problem with the fact that the suffering of the righteous seems to contradict

66   *The Destiny of the Righteous in the Psalms*

the core belief that God is good to the "pure in heart." But the suffering of the righteous is most problematic set over against the "prosperity" (šālôm, v. 3) of the wicked. The problem is important for understanding the shape of the Psalter, since Psalm 73, with its central location, seems to call into question the statement that concluded Psalm 1: "The LORD watches over the way of the righteous, / but the way of the wicked will perish" (v. 6). Indeed, Psalm 73:1 basically restates Psalm 1's confident assertion about the future of the righteous and wicked. The following verses, however, call that assertion into question. They also call into question the descriptions of the end of the wicked in Book 2 (Ps. 52:5–7 [6–8]).

Psalm 73 is central to the Psalter's concern over the destiny of the righteous by the way it wrestles with the truth of Psalm 1:6 and other promises that the wicked will not stand forever in their prosperity. Psalm 73 ends with a confident assertion that eventually the wicked will get what they deserve, a truth the psalmist has gained in the sanctuary (v. 17), but the question of God's justice to the "upright," to Israel, has been raised. In its exilic context, the question has to do with why tyrants and tyrannical nations are allowed to dominate the weak and powerless, as well as why ruthless individuals so often have their way in life. Such questions will continue, and the communal cast to the questions will increase as Book 3 unfolds.

Psalm 74

Psalm 74 occupies a place in Book 3 similar to that of Psalm 44 in Book 2. As with Psalm 44, Psalm 74 is a community lament in which the people complain of being "cast…off" (zānah) by God (v. 1). This psalm represents the growing question of theodicy: Where is God in the midst of the suffering of the righteous? Also as in Psalm 44, this psalm follows a psalm spoken by an individual, but it has significant ties to the previous psalm in parallel vocabulary and theological concerns. The sanctuary in which the psalmist in Psalm 73:17 envisions the downfall of the wicked (miqdĕšê-'ēl; "sanctuaries of God") lies in ruins in Psalm 74:3 (baqqōdeš; "in the sanctuary").

Violence is a problem in both psalms (hāmas in Ps. 73:6; 74:20). In Psalm 73:18 the wicked "fall to ruin." The same term is used to describe the decimated sanctuary in Psalm 74:3 (maššu'ôt).[36] Another important link between these two psalms is the identification of Israel as the righteous who are oppressed by enemies. As noted above, Psalm 73 begins with such a designation by referring to Israel as the "pure in heart" (v. 1). In that psalm a plural reference (Israel) appears where a reference to an individual is expected. In Psalm 74 the opposite is true. Where plural terms might be expected, singular words appear to identify the people of Israel as the righteous. They are called "poor" ('ānî; see "your poor" in v. 19 and "the poor" in v. 21b), "downtrodden" (dak, v. 21a), and "needy" ('ebyôn, v. 21b). The righteous who suffer are Israel–Israel, the servants of God who are now oppressed by the nations. This identification of the righteous as Israel is enhanced in the final psalms in Book 3.

Psalms 88 and 89

Book 3 of the Psalter ends on a note so stark, it almost appears that the psalmist has lost faith completely. Psalms 88 and 89 are tied to each other by their common complaint that God has "cast...off" his people (Ps. 88:14 [15]; cf. 89:38 [39]).[37] Thus the complaint that began in Psalms 42–43 comes to its greatest expression here at the end of Book 3. Psalm 88 for its part is perhaps the most despairing psalm in the Psalter. The righteous person who prays this psalm prays with words and images known in many other psalms, but with a pessimism hardly known elsewhere. The speaker here cries out with concerns about God's presence, but with no assurance that God is near. Indeed, the psalmist cries out "in your presence" (v. 1 [2]), attempting to find a place near God in prayer. (See chapter 1.) Yet the psalmist feels that God now hides God's face and has cast him off (v. 14 [15]). The prayer is similar to Psalm 3 in that it raises the issue of God's "help" for the one who prays (see the term *yĕšû'â* in Ps. 3:2 [3]; 88:1[2]). In Psalm 88, however, the psalmist prays "like those who have no help" (v. 4 [5]). The presence of God, the comfort of "being near God" that the righteous cherish and long for, seems in Psalm 88 to be completely missing.

Psalm 89 also pleads concerning God's presence, but it uses a particular expression to characterize divine nearness: God's "steadfast love" (*ḥesed*). The term *ḥesed* has to do with covenant faithfulness. The covenant is the formal agreement that God made to establish David's line forever; the covenant is upheld by God's *ḥesed*, God's steadfast love, that aspect of God's character that characterizes God as a covenant partner.

The problem in Psalm 89 is precisely that God promised, unconditionally, "I will not remove from him [David] my steadfast love" (v. 33 [34]), and, "I will not violate my covenant" (v. 34), regardless of how David's descendants violate God's statutes (vv. 30–32 [31–33]). But it seems that God has broken the covenant. Therefore, the psalmist asks, "Lord, where is your steadfast love of old, / which by your faithfulness you swore to David?" (v. 49 [50]). With this question Psalm 89 raises the question of theodicy, just as Psalms 42–43, 44, and 74 raised it earlier. Is God being unfaithful to the covenant? Is God unable to uphold it in the face of enemy threats?

This psalm is similar to Psalms 42–43, 44, and 88. The problem of God's steadfast love is linked in Psalm 89 to the complaint that God "cast off" his people. Both terms that communicate this complaint in the Psalter appear in verse 38: *zānaḥ*, here translated "spurned," and *mā'as*, rendered "rejected." But most important is how the psalmist focuses the complaint. The specific problem here is that God has "spurned" and "rejected" the anointed. True to the references to him in the rest of the Psalter, the anointed is referred to as David (vv. 3 [4], 20 [21], 35 [36], 49 [50]). The one who was enthroned on Zion as the representative of God's reign in Psalm 2 and the one who prayed to God for deliverance in the face of enemies throughout Books 1 and 2 (see especially Ps. 3) has now been rejected by God, or so it seems to the psalmist.

It will become obvious in Book 4 that this question is a question of God's ability and willingness to secure the destiny of the righteous people, not simply a question of the maintenance of a particular ruling house. There the question about what God is doing with his servant David will be answered by speaking of what God will do with and for his servants, Israel. But this identity of David with the people is present in Psalm 89, albeit in subtle ways.

In two verses of Psalm 89, the Masoretic Text has plural terms (referring to the people) where one expects singular references to the anointed. In verse 19 (20), MT reads, "you spoke in a vision to your faithful *ones.*" NRSV determined that other witnesses to the text of this verse, which have a singular term, probably have it right. The faithful one who received the vision was Nathan the prophet (2 Sam. 7:17). Similarly, verse 50 (51) of the MT pleads to God, "Remember, O Lord, how your *servants* are taunted." Again, NRSV opts to translate a singular ("servant") with other witnesses to this verse, thinking that the servant is the anointed one (David) who has been rejected. NRSV may well be right in its assessment of the original wording of Psalm 89. However, it is interesting that in the best Hebrew manuscript, these two verses have plural terms. It seems to indicate that, at the least, an early interpreter read the references to the anointed and to the one entrusted with his appointment as references to Israel in exile. The association is not surprising. This psalm raises in the most pointed way that God's faithfulness to David is wrapped up in God's care for Israel, the righteous people.

Conclusion

Psalms 1–89 unfold as a kind of tragic drama in which the destiny of the righteous hangs in the balance. Beginning with grand assurances that "the LORD watches over the way of the righteous, / but the way of the wicked will perish " (Ps. 1:6), and that the Lord will give shelter to "all who take refuge in him" (Ps. 2:12), this segment of the Psalter moves to profound questions about what God is doing with the righteous. The righteous complain that though they have trusted in God alone (Ps. 44:6 [7]), nevertheless it seems that God has cast them off (Ps. 44:9 [10]; 74:1). The doubts about God's faithfulness to the righteous focus particularly on David, the anointed of the Lord. Though he was enthroned on Zion as the representative of God's reign (Ps. 2:6), and though he trusted in God's salvation when beset by enemies (Ps. 3), it seems that now God has "spurned and rejected him" (Ps. 89:38 [39]).

The righteous are left asking, "Where is your steadfast love of old?" (Ps. 89:49 [50]). Such questions are posed, however, with the belief that God has not forgotten the righteous. Indeed, Psalms 1–89 are like the first portion of a complaint psalm writ large. This initial portion, with its complaints and questions, anticipates and provides the context for the conclusion in which God's faithfulness will be affirmed. The next chapter will examine the final portion of the Psalter (Ps. 90–150), which provides that affirmation in the declaration, "The Lord reigns!" But for now it is important to note that Psalms 1–89 illustrate an important truth about the faith of the righteous: their faith does not ward off trouble, but helps them to live rightly in the midst of it. Or, to put it in terms used earlier, the hope for a better future gives shape to life in the present.

5

The Suffering Servants as the Lord's Anointed

Psalms 90–150

Lord, where is your steadfast love of old, which by your faithfulness you swore to David? (Ps. 89:49 [50])

Psalm 89 concludes Book 3 of the Psalter by questioning God's faithfulness to his anointed. The dynasty that once ruled in Jerusalem lies in ruins with no sign of immediate restoration. As the last chapter indicated, however, Psalm 89 speaks of David as the defender and the symbolic head of God's people, not a solitary historical and political figure. Thus, the complaint of Psalm 89 is really a complaint about what God is doing with and for the righteous.

Moreover, when Psalm 89 is read together with the psalm that precedes it, the question about the destiny of the righteous appears in language that recurs throughout Books 1–3. Psalm 88 puts the question about God's *ḥesed* in terms of God's presence with the psalmist: "Why do you hide your face from me?" (v. 14b [v. 15b]; cf. v. 11 [12]) As seen in chapter 3, being near God is what the righteous seek more than anything else.

Despite the stark complaint that ends Book 3, however, signs of hope for the future appear already in Psalm 89. As noted in the last chapter, Psalm 89:50 (51) refers to God's servants, the suffering community, at a place one expects a reference to David, the servant of the Lord. This subtle shift from emphasis on an individual ruler to focus on a chosen people anticipates at least part of the answer to the problem of the destruction of monarchy: the people as a whole will inherit the promises made to David; Israel becomes David's "offspring" (Jer. 33:19–22). By this shift from king to people, the Psalter will assure Israel that the promises to David, and to the righteous, have not been abandoned. Instead, they have been redirected and reshaped. What is more, in its refashioned state, the Davidic covenant has room for hope that a new David will one day arise.[1] This chapter will explore further how the shape of the Psalter shows this revamped hope for the righteous.

Recent scholarly discussions of Books 4 and 5 of the Psalter have focused on how the psalms in these sections of the book work together to "answer" the problem of exile. To understand this modulation of faith more fully, this chapter focuses on how Psalms 90–150 address the traumatic circumstances of the righteous presented in Psalm 89, circumstances symbolized by the suffering of the anointed (David) and the exile of God's people. The discussion here will not so much examine individual psalms as it will look at Books 4 and 5 as units. The first feature of Psalms 90–150 to be examined is the noticeable shift from David to Moses as the primary "voice" in Book 4 of the Psalter, and the role Moses plays in this portion of the Psalter.

Book 4 (Ps. 90–106) as an Answer to Psalm 89

Gerald Wilson labels Psalms 90–106 the editorial "center" of the Psalter.[2] These psalms follow upon and "answer" the complaint of Psalm 89. There seems little doubt that this portion of the Psalter contains the most self-conscious theological portion of the book of Psalms. Psalm 89 concludes three books that have wrestled with the destiny of the righteous with a complaint that David, the righteous' representative, has been rejected. Now Book 4 follows the lament of Psalm 89 with reassurance that "the Lord reigns." (NRSV has "the LORD is king;" Ps. 93:1; 96:10; 97:1; 99:1.) But what does that proclamation mean in the context of Book 4 of the Psalter? Does it imply, as Wilson concludes, that God reigns to the exclusion of a Davidic king? Has the Lord's anointed become unnecessary?[3]

Psalm 90: Moses' Prayer for the Righteous

One of the most striking features of Book 4 is the dominating presence of Moses. Moses' name appears seven times in Psalms 90–106 (Ps. 90 [superscription]; 99:6; 103:7; 105:26; 106:16, 23, 32), but only one time in the rest of the Psalter (Ps. 77:20). Instead of repudiating Israel's confidence in the Davidic king, Moses here seems to comfort the righteous people whom David represented.

The comfort Moses offers Israel comes first in Psalm 90, the only psalm in the Psalter that is attributed to Moses. In this psalm Moses plays a role for Israel in exile like the role he played for Israel in the exodus; namely, he stands between the people and God and pleads to God on the people's behalf.[4] As he does, he addresses the complaints that Psalms 88 and 89 raised at the end of Book 3: God is absent (Ps. 88:14b [15b]); God has "cast...off" his people and his anointed (Ps. 88:14a [15a]; 89:38 [39]); the covenant with David is broken (Ps. 89:49 [50]).

Psalm 90 opens with a statement about the place of God's people in God's presence:

> Lord, you have been our dwelling place
>   in all generations.
> Before the mountains were brought forth,
>   or ever you had formed the earth and the world,
>   from everlasting to everlasting you are God. (vv. 1–2)

The word translated "dwelling place" ($mā\,^{\subset}\hat{o}n$) is closely related to other terms such as "refuge," "fortress," "hiding place," and "shade," all of which are frequent labels for God in the Psalter (see chapter 1).[5] This psalm declares that "in all generations," including the present generation that has suffered exile, God's presence is available in unmediated form. The king, the temple, and the land could all be lost, but God would remain a dwelling place, a refuge for his people.

The Mortality of the King and the Suffering of Israel

Perhaps most importantly, Moses in Psalm 90 seems to address the complaint over the fall of the monarchy by bringing the plight of king and people together through a description of both as having a fleeting existence.

Just before the prayer of Moses in Psalm 90, the king in Psalm 89 complained of his own mortality saying:

> Remember how short my time is–
>   for what vanity you have created all mortals!
> Who can live and never see death?
>   Who can escape the power of Sheol? (vv. 47–48 [48–49])[6]

In Psalm 90 Moses prays about mortality with much the same language as Psalm 89:47–48 (48–49). Psalm 90 could well be taken as a reflection on the cry of the king in Psalm 89:47–48 (48–49). The motivation Moses cites for God's mercy in this psalm is specifically the mortality of the servant people, Israel.

Moses' petition for Israel in Psalm 90 is drawn from Exodus 32: "Turn, O LORD! How long? / Have compassion on your servants!" (Ps. 90:13; cf. Ex. 32:12). In both Psalm 90 and Exodus 32 Moses cries to God because of the anger ($^{\supset}ap$) and wrath ($ḥēmâ$) God displays toward Israel (Ex. 32:10,

11, 12; Ps. 90: 7, 9, 11). The Exodus account shows the divine rage as a response to Israel's sin in making the golden calf.

In Psalm 90, however, no specific sin is in view. Rather, the emphasis of the psalm, and the subject of Moses' prayer, is the connection between divine wrath and the brevity of life. Mortality is a sign of God's judgment, it seems (vv. 3–6, 7–8). It also seems that the failure to confess one's mortal limitations is the gravest of sins, the primary sin from which one must repent. So, verse 12 declares, in light of God's wrath, "teach us to count our days / that we may gain a wise heart." Moses' seeks God's compassion (v. 13) then in light of Israel's mortal weakness. The hope Moses puts forward for Israel is for its limited days to be useful and filled with joy and purpose:

> Satisfy us in the morning with your steadfast love,
>   so that we may rejoice and be glad all our days.
> Make us glad as many days as you have afflicted us,
>   and as many years as we have seen evil.
> Let your work be manifest to your servants,
>   and your glorious power to their children.
> Let the favor of the Lord our God be upon us,
>   and prosper the work of our hands—
>   O prosper the work of our hands! (vv. 14–17)

The extended reflection in Psalm 90 has important implications for reading the king's confession of mortality in Psalm 89:47–48 (48–49). Indeed, it seems more than accidental that Psalm 89 also speaks of God's wrath and anger directed against his anointed. Now it is the righteous people, God's servants, who suffer under the reality of their mortal limits.

Moses' prayer for God's mercy is based on the fact that Israel is the victim of God's "wrath" and "anger" due to its mortal limits, but this prayer seems to "answer" a prayer for the king who, as an individual, has experienced God's wrath and anger because of *his* mortality. Based on this pairing of psalms and the way the theme of mortality appears in them, it seems that the king is being understood as a representative or a symbol of Israel in its suffering. When looking further at these two psalms and other psalms in close proximity, there seems little doubt that David has become not only a symbol of the monarchy but a symbol for Israel. David is the one who bears the sins and shame of the nation.

Servant and Servants of the Lord

Another sign that in Psalm 90 David becomes a cipher for Israel in the Psalter is the nature of references to God's servant(s) in Psalms 89 and 90. Two times in Psalm 89, David is referred to as God's servant. In verse 3 (4) God calls him "my servant" as he recollects the establishment of the covenant. In verse 39 (40) the psalmist complains, "you have renounced the covenant with your servant." Thus, David is identified by this label, as he is more often than anyone else in the Old Testament. Moses' prayer in Psalm 90 petitions God with the same language, but it asks God to have compassion on the Israelites who have suffered exile; they are called "your servants" in verse 13. But as already noted, this servant/servants interplay is at work already in Psalm 89. As the psalm concludes, the psalmist asks God to remember the covenant with David:

> Lord, where is your steadfast love of old,
>   which by your faithfulness you swore to David?
> Remember, O Lord, how your servant is taunted;
>   how I bear in my bosom the insults of the peoples.
>   (vv. 49–50 [50–51])

As noted already, in the Masoretic Text, the expression "your servant" in verse 50 (51) is plural, "your servants." Although there is evidence in other Hebrew manuscripts, in the Greek version, and in the Syriac version that leads NRSV to take the singular form as most original, the plural form may well be due to a tradition of interpretation in which David is understood as a cipher for Israel. The suffering and humiliation of the nation in exile is portrayed as the suffering of its great king. There is further evidence that makes this view compelling.

Psalm 89 places two other labels on David that subsequent psalms apply to Israel. Psalm 89 twice calls David "my chosen one." In Psalm 89:3 (4) God calls David, "my chosen one" (Hebrew *běḥîrî*), and similarly in verse 19 the psalmist reports a divine oracle in which the Lord speaks of David as "one chosen from the people" (*bāḥûr mēʿam*). The final two psalms in Book 4 use this term in the plural to refer to Israel, Israel now in exile:

> O offspring of his servant, Abraham,
>   children of Jacob, his chosen Ones… (*běḥîrāw*, Ps. 105:6)

> Remember me, O Lord, when you show favor to your people;
>   help me when you deliver them;
> that I may see the prosperity of Your chosen ones (*běḥîrêkā*),
>   that I may rejoice in the gladness of your nation,
>   that I may glory in your heritage. (Ps. 106:4–5)

Perhaps the most arresting title transferred from David to Israel, however, is "anointed" (Hebrew *měšîaḥ*). The label is reserved almost exclusively for royal figures who were anointed with oil at coronation to mark them as God's choice to carry out the unique tasks of monarchy (1 Sam. 16:1–13). Again, Psalm 89 twice uses this term in reference to the king (vv. 38 [39] and 51 [52]). Psalm 105:14–15, however, uses the term in a much broader sense:

> He allowed no one to oppress them;
> 	he rebuked kings on their account,
> saying, "Do not touch my anointed ones;
> 	do my prophets no harm."

Uncertainties remain as to the antecedent of "anointed ones" in this passage. The larger context in verses 12–15 suggests this label refers to Abraham and his company as they wandered "few in number" from Mesopotamia (v. 12). The parallel reference, "my prophets," could also be a label for Abraham's people, since Abraham is called a prophet in Genesis 20:7. But several features of this passage suggest that, instead, these two labels are applied again to the Israelites who, at the time of the psalm's composition, are in exile. Psalms 105 and 106 are placed together and were perhaps edited as "twin psalms" to close Book 4. Therefore, it would not be surprising if Psalm 105, as with Psalm 106, included intentional references back to Psalm 89. That seems to be the case with the term "anointed ones" in Psalm 105:15. Although the context does refer to the Abrahamic era, Abraham is nowhere else labeled God's anointed. It is much easier to argue that the title in Psalm 105:15 is influenced by the use of the term in Psalm 89. Psalm 105:15 transfers the title "anointed" from the monarch to the people, just as Psalm 106:5 applies the label "chosen" to Israel, while it had previously referred to David. The larger context of Abraham's life suggests the poet here views Abraham much as he does David: not so much as an historical figure as a symbol of the people.

Although Abraham is famously dubbed a prophet in the one Genesis text cited above, neither the larger group with him nor the early Israelites are ever called by that name. In the book of Psalms, the word for "prophet" (*nābī'*) occurs only three times: in the historical title of Psalm 51 ("when Nathan the prophet came to him, after he had gone in to Bathsheba"), in Psalm 74:9, and here in Psalm 105:15. Psalm 74:9 is an interesting parallel since it appears within a psalm likely composed shortly after the destruction of Jerusalem: "We do not see our emblems; / there is no longer any prophet, / and there is no one among us who knows how long."

The word "prophet" is used here to lament that divine revelation is not available to Israel in the wake of the destruction of Jerusalem. Bernard Gosse suggests that Psalm 105:15 applies the label "prophet" to the whole people, or to a representative group within Israel, as a "response" to Psalm 74:9. He believes Psalm 105:15's use of both "prophets" and "anointed ones" is part of a larger pattern of reinterpreting such titles in the exilic period.[7] If the label has a representative group in mind, the likely candidates are the Levites, who had responsibility for leading worship in the restored temple in Jerusalem. In Chronicles these figures are indeed said to have prophetic gifts and "prophesy" through the music of the cult. Whether or not the words "prophet" and "anointed" have been recast as labels for exilic Israel, it seems clear that the other terms discussed ("chosen," "servant") have been so reinterpreted and now apply to David as representative of Israel.

Psalms 91 and 92: "The Righteous Flourish"

After Psalm 90, two more psalms appear that also speak to the problem of mortality as a way of comforting those who have experienced defeat and exile. By virtue of the fact that these psalms do not have titles, they seem intended to be read as prayers of Moses as well. Hence, Moses' appeal to the Lord on behalf of God's servants continues in Psalms 91 and 92.[8]

Psalm 91 speaks to those "who live in the shelter of the Most High, / who abide in the shadow of the Almighty" (v. 1). These images are related closely to that which appears in Ps. 90:1 ("you have been our dwelling place / in all generations"). Those who place their trust in the Lord are assured divine protection. Psalm 91 continues this theme and concludes with a divine promise to provide longevity to those who seek him: "With long life I will satisfy them, / and show them my salvation" (v. 16). Psalm 92 addresses the same concern of the brevity and insecurity of life by comparing the destinies of the wicked and righteous:

> Though the wicked sprout like grass
>   and all evildoers flourish,
> They are doomed to destruction forever,
>   but you, O Lord, are on high forever. (vv. 7–8 [8–9])

> The righteous flourish like the palm tree,
>   and grow like a cedar in Lebanon.
> They are planted in the house of the Lord;
>   they flourish in the courts of our God.
> In old age they still produce fruit;
>   They are always green and full of sap. (vv. 12–14 [13–15])

Psalms 90–92 are connected by their common interests in the ephemeral nature of the human and the willingness of God to preserve and prolong the lives of those who trust in him. On the lips of Moses, as it were, these psalms address the lament of Psalm 89 with a clear message: when mortal limits overwhelm, trust in God, the eternal Sovereign, who is able to satisfy with steadfast love and make "glad all our days" (Ps. 90:14). The Lord, who has been Israel's refuge in all generations, is held up in these psalms as the secure refuge for those who face humiliation and death (Pss. 90:1; 91:1–4, 9–12, 14–16; 92:16 [17]).[9]

Psalms 93–100: "The Lord Reigns!"

Psalms 93–100 follow the psalms that deal with human morality with the repeated claim, "The Lord reigns!" Psalm 100 serves as a conclusion to this grouping by summing up and repeating many of the emphases of

Psalms 93–99, repeating particularly the vocabulary of Psalm 95.[10] Psalms 93–99 themselves are united thematically perhaps more than any other grouping of psalms in the Psalter. They have in common the claim that "the Lord reigns" "–or, as some translations have it, "the Lord is king" "–and the celebration of that claim. Even Psalm 94, which does not contain this statement, highlights God's kingship by its portrayal of the Lord as judge of the earth (vv. 2, 12–15, 23).Psalm 93 introduces another sign of God's sovereignty in the past, particularly in the era of Moses: torah.Psalm 93:5 reads, "Your decrees (ʿēdōt) are very sure; / Holiness holiness befits your house, / O Lord, forevermore" (v. 5). Then at the end of the group of psalms that celebrate God's kingship, another reference to divine instruction appears. Psalm 99 combines the themes of Yahweh's kingship ("Mighty King, lover of justice," v. 4) and the law given through Moses: "Moses and Aaron were among his priests, / Samuel also was among those who called on his name. / They cried to the LORD, and he answered them" (v. 6).The faithfulness of Moses, Aaron, and Samuel is then described in terms of torah obedience: "He spoke to them in the pillar of cloud; / they kept his decrees (ʿēdōt), / and the statutes that he gave them" (v. 7). Psalms 93–99 bracket the sections of psalms that declare, "The Lord reigns" with reminders that the law of Moses is a primary sign of that reign.[11] With these words Israel in exile is offered assurance that God is still in control and has not abandoned God's righteous people.

Psalms 105–106: "Gather Your People"

At the other end of Book 4, Moses appears again with a message similar to that in Psalm 90. Here the prayer is that God will gather God's people who have been scattered among the nations (Ps. 106:47). As the psalmist employs Psalms 105–106 to pray for Israel in exile, they receive assurance as they remember how God cared for them in the past through the leadership of Moses. Moses appears in these psalms in a way similar to that in Psalm 90. As noted above, Psalm 90, cast as a prayer of Moses for Israel in exile, harks back to his intervention for Israel during the golden calf episode in Exodus 32. Psalms 105–106 form a unit at the other end of Book 4 that highlights the same work of Moses. Psalm 105:26–45 notes that God sent Moses and Aaron to perform signs in Egypt that would precipitate Israel's release from captivity. Psalm 106 then picks up the story of Israel's salvation where Psalm 105 left off. When this final psalm of Book 4 begins its rehearsal of Israel's history, however, it focuses from the beginning on Israel's rebellion. The ancestors "did not consider your wonderful works" in Egypt, but "rebelled against the Most High at the Red Sea" (v. 7). "They were jealous of Moses in the camp, / and of Aaron, the holy one of the LORD" (v. 16). The golden calf incident gets particular attention: "they made a calf at Horeb / and worshiped a cast image" (v. 19; cf. vv. 20–23). This sets the stage for Moses' intercession: "Therefore he said he would destroy them– / had not Moses, his chosen one, / stood in the breach before him, / to turn away his wrath from destroying them" (v. 23). This text recalls the same occasion of Moses' prayer for Israel as Psalm 90, and uses the same language as well. In both passages Moses acts to turn (Hebrew root *šûb*) God's wrath (Hebrew *hēmâ*) away from his people (Ps. 90:7, 9, 11, 13). With memory of God's action through Moses in the wilderness, Israel now in exile is offered hope that God will gather them again as a people.

Reenter David: Psalms 101, 103, 104

The pronounced emphasis on Moses and the wilderness period in Israel's history, combined with the concentrated statements about divine kingship, leads some scholars to conclude that these psalms "answer" Psalm 89 with what amounts to a repudiation of monarchy. In their opinion these psalms look to the age of Moses, when there was no king, as the ideal age. According to this view Psalm 90:1 should be heard as "Lord, *you* [and not a human monarch] have been our dwelling place / in all generations" (Ps. 90:1).[12] But what is to be made of David? What place does he have now in the Psalter's concern for the righteous? Has David been rejected? Was Psalm 89 intended as a death knell for monarchy? The point could be made, perhaps, that Psalms 90–106 were intended to communicate that message–if it were not for Psalms 101 and 103. David appears again in the heading of these two psalms, and the psalms themselves fit the identification of David in the rest of the Psalter. In Psalm 101 David speaks in familiar tones about his role in establishing justice. His relationship to the righteous and his central place in their destiny is as sure as ever: "I will look with favor on the faithful in the land, so that they may live with me; whoever walks in the way that is blameless shall minister to me" (v. 6). "Morning by morning I will destroy all the wicked in the land, cutting off all evildoers from the city of the LORD" (v. 8). These verses make clear that hope in the human king is far from dead. Judging from this psalm, Book 4 seems to retain the central role of the king in God's system of justice. Indeed, Psalm 101 presents the king just as Psalms 41 and 72, as the champion of the poor and downtrodden and as the defender of the righteous. Chapter 7 will deal with this matter in more detail.

In Psalm 103 David proclaims a message parallel to that of Moses at the beginning of Book 4. Like Psalm 90, this psalm deals with the sinfulness of the people in terms of mortality (see esp. vv. 15–18), making the specific point that the Lord has compassion for his people because "he remembers that we are dust" (v. 14). Also as in the first psalm in Book 4, Psalm 103 focuses on God's steadfast love, assuring Israel that the Lord's *hesed* outstrips their sinfulness (vv. 7–14). This psalm also makes clear that God's steadfast love is reserved for the righteous: God "works vindication / and justice for all who are oppressed" (v. 6); "the LORD has compassion on those who fear him" (v. 13); "the steadfast love of the LORD is from everlasting to everlasting / on those who fear him, / and his righteousness to children's children" (v. 17). In this psalm David speaks as Moses does earlier in Book 4; he proclaims hope for the righteous community and promises that God's steadfast love will sustain them.

The beginning and ending expression, "Bless the LORD, O my soul" (Ps. 103:22; 104:1, 35b) holds Psalms 103 and 104 together as a pair. Since Psalm 104 does not have a superscription, it is probably to be heard as the words of David as well. However, Psalm 104 is very different from Psalm 103 in that it focuses on the magnificence of God's creative work. This attention to creation, though, culminates in a statement about God's justice for the righteous: "Let sinners be consumed from the earth, / and let the wicked be no more" (v. 35a). David not only represents hope for the righteous; he, as does Moses, also prays for God's justice and mercy on their behalf.

Given the way David appears in Book 4, therefore, the presence of Moses in Psalms 90–106 was probably not intended to place Moses over David. Nor does Book 4 reject the monarchical period in favor of the "pristine" wilderness epoch. On the contrary, the time between exodus and entry into Canaan is not romanticized here at all. (In Ps. 106:6–39 it is precisely the wilderness period that illustrates Israel's sinfulness; see also Ps 95:7–11.)

Instead of establishing Moses over David, Book 4 rather seems to bring them together to enhance the idea that the Psalter is torah, divine instruction. The doxology at Psalm 106:48 divides the Psalms into five sections with a line that recalls Moses' words in Deuteronomy 27. This fivefold division was most likely intended to communicate the idea that both Moses and David speak across the ages with words of comfort to the righteous, and that David gave torah just as Moses did.[13]

In Book 4 the king remains a tangible sign of hope for the righteous. Their destiny is to be realized in the context of his reign as he establishes an administration that reflects the justice of God (Ps. 101). A change in the conception of monarchy does seem to occur here, however. The complaint in Psalm 89:39 (40) that God renounced God's covenant with his *servant* (David) gives way in Book 4 to promises of restoration to the Lord's *servants* (the exiled people; Ps. 90:13).

When Book 4 assures that God honors God's covenant (Ps 106:45), it does not identify the covenant. In the immediate context, however, are references to the covenant with Abraham (Ps. 105: 10, 42).[14] It seems that here the Davidic and Abrahamic covenants have been conflated, as in Jeremiah 33:19–22 (see also the Aramaic Targum on Ps 89:4 [5] and see Mt. 1:1). The promises once given to David have now been applied to the whole people.[15] This idea will be addressed further in chapter 7.

Book 5 (Psalms 107–145)

The first verse in Book 5 (Ps. 107:1) is nearly identical to Psalm 106:1: "O give thanks to the LORD, for he is good; / for his steadfast love endures forever." This leads Erich Zenger to conclude that Book 5 is a kind of commentary on Books 1–4, which are being read as a single unit.[16] Whether that was the intention of psalm editors or not, Book 5 does continue the themes already observed in Books 1–4. These final psalms give a particular cast to the problem of the destiny of the righteous.

Book 5 is usually counted as Psalms 107–150, but the final five psalms should probably be considered a conclusion that stands outside the "book" structure in the same way Psalms 1–2 form an introduction. Psalms 107 and 145, then, provide the frame for Book 5. Both of these psalms highlight God's goodness to the righteous, for whom he extends his steadfast love. Recall that the question of God's *hesed* ("steadfast love") to his anointed was raised in Psalm 89:49 (50) and "answered" in Psalms 90:14; 92:2 (3); 103:4, 17; 106:1, 45.

In the two psalms that frame Book 5, the Lord's steadfast love to the righteous appears again as the main subject. The term appears six times in Psalm 107 (vv. 1, 8, 15, 21, 31, 43). It appears in the first and last verses of the psalm and in a fourfold refrain that structures the poem (vv. 8, 15, 21, 31). *Ḥesed* is also prominent in Psalm 145 in the declaration, "The LORD is gracious and merciful, / slow to anger and abounding in steadfast love" (v. 8).

Psalms 107 and 145 likewise declare God's care for the righteous and God's certain provision for a secure future. Psalm 107 emphasizes throughout that God cares for those in distress (for example, v. 9 declares that he "satisfies the thirsty" and "the hungry he fills"), and verses 41–42 put this in the familiar language of the destiny of the righteous:

> But he raises up the needy out of distress,
>   and makes their families like flocks.
> The upright see it and are glad;
>   and all wickedness stops its mouth.

In a similar way Psalm 145:19–20 states:

> He fulfills the desire of all who fear him;
>   he also hears their cry, and saves them.
> The Lord watches over all who love him,
>   but all the wicked he will destroy.

Book 5 begins and ends with promises that God will make the righteous flourish and will bring the wicked to an end. And, at the beginning and end of Book 5, David appears again as the representative of the righteous.

After the initial introductory psalm (Ps. 107) in this section, three psalms of David present David in this manner. Psalms 108–110 illustrate well the point made numerous times already: the anointed of the Lord, who is charged to establish God's justice, is one of the righteous who suffers. As one of the righteous, he cries out to God in his distress; and God hears him. As the anointed, he petitions God for and anticipates the renewal of his vigor that allows him to carry out God's will.

The composition of Psalm 108 shows that Psalms 108–110 are placed at the beginning of Book 5 to reiterate these ideas. This psalm is a combination of Psalm 57:7-11 (8–12)–which forms Psalm 108:1-5 (2–6)–and Psalm 60:5-12 (7–14)–which makes up Psalm 108:6-13 (7–14). The portion of Psalm 57 that was borrowed to form Psalm 108:1-5 (2–6) follows particularly well upon Psalm 107. Psalm 107 called for those God delivered to "thank the LORD" (v. 31); now in Psalm 108:3-4 (4–5) David indeed gives thanks for God's steadfast love. Hebrew *yāhâ*, "to give thanks," is used in both cases. Indeed, the steadfast love of God that was celebrated in Psalm 107 (vv. 1, 8, 15, 21–22, 31–32) is now cited as the reason for praise in Psalm 108:4 (5). So, in Psalm 108 David leads the thanksgiving and praise for which Psalm 107 called.[17] Psalm 107 presented God's salvation in terms of God's deliverance of the righteous: "he raises up the needy out of distress" (v. 41). In Psalm 108 David speaks again as one of them and on their behalf.

The portions of Psalms 57 and 60 that are joined to form Psalm 108 come together in Psalm 108:5-6 (6–7). Verse 5 (6) is from Psalm 57 (v. 11 [12]) and verse 6 (7) is from Psalm 60 (v. 5 [7]). These two verses formed from portions of Psalms 57 and 60 include a petition that is the linchpin of Psalm 108. These verses show the continuing struggle over the effects of exile for the righteous (verse 6: "Give victory… / so that those whom you love may be rescued"). Moreover, the identification of community concerns is particularly appropriate here.

David represents the righteous community who has suffered defeat and humiliation in exile. One of the lingering pains, seen later in Psalm 137:7, is that Israel's neighbor (and brother) Edom participated in their downfall. In Psalm 108 Edom is highlighted (v. 10 [11]) as a foe that is not yet overcome.[18] David's complaint, therefore, is a complaint over the opposition to the righteous in the larger sense of God's people and as represented by the anointed.

On the other end of Book 5, David "speaks" the final word in Psalm 145:20, which echoes the sure promise of Psalm 1 that the righteous will flourish and the wicked will perish (Ps 1:6). In both of these Davidic collections in Book 5, David appears as he did earlier in the Psalter, as one who calls on the Lord when oppressed by enemies. (See especially Ps 109.). Therefore, as the Psalter comes to a conclusion the anointed is still the representative of the righteous, the model of the one Yahweh saves.

"Praise the Lord" (Psalms 146–150)

Psalms 146–150 conclude the Psalter with a crescendo of praise. These five psalms are linked by the words, "Praise the LORD" (Hebrew *hallû yāh*) which appear at the beginning and end of each. Psalm 150 begins each line with these words. Before these concluding psalms give way to the pure praise in the final psalm, however, they state again what is perhaps the central message of the Psalter: "The Lord watches over the strangers; / he upholds the orphans and the widow, / but the way of the wicked he brings to ruin" (Ps. 146:9).

Therefore, the Psalter's final concatenation of praise is offered specifically on the belief that God will right the wrongs done to the righteous. But the context of this concluding praise gives a particular cast to the celebration. Spoken while the righteous continue to suffer, the final word of praise looks toward the future. Praise in this case is not triumphal assurance that all is well now, but hope-full claims that God is still in control of the world and that faith provides the strength to live in the midst of suffering.

Conclusion

The conclusion to the last chapter suggested that Psalms 1–89 constitute a grand liturgical drama that calls into question God's faithfulness to the righteous. If that is an accurate description of Books 1–3 of the Psalter, then Books 4 and 5 might be characterized as a chorus of voices meant to assure the righteous that "the Lord [still] reigns" and that the Lord will keep his promises. In these psalms Moses and David are the main speakers. Moses begins with the reminder that the Lord was Israel's "dwelling place" throughout all generations (Ps. 90:1–2). He continues with the promise that "the righteous flourish like the palm tree, / and grow like a cedar in Lebanon" (Ps 92:12 [13]). Even in the face of the greatest opposition, even in exile, it seems, God has not lost sight of the righteous. David also offers words of encouragement. Significantly, his last word before the Psalter concludes is a promise concerning the destiny of the righteous: "The LORD watches over all who love him, but all the wicked he will destroy" (Ps. 145:20). That said, David then promises to praise God "forever and ever" (Ps. 145:21). David then bursts forth into a concatenation of praise that ends the book (Ps. 146–150). This praise is not a jubilant cry that arises from a carefree life. Rather, it is a confident cry, in the midst of suffering, that God still reigns and that God will make things right for the righteous. That hope, in turn, gives shape to life and faith in the present.

This recasting and reshaping of Israel's faith can serve as an important model for people of faith today. Although faith must be grounded in certain tenets that do not disappear when challenged, faith is never static adherence to the past. Rather, it responds to new circumstances by applying the traditional beliefs in fresh ways. As Books 4 and 5 of the Psalter make clear, exile, with the loss of the land, temple, and the Davidic monarchy, did not make these concrete expressions of faith unnecessary. But it did require a different view of them than Israel had before the trauma of 587 B.C.E. For Christians this modulation of faith should seem quite appropriate. After all, the church has participated directly in these fresh appropriations of old beliefs. The monarch that was lost in the Babylonian defeat was recast as a future hope, and the church found fulfillment of that hope in Jesus of Nazareth. In other words, the Christian faith is the direct heir of the shift in thinking and the continuing hope that appears in Books 4 and 5 of the Psalter.

PART III

The Embodied Hope of the Righteous

David, Zion, and Torah

6

David

Defender of the Righteous

> *The LORD is king, he is robed in majesty;*
> *the LORD is robed, he is girded with strength.*
> *He has established the world; it shall never be moved;*
> *your throne is established from of old;*
> *you are from everlasting.* (Ps. 93:1–2)

Is such a confession realistic? Can it truly be said that God is king, reigning over all the world, when suffering and heartache seem to be the plight of the righteous?

The last two chapters considered how the concern for the destiny of the righteous appears throughout the Psalter and how the subject contributes to the shape of the book. The survey of the Psalter's shape revealed that the righteous' faith is extremely resilient. The righteous express confidence in God's goodness and justice even when the wicked persecute the righteous and cause them to suffer.

"The Lord Reigns"

In Psalms 90–150 this faith is expressed in the claim that "the Lord reigns!" This declaration is a confession that God ultimately is in control of the world. Whatever form the suffering of the righteous takes—persecution at the hands of personal enemies, the death-threatening work of the anointed's political foes, or the exile of the righteous people—the words, finally, resound, "all the wicked he will destroy" (Ps. 145:20), "Praise the LORD" (Ps. 146:1).

The claim that "the Lord reigns," however, raises the question, On what basis do the righteous make that claim? Although faith is an expression of belief in how the world will be one day, the future must be seen in the present, in some limited way at least, for such faith to be meaningful. As Samuel Terrien has shown, God's "elusive presence" must be made manifest in concrete expressions. In other words, the faith of the Bible is inherently incarnational, culminating in the "word became flesh" (Jn. 1:1–18), *the* Incarnation. The Psalms also treat the faith of the righteous as incarnational. It has already been shown that the righteous know God's presence, locating themselves "near God" in part by bringing themselves near certain tangible expressions of God's will.[1] This section (chapters 6–10) probes further into those signs of God's reign that appear in the Psalter and asks how the righteous' faith in relation to them was modified in light of the experience with the wicked.

Specifically, this section will examine three sources of, and witnesses to, divine presence and protection: David (the anointed of the Lord), Mount Zion (the dwelling place of God), and torah (the word of God). Each of these three is important for the destiny of the righteous in the way it makes God's justice known and gives access to God's presence. It is perhaps not by chance that all three are prominent in Psalms 1 and 2, which introduce the Psalter. From the very beginning the reader of the Psalms is presented with these means by which the righteous know God's deliverance. As this section explores the significance of the king, Zion, and torah for the righteous' destiny, it will try to come to terms with the particular problem of how each of these provided security for the righteous during and after the exile.

The King and the Security of the Righteous

One of the most important features of the Psalter's concern for the righteous is the close association of the security of the righteous with the human king, identified almost exclusively with David. The Lord's anointed represents the suffering righteous, as Psalm 3 illustrates. But the king also appears in the Psalms as the defender of the righteous, as the one through whom God works to make their way safe and prosperous. This chapter and the next take up this aspect of the Psalter's concern for the destiny of the righteous.

The chapter will consider briefly some key psalms that focus on the king; most importantly, the discussion will focus on how these psalms show the king's essential role in defending the righteous. These psalms will be treated under two headings: Psalms 2 and 89:1-37 (2-38) are examined together because they speak of the king as the "son of God." This label indicates the king's unique role as God's representative on earth; the righteous look to him as a sign of the Lord's cosmic stability. Psalms 72 and 101 depict the king more specifically as defender of the righteous or, in the language of the Psalms, as their "shepherd"; he is the righteous judge who looks out for the welfare of the helpless and afflicted; in this role the king expresses God's justice on earth for the sake of the righteous.

Throughout this discussion it will be obvious that the view of the king in the Psalms is elevated and idealized. Neither David nor any of his descendants came close to delivering on these expectations. For both Christians and Jews, however, the idealized portrait of the king is crucially important. It helped create a structure of faith that would redefine the nature of human rule and would be the foundation of expectations for a ruler in days to come, expectations for a Messiah, an "anointed one" who would usher in God's kingdom and bring about God's perfect rule. For Christians this expectation would be met in the life and ministry of Jesus of Nazareth. The psalms at the center of this chapter and the next are an appropriate starting point for reflection on his mission, a mission that was also closely connected to the plight of the righteous (Matt 6:25–34).

The Royal Psalms and Israel's Expectations for the King

A common starting point for a discussion of the king in the Psalms is a group of psalms that Hermann Gunkel called "royal psalms."[2] Gunkel used this label to identify nine psalms (Ps. 2; 18; 20; 21; 45; 72; 101; 110; and 132) that focus on some aspect of the human king or some event in the life of the monarch. Scholars before the nineteenth century generally interpreted these psalms as eschatological poems about a future Messiah.[3] Gunkel argued, however, that these psalms had their origins in the life events of actual kings of Israel or Judah. He saw that the lofty language these psalms used for the king was due to a "court style" typical of ancient Near Eastern scribes who praised their lord on high occasions of import to the nation (coronation, victory in war, establishment of a new temple).[4]

Psalm 2 is a good example of a psalm that came to be read in a dramatically different way with this new perspective. Once thought to contain a description of a future, idealistic ruler, this psalm was read in Gunkel's schema as liturgy for a king at his coronation. It is not hard to imagine how Psalm 2 might have functioned on such an occasion. A priest or prophet perhaps delivered the words of God to God's "anointed" in verse 6: "I have set my king on Zion, my holy hill." To this the king then responded, "I will tell of the decree of the LORD: / He said to me, 'You are my son; / today I have begotten you'" (v. 7). The warning to the "rulers of the earth" to do obeisance (vv. 10–12a) may be explained as an address to the leaders of subject peoples who attended the coronation, since suzerains in the ancient Near East typically required their vassals to pay tribute each year (2 Sam. 8:2, 6, 10–12).[5]

Gunkel's student, Sigmund Mowinckel, solidified the view that the so-called royal psalms arose from events in the life of Judean kings. He insisted that practically all the psalms in the Psalter had a cultic setting–they were used in worship in the preexilic period. In line with this view, the psalms about the king were all psalms by or about historical kings who ruled on Mount Zion.[6] Mowinckel's greatest contribution was his theory that the royal psalms had their origins in a yearly festival that celebrated God's kingship and the concomitant rule of the Judean monarch. He noticed that a group of psalms in the Psalter celebrated God's kingship with the declaration, "The LORD is king" (Hebrew Yahweh mālak; Ps. 93:1; 95:10; 97:1; 99:1). This line sounded to Mowinckel like the proclamation of Marduk's kingship that capped off the Babylonian *akitu* festival, which marked the Babylonian New Year.[7] Based on this similarity, Mowinckel proposed that Israel held a similar festival in which Yahweh's kingship was celebrated.

Since a prominent part of the Babylonian rite was a reaffirmation of the human king, and the royal psalms gave evidence of the monarch being affirmed and praised, Mowinckel reasoned that such a reaffirmation of the Davidic ruler must have occurred in Israel's festival as well. Mowinckel thought the king was the center of the worship life of the people, given the centrality of monarchs in other ancient societies. For Mowinckel, the king was the primary agent by whom God communicated blessings to the people, a role celebrated in the royal psalms.[8]

Modern scholars, like some Old Testament authors who saw the dangers of human rule, have criticized Israel's monarchy for its abuses. Some modern scholars have read into the account of monarchy's beginnings quite narrow interests—namely, that the wealthy in Israel wanted a centralized government to protect their interests.[9] Certain Old Testament texts register warnings about this human claim to power as well (Deut. 17:14–20; 1 Sam. 8:10–18). These criticisms of human kingship are right in so far as Israel's monarchy was punctuated by rulers who abused their power and acted on behalf of the privileged (1 Kings 21).

This sketch of Israel's kingship may be true historically in regards to the origins of the institutions and to some negative realities of human rule. The Psalms in their present form, however, present a decidedly different picture of human kingship. In the Psalter the king ensures the cosmic order of God's reign and ensures God's justice is meted out on earth. This order is particularly focused on the plight of the righteous before the wicked. The king's main purpose is to ensure justice, to offer protection for the righteous, to vouchsafe the proliferation of righteousness in the land (Ps. 72). In sum, the king's primary task is to look out for the destiny of the righteous (Ps. 101).

The King as Son of God

"You Are My Son:" David and the Order of the Cosmos

In the Psalms, the Lord's anointed represents the rule on earth of one who defends and maintains the order of the cosmos by which the righteous find security. This relationship between God's reign and the anointed's reign is expressed by the designation of the anointed as God's son. The conception of the anointed as God's son is influenced by the idea in the ancient Near East that gods rule from the heavens by means of terrestrial agents. Psalms 2:7 and 89:26 (27) record directly God's proclamation that the king is God's son.[10] This view of the monarch frames the first half of the book of Psalms.

One aspect of the king's provision of security for the righteous was his representation of God's reign over and establishment of order in the cosmos. In the Psalter's view of God's kingship, "The stability of the world is the reality of his reign."[11] One sign of that stability is the presence of the king enthroned on Mount Zion.

The Lord's cosmic order has two dimensions, both of which involve the king. First, an order to the natural elements testifies to God's control. Many of the references to this aspect of God's reign involve God's taming or directing the waters that represented chaos to ancient people. When Psalm 104:2b says that God "stretch[ed] out the heavens like a tent," it refers to the establishment of a vault in the heavens to hold back the heavenly sea (Gen. 1:6). Other references more directly speak of God directing the chaotic waters into their proper places (Ps. 104:5–9) and exercising control over the creatures of the sea that represented chaos (Ps. 74:13–14).

Second, God put nations into their places as well (Ps. 47). Modern Western people sometimes divide these dimensions of God's reign into categories of nature and history. In the Psalter the two belong together. They both illustrate forces that Yahweh controls. For the righteous the two dimensions of God's sovereignty work together to assure them that the wicked will not prevail over them. Just as God did not create the world as chaos, so, too, God does not allow the wicked to have their way forever (Isa. 45:18–19).

Psalm 2 and the Order of the Nations

Psalm 2 presents an historical scenario of the rebellion of the nations, whose kings "take counsel together, / against the LORD and his anointed" (v. 2). God looks down from heaven unconcerned about their recalcitrance (v. 4).[12] He has placed his king on Mount Zion as the instrument of his wrath and the sign of his rule over them (v. 6). As a world sovereign, the Davidic monarch will express the universal sovereignty of God. God declares to him, "I will make the nations your heritage, / and the ends of the earth your possession" (v. 8). The kings of the earth are called to submit to Yahweh's rule and, by extension, to the rule of the Davidic ruler. The call of the nations to submit to the Lord's reign is put in concrete terms in verse 12: "Kiss his feet, / or he will be angry, and you will perish in the way, / for his wrath is quickly kindled. / Happy are all who take refuge in him."

The first portion of this verse may suggest that the kings of the earth are to express their submission to God by doing obeisance to the king of Judah.

NIV offers what is arguably a better translation in which the claim is clearer. The crux of the problem is that after the word "kiss," a word appears that has two consonants, *br* that do not signify a Hebrew term that is coherent in this context. Therefore, some scholars (such as the translators of NRSV) believe there was an error in the transmission of the text. They propose that four letters at the end of verse 11 (*glyw*) were misplaced (these letters as they now stand form an imperative, "shout," as with joy in worship, which makes sense as a parallel to "serve the Lord" that precedes it). According to this theory, these letters should appear after the letters *br* to make the common expression, "his feet" (*brglyw*), the first letter being understood as a preposition that sometimes introduces the direct object.

While this argument is certainly plausible, the letters *br* do signify a well-known *Aramaic* word (a closely related language that appears in portions of Daniel and Ezra). In Aramaic *bar* is the common word meaning "son." NIV thus understands this word as a reference to the king, the "son of God" referred to earlier in the psalm by the Hebrew term for son, *bēn* (v. 7). In this way of reading the verse the foreign rulers are called to "kiss the son," that is, the king of Judah, as a sign of obedience to God. If this understanding is correct, the parallel between God and the king of Judah is striking. The kings of the earth are called to show their allegiance to God, the universal sovereign, by doing obeisance to the Davidic ruler. The reign of the earthly king is the primary sign of God's ordering of the nations and of Israel's central place in that order.

As already observed, the nations who oppose God's will and God's anointed are identified in the Psalter at certain points as the wicked. The New Testament read these psalms accordingly. (See especially Acts 4:23–30.) The righteous are those who, by contrast, submit to God's reign and align themselves with the Lord's anointed. Given this worldview, the reign of the anointed over his enemies has a direct positive impact on the righteous. The enemies of the anointed are also the enemies of God; they are the wicked who oppress and persecute the righteous. The righteous' destiny–their safety and prosperity–is vouchsafed by the presence of the king on Zion, filling the role of "son of God."

Psalm 89:1–37 (2–38)

Psalm 89 is similar to Psalm 2 in its presentation of the Davidic king as God's earthly regent who symbolizes God's universal reign. But Psalm 89 expresses the significance of the king in maintaining the order of creation more than does Psalm 2. The first two-thirds of the poem (vv. 1–37 [2–38]) consists of three subdivisions: verses 1–4 (2–5) recall God's faithfulness to the Davidic monarch; verses 5–18 (6–19) celebrate God's eternal kingship; and verses 19–37 (20–38) recount God's election of David and his line to rule into perpetuity. (See especially v. 36 [37].) Some scholars have seen Psalm 89:1–37 (2–38) as an amalgamation of once separate elements, some of which focused on the election of the Davidic monarchy (vv. 3–4 [4–5], 19–37 [20–38]) while others praised God for his universal sovereignty (vv. 1–2 [2–3], 5–18 [6–19]). But a close reading of the psalm suggests rather that the various subdivisions are a unit, the purpose of which is to highlight the choice of the Davidic king as "the firstborn, / the highest of the kings of the earth" (v. 27 [28]). Psalm 89:5–18 (6–19) presents God's reign with language and imagery that reappear in verses 19–37 (20–38). In verses 5–18 (6–19) Yahweh is the cosmic sovereign who has no equal among the divine beings:

> For who in the skies can be compared to the Lord?
>   Who among the heavenly beings is like the Lord,
> a God feared in the council of the holy ones,
>   great and awesome above all that are around him?
>   (vv. 6–7 [7–8])

A primary illustration of God's power as king is his command over the chaotic waters:

> You rule the raging of the sea;
>   when its waves rise, you still them.
> You crushed Rahab like a carcass;
>   you scattered your enemies with your mighty arm.
>   (vv. 9–10 [10–11])

Verses 13–18 (14–19) conclude this segment of the psalm with declarations of praise. The people praise God because his might is channeled through righteousness and justice, and because he is characterized by faithfulness and steadfast love (vv. 13–14 [14–15]). The final verse of this portion of the psalm, moreover, emphatically declares God's exclusive prerogative over Israel (v. 18 [19]). It sets the stage for the introduction of the human monarch as the Lord's special representative.[13]

Verses 19–37 (20–38) present the Davidic king in terms remarkably parallel to those that exalt the Divine King in verses 5–18 (6–19). The human king is established by Israel's God as the concrete expression of divine rule on earth: the strong right hand of God that is seen in his rule over the chaotic waters (v. 13 [14]) strengthens the Davidide (v. 21 [22]) so that his enemies will never overpower him (vv. 22–23 [23–24]); the king will participate in the Lord's hegemony over the waters as God sets "his [the earthly king's] hand on the sea / and his right hand on the rivers" (v. 24 [25]); just as God is the highest of all divine beings, so also the Davidic king is named "the firstborn, / the highest of the kings of the earth" (v. 27 [28]).

Whatever divine royal functions appear as the military and administrative duties of earthly kings, they represent expressions of God's universal hegemony. Human rule is also presented in the Psalms as more than a set of practical protective tasks. Human kingship is an expression on earth of

God's rule in the heavens. That is, as part of God's establishment of the world's stability, the human king has a cosmic significance as well.

The parallel between the Davidic king's rule on earth and God's rule in heaven reflects a belief seen in other parts of the Old Testament regarding the relationship between divine and earthly realms. For example, this is likely the idea that stands behind the lamentation over the prince and king of Tyre in Ezekiel 28:1–19. The prince is probably the earthly ruler (Ezek. 28:1–10) who is empowered by and does the bidding of the city's patron deity, referred to as its "king" (Ezek. 28:11–19). This idea is also known from the cache of written materials discovered in Ras Shamra (ancient Ugarit) in 1929.[14] From what can be ascertained from the Baal-Anat-Mot cycle of stories recovered there, it seems that these neighbors of Israel imagined a heavenly court that mirrored the power structure on earth. It seems that the struggle of Baal for a dominant place in the pantheon reflects the efforts of Baal's followers to gain a place of power in the political system of their society. In other words, the Canaanites' belief about Baal's sovereignty legitimated their support for particular human rulers.[15]

This inextricable link between divine and human kings at Ugarit provides in turn a helpful analogy for descriptions of the Davidic king's relationship to Yahweh. Indeed, the king in Jerusalem was not only chosen by Israel's God, but was also a tangible sign of the Lord's cosmic reign. God appoints and empowers the earthly monarch to exercise authority on God's behalf in both mythic and historical scenarios.

"To Be the Shepherd of His People": David as Protector of the Righteous

If the identification of the king as God's son marks him as the keeper of cosmic order, the identification of the ruler as "shepherd" identifies him even more directly as the defender of the righteous. As God's representative, the king provides for the righteous tangible signs of God's protective power.

The shepherd role for Israel's king appears in the culmination of Psalm 78. This psalm rehearses Israel's history from the time God spoke to Abram, through the exodus and wilderness wandering, to the beginning of monarchy in the land of Canaan. The psalm ends with God's appointment of David to care for God's flock:

> He chose his servant David,
>   and took him from the sheepfolds;
> from tending and nursing ewes he brought him
>   To be the shepherd of his people Jacob,
>   of Israel, his inheritance. (vv. 70–71)

Although the shepherd image is common for kings and other leaders in the ancient Near East, it is particularly appropriate as a symbol for Israel's conception of its king, one who protects the helpless and ensures justice for the righteous. The subtle but powerful message of the image was that the ruler of the people would be like the shepherd who guarded the helpless sheep and protected them from predators. This link between the activity of shepherds and the beneficial rule of the monarch is particularly prominent in a version of Psalm 151 (that appears in the Greek Psalter) in a scroll from Qumran cave 11 (11QPs^a). The psalm is presented as David's testimony to how God made him king over Israel. It begins with David's account of how his father gave him charge of the sheep: "He appointed me shepherd over his flock, / and ruler over his kids."[16]

Then, as the psalm closes, it uses the same language to recount David's charge as king: "He sent and took me from following the flock and anointed me with holy oil; / he appointed me as prince over his people, / and as ruler over the sons of his covenant."[17]

To be Israel's ruler was to be Israel's shepherd, to care for a people who needed protection. To be sure, the notion that the king was a shepherd to the people could be, and undoubtedly was, used as propaganda to maintain the monarch's power.[18] The king was not always shepherd in the ideal sense. Nevertheless as Judah formulated its view of kingship, even if as a hope for what could be, it modulated the typical understanding of human rule so as to emphasize the establishment of justice for the poor. Mays expresses this particularly well: "Justice and righteousness became the first and organizing responsibility of the king upon which all else depended. They are not one item in a list but the foundation on which all other possibilities rest."[19]

This is borne out in Psalms 72 and 101, two royal psalms that focus on the king's role as defender of the righteous.

"May He Defend the Poor": Psalm 72

Psalm 72 in its content and structure reflects the king's identity as defender of the righteous. The psalm divides naturally into two parts, verses 2–11 and 12–17, with verse 1 as an introduction to the whole, verses 18–20 a closing doxology, and verse 20 a colophon identifying the psalm (and previous psalms) with David. Verse 1 opens with an address to God that features an imperative "give." The one who prays petitions God to give the king "your justice" and "your righteousness." Justice and righteousness are elsewhere said to be the foundation of the Lord's throne (Ps. 89:14 [15]; 87:2). Amos typically pairs these two words to describe the principles on which a just society is founded (Am. 5:24). Justice is the administration of what is right. Righteousness is "the rightness that belongs to those who fulfill the responsibilities which their relationships to others involve."[20]

At the beginning of Psalm 72, God is recognized as the one who exercises perfect justice. Because of that fact, God is characterized by righteousness. The psalmist thus asks for these essential features of God's character to be bestowed upon the king. Here, as in Psalms 2 and 89, the king is understood as an earthly expression of the cosmic order. That order is focused, however, on the king's provision for the poor.

Whereas verse 1 includes an imperative addressed to God ("give"), verses 2–11 are linked by verbs that express wishes for the king. The wishes are grouped in three sections; the first section (vv. 2–4) wills for the king to administer justice; the second (vv. 5–7) calls for his long life, fame, and peaceful reign; the third (vv. 8–11) wishes for him worldwide dominion and acclaim. All three sections are related to the theme of justice for the poor in one way or another. The fact that verses 2–4 emphasize this point at the outset sets this as the primary agenda for what follows. Verse 2 picks up on the qualities of God that the psalmist asked God to give the king: "May he judge your people with righteousness, / and your poor with justice" (v. 2). The word "judge" here translates a Hebrew term (*dîn*) that in some contexts has the sense of "plead for" (Jer. 30:13). Followed by the expression "with righteousness," the wish is for the king to stand decidedly on the side of the poor and oppressed. This section ends (v. 4) by filling out that wish with additional detail: "May he defend the cause of the poor of the people, / give deliverance to the needy, / and crush the oppressor." "Defend the cause" here renders a form of the verb *šāpat*, which harks back to the justice of God in verse 1. "Deliverance" stands for the word *yôšia'*, which in other psalms refers to the salvation of God (Ps. 3:2, 8 [3, 9]). These words indicate again that the psalmist wishes for the king to express on behalf of the righteous the qualities that characterize God's reign.

The verse at the center of this section (v. 3) appropriately ties righteousness to *šālôm*. Though the NRSV translates the word as "prosperity," it probably connotes here a wholeness and completeness that is possible only when justice and righteousness hold the day. The verse may be saying that *šālôm* (which the "mountains yield") is evinced by righteousness.[21]

Verses 5–7 are linked also to the concern for the righteous, specifically as a sign of the cosmic order the monarch upholds. Verse five wishes long life for the king; indeed, life that extends far beyond human limits.[22] The most important hope for the king is that he will be a conduit of fertility, expressed in verse 6: "May he be like rain that falls on the mown grass, like showers that water the earth."

In the final verse of this section these wishes for the king to show the blessings of the natural realm coincide again with the well-being of the righteous. Verse 7 ends with the hope that "peace (*šālôm*) abound." The previous portion of the verse is typically translated, "In his days may righteousness flourish." Again righteousness and *šālôm* (well-being) are paired as signs of the just rule of the king. The term rendered "righteousness" is actually a form (*ṣaddîq*) that typically refers to a person or type of person, that is, to the righteous. This form has seemed difficult to many translators, as it must have seemed to the Greek version, which translated with a word meaning righteousness. Nevertheless, the word "righteous" would make sense here and would be consistent with the message of the rest of the psalm. Under the reign of the king described here, the righteous flourish. All cosmic signs of the king's right rule converge on this one primary concern, that the righteous find their place under his reign.[23]

The verbs in verses 8–11 invite a recognition of the righteous king's worldwide dominion ("from sea to sea, / and from the River to the ends of the earth," v. 8). Rulers will come from distant and famous lands and render tribute (vv. 10–11), but the reason for the king's place of superiority is his concern for the poor. The second major segment of the psalm makes this clear. Verses 12–14, which detail the depth and intensity of the king's care for the poor, begin with the Hebrew particle *kî*. This particle sometimes serves as a causative ("for"/"because") and at other times as an intensive ("indeed!"). Taken either way here, the word makes clear that the praise to be offered the king is due to his character as defender of the helpless.

Verses 12–14 present the monarch's supreme concern for the poor in even more detail than verses 2–4. He "delivers the needy" (v. 12), "has pity on the weak and the needy," and "saves the lives of the needy" (v. 13). Verse 14 brings this section to a strong conclusion with a statement about the king's care for the righteous. It says the king redeems (*yigʾal*) their lives "from oppression and violence." The term "oppression" probably refers to economic servitude (Prov. 29:13), and "violence" may have this connotation as well (2 Sam. 22:49; Ezek. 28:16). Perhaps most important, however, is the king's intimate relationship to the poor. He "has pity" on them (v. 13), and "precious is their blood in his sight" (v. 14). They are not a distant concern of his administration; indeed, their needs are his first concern.

The close relationship between king and poor is perhaps best illustrated by the description of his action on their behalf as "redemption" (v. 14). This is the language of kinship. Only a near kinsman would have such responsibility (Ruth 3:13; 4:4, 6).[24] Therefore, the king portrayed here is one who sees the poor as part of his own family and acts in loyalty to them, as a kinsman toward a close relative in need. In other words, the king is responsible for bringing people under his care into the "household of God" that they might know God's protection and care.

"I Will Destroy All the Wicked": Psalm 101

Psalm 101, like Psalm 72, is based on the assumption that the king provides a system of justice in which the righteous find a secure place. Although this psalm does not mention the king specifically, its testimony of commitment to righteousness and justice suggests the monarch is speaking. This has long been recognized. John Calvin characterized Psalm 101 this way:

> What David here says concerning singing must be understood by the reader as intimating that this psalm contains the substance of his meditations with himself, as to what kind of king he would be whenever he should be put in possession of the sovereign power which had been promised him.[25]

This psalm is concerned with justice from beginning to end. More than that, the one speaking is committed to forming a righteous character as well as establishing what is right in the legal sense.[26] Indeed, the king is concerned with having "integrity of heart," as he says in verse 2b.

Psalm 101 is not easy to outline, primarily because of the question at the end of verse 2a ("When shall I attain it?"). This problem will be considered in the next chapter. One way to conceive the rhetorical movement of the psalm is as follows: verses 1–2 set forth the king's claims concerning the integrity he wishes to maintain. These two verses begin with his intentions to focus on and know God's character: "I will sing of loyalty and of justice" (v. 1); "I will study the way that is blameless" (v. 2). "Loyalty and…justice" describe the faithfulness of God. Psalm 89 begins (v. 1 [2]) with similar words ("I will sing of your steadfast love"; (translating Hebrew ḥesed, the same word translated loyalty in 101:1). These words seem to refer to God's goodness toward David.

As observed already, "justice" is a key feature of God's reign that is acknowledged at the beginning of Psalm 72. After pledging to sing and meditate on these things (vv. 1–2a), the king then promises to model the "integrity" (NRSV "blameless"; Hebrew *tāmîm* in v. 2a, *tām* in v. 2b) of God in his own life and within his own "house." "Integrity" has to do with what is whole or complete. It refers to the ideals of government established by God, ideals already described in relation to Psalm 72.[27] The term "house" represents his kingdom, the whole extent of his rule. (See 2 Sam. 7). In other words, the king has in mind not just a commitment for his personal life, but for his administration as well.

In verses 3–5 the king gives a set of promises cast as negative actions. There are things and people the king will not do and will not tolerate. These statements speak of the king's character formation by means of his removal of nefarious elements from his realm and separation of himself from their influences. For example, the statement of verse 4a puts in negative terms what was spoken of positively in verse 2b: "Perverseness of heart shall be far from me" (v. 4a); "I will walk in integrity of heart" (v. 2b).

The positive counterpart to these statements appears in verse 6: The "faithful in the land" shall "live with me"; "whoever walks in the way that is blameless / shall minister to me." "Blameless" is again the term *tāmîm* (translated "integrity" in NAB); the key feature of God's character the king has pledged to embrace.

The psalm concludes with another set of negative declarations similar to those in verses 3–5. Verse 7 has the same emphasis on the king's "house" (communicated also by the expression "shall continue in my presence" in the second half of the verse) that is present in verse 2b. The royal administration shall be free of those who are merely looking out for themselves. The righteous, and the way of righteousness ("integrity") will characterize the king's "house." The psalm then concludes with a sweeping summary of how the king will remove those who are not out for justice: "I will destroy / all the wicked from the land, / cutting off all evildoers / from the city of the LORD." Those to be cut off are here identified as those who oppose and persecute the righteous. It is also interesting that at the close of the psalm the scope of the king's "purge" changes, from his "house" to "the city of the LORD." The change is not surprising, since the king's house has Zion as its central location. Moreover, as chapter 8 will observe, Zion is a place free from wickedness, at least in its ideal portrayal.

Conclusion

The psalms at the center of this chapter—the so-called "royal psalms"—may have drawn their language from poems originally meant to support the rule and political agenda of Judean kings. In their present form, however, these psalms seem to have a different agenda. First and foremost, they present the responsibility of the king to make evident God's reign. As Psalms 2 and 89:1–37 (2–38) show, the monarch is the son of God who represents the sovereignty of God on earth. This means particularly that as the representative of God, he establishes justice for the poor. The earthly monarch is to show an intimate connection to the righteous. As Psalm 72 indicates, he is expected to embody the righteousness of God (v. 1) and, in turn, to be like a near kinsman to the righteous by redeeming them from their trouble (v. 14). As the king testifies in Psalm 101, he commits to forming an administration in which the values of the righteous flourish. He has a righteous habit of mind—an integrity—that creates an environment in which they prosper.

It is no wonder that some of the psalms examined here—Psalm 2 particularly—were primary texts the early church used to describe the royal character of Jesus. Jesus was understood, as was his ancestor David, as one whose life embodied the presence of God and rule of God on earth. Through his life and work, and through his future work, he fulfills the role of defender of the righteous. In moving from the Psalms' expectation of the king to the New Testament's portrayal of Jesus as king, however, it is important to understand what became of the expectations for the king in light of the loss of monarchy in Israel. That is a primary concern of the Psalms and of the Psalter's concern for the righteous. The next chapter takes us to that most important matter.

7

David

The Enduring Hope

The LORD answer you in the day of trouble! (Ps. 20:1)

The last chapter showed that the king in the Psalms is identified largely by his role as protector of the righteous. He stands with those who are helpless and redeems them from their trouble, as a near kinsman would do (Ps. 72:14). The Psalter received its present shape, however, during and in the wake of the Babylonian exile, when there was no king in Judah. That raises the question, How were the expectations about the king understood in light of this trauma? What became of the hopes of the righteous that were vested in the Davidic monarch? How did the righteous conceive the king's role in their destiny during and after the exile?

These questions are in large part questions about the reign of God and how it was expressed in the human ruler. In light of the Babylonian defeat and the loss of the Davidic monarchy, how could Israel claim, "The Lord reigns!"? As Book 4 of the Psalter makes clear, Israel not only continued to make this claim, but it perhaps became the central tenet of their faith. To continue the belief in God's sovereignty, however, Israel had to come to terms with the promises made to David and the nature of the role of the king in the destiny of the righteous. This chapter looks further at how the Psalter addresses the role of the king in light of exile.

Central to this subject is the positioning of the royal psalms in the Psalter. It may be helpful for the reader to look back at the overview of

Psalms 90–150 presented in chapter 5. The discussion that follows builds on and expands certain portions of that chapter. A primary subject will be the relationship between Psalm 89 and the psalms that immediately follow it in Book 4 (Ps. 90–106). This chapter will attempt to come to terms with the fact that what is said of David in Psalm 89 is said of Israel in subsequent psalms: David, like Israel, has become the object of God's wrath (Ps. 89:38 [39]; 90:7–8) and bears painful signs of mortality; David, the Lord's servant, has passed from the scene, and now the Lord's servants, Israel, are left to discern the meaning of this loss (Ps. 90:13).

As already noted, Gerald H. Wilson put forward one of the most influential theories about the role of the royal psalms in the structure of the Psalter. Wilson supposes that the royal psalms actually serve as a kind of historical memory of the monarchy, recalling how kingship in Israel failed.[1] Specifically, he believes Psalms 2; 72; and 89 were placed at the "seams" of Books 1–3 to communicate this point.[2] These psalms, Wilson avers, frame Books 1–3 and "rehearse" the events of the Davidic monarchy, from inception at the first king's coronation (Ps. 2:7), through succession at his death (Ps. 72), to its culmination in the failure of monarchy in the Babylonian exile (Ps. 89). Book 4 then "responds" to the failed monarchy with an old message drawn from the age of Moses: "The Lord reigns" (Ps. 93:1; 96:10; 96:1; 99:1; cf. 95:3; 98:6). Wilson notes further that after this point in the Psalter, the human ruler is never called "king" (*melek*). That term is reserved for God alone. Moreover, some references to the human ruler using other terms amount to a negative critique (Ps. 118:8–9; 146:3–4). Together these features of Book 4 (and Book 5) of the Psalter point to a rejection of human kingship in favor of divine rule. The Psalter's "answer" to the loss of monarchy, Wilson avers, is that monarchy is not really necessary anyway, since Israel lived without a human king in their formative period in the wilderness under the leadership of Moses.[3] "The Lord reigns" is the final word for those who have experienced exile. By implication, Wilson proposes that the righteous are now to put their trust directly in God and not in the human agent, the king, who had previously served as an earthly symbol of God's justice on their behalf.

For Christians the question of what became of the expectations for the king is absolutely crucial. If the Psalter intends to communicate the notion that royal expectations were null and void, as Wilson says, then the New Testament's presentation of Jesus as a royal figure must go against the Psalter's understanding of human rule. But this chapter will propose that, to the contrary, the early church thought of Jesus much as the Psalms present the Davidic king. The view of the king in the Psalter, which anticipates that in the New Testament, becomes most clear when the royal psalms are read in relationship to the righteous in exile and their expectations for the king.

Who Can Save the Righteous?

Psalm 20 and the Identity of the True King

Psalm 20 shows the uncertainties about the human king that developed in the aftermath of the exile. On the one hand, this psalm shows the central importance of the king to the hope of the righteous by its inclusion of the king in the righteous' prayers. The psalm focuses on the king's ultimate benefit to the righteous and his responsibility to ensure their welfare. The king is not the protector of the people of his own accord; he is the Lord's instrument, the one who brings about God's will on earth. The righteous pray that the king exercise this role faithfully, for it is essential for their well-being that he does. On the other hand, the psalm seems to show an awareness that ultimately only God is king. The righteous, and the human king, can only rely on the Divine Ruler for their protection.

Psalm 20:1–5 (2–6) records the righteous' petitions made for the human king. These verses consist of pleas to God that indicate speech in the king's presence (for example, "The LORD answer you," v. 1 [2]; "May he send you help," v. 2 [3]). In verses 6–8 (7–9) the mode of address changes, from petition to declaration. The psalmist speaks with assurance that God will help the anointed (v. 6 [7]); then the speaker declares the people's ultimate confidence in God alone: "Some take pride in chariots, and some in horses, / but our pride is in the name of the LORD our God" (v. 7 [8]). The king here "is not the savior but the saved."[4] This aspect of the prayer makes clear that the Lord is the object of trust, not the king. Nevertheless, the king's salvation is the object of joy for the righteous who pray the prayer. They recognize that their future is linked closely to the future of the anointed.

The last verse of Psalm 20 returns to the mode of petition, but it is not clear what exactly it asks of God. It is possible that Psalm 20:9a (10a) was intended as a petition to God on behalf of the human king: "Give victory to the king."[5] If that were the case, the final portion of the verse would then read, "let him [the human king] answer us when we call" (v. 9b [10b]). Such a translation would recognize the human king's essential role in establishing God's justice on behalf of those who call out to God for deliverance.

The verse may be better translated, however, with JPS: "O Lord, grant victory! May the King answer us when we call" (v. 9 [10]). If this is the correct understanding of the words, the king in this verse is probably not the anointed for whom the psalmist prayed in verses 1–5 (2–6). Rather, it is more likely the Lord who, according to verses 6–8 (7–9), is the sole defender of the people. If this is the correct interpretation of these verses, the end of the psalm reflects Israel's struggle over how human kings should be understood in light of Yahweh's identity as King (Ex. 15:18). It reflects the idea that kingship has been democratized and now the promises once made to the monarchy are inherited by the people as a whole.[6]

Regardless of which reading of Psalm 20 is right, it is clear that human kingship in this psalm has become ambiguous. The king's office remained crucially important to the hopes of the righteous. His attention to the righteous was an expression of God's salvation. But the king's success depends on God's salvation. The monarch was as dependent on God's reign as any other subject of the Divine King.

The Throne of Justice: Who Can Protect the Righteous?

Another sign of the ambiguity over the power of the human king in the Psalter is the apparent shift away from the king's role as one who brings justice for the righteous. Book 2 of the Psalter and the "prayers of David, son of Jesse," end with a grand prayer for the king to ensure justice for the righteous and to cause righteousness to flourish in his domain. As the last chapter showed, Psalm 72 is a prayer for the king to act as defender of the righteous. He is to judge the people "with righteousness" (v. 2), even as God does. Under his reign the poor and oppressed are to find protection, for he defends their cause (v. 4).

If Psalm 72 presents the grandest hopes for and confidence in the Davidic king, Psalm 89 expresses the most profound disappointment. Book 3 ends with a psalm that seems to express a direct contradiction, or at least a diametrically opposite perspective, on the king than that of Psalm 72. Psalm 89 laments that the hopes expressed in Psalm 72 are now dashed. To be sure, the hopes for the king to defend the poor and oppressed are not mentioned explicitly in Psalm 89. What is mentioned—indeed what is emphasized—is that the king's largesse, through which Psalm 72 says he would have capacity to act in that role, has been reduced to nothing. The parallel language of the two psalms suggests they are working in tandem—at the ends of Books 2 and 3—to communicate this sad fact. In both psalms the monarch's rule is promised to last like the sun and moon (72:5; 89:36–37 [37–38]); in both psalms the king's dominion will cover an expanse from sea to river (72:8; 89:25 [26]); also in both psalms the king is offered longevity and a name that will endure (72:15, 17; 89:4 [5], 29 [30], 36 [37]). The parallels in language in the two psalms shows that they operate with the same set of expectations for the king.

In Psalm 72 these signs of successful rule and political vigor are specifically for the purpose of establishing justice for the poor. In the ideal view of the Psalter, monarchy was "an attempt to implement very concretely God's policies of justice and righteousness."[7] Indeed, Psalm 72 opens with the hope that the king will rule with "justice" and "righteousness," the very qualities at the center of God's reign. Psalm 72:1 suggests, therefore, that the king is one through whom God's protection of the poor will be expressed on earth. Psalm 89 does not mention the loss that comes for the righteous, but such explicit reference is not necessary. That has been the benefit of the monarch to this point in the Psalter, as Psalm 72 highlights so pointedly.

Psalm 89 laments the fact that the king's political prowess, which would allow such concrete expression of God's reign, is reduced to nothing.

From what has been observed thus far about the concern for the destiny of the righteous in the Psalter, one would expect Book 4's "response" to Psalm 89 to be directed in large part toward the king's inability to establish justice for the righteous. That does seem to be an important part of Psalms 90–106. While the general notion that Psalms 90–106 reject human rule is untenable (for reasons spelled out earlier), these psalms do implicitly declare that certain prerogatives of the king are limited. Chief among them is the establishment of a just rule in which the righteous are given the protection they deserve. As a result, the responsibility of the monarch to establish justice for the poor, to ensure the destiny of the righteous, is transferred from human king to Divine King, at least temporarily.

This "transfer" is accomplished by the presence of certain vocabulary in Psalm 89 that is then repeated, but applied to God (instead of the human king), in Book 4. It has been observed already that the Hebrew root *mlk*, from which derive the noun *melek* (king) and the verb *mālak* ("to reign" or "to be king"), is used of God in Book 4 and that the label "king" is not applied to a human ruler beyond this point in the Psalms. As Wilson argues, something has changed in the perception of the human king. Perhaps the greatest clue to the psalmist's interests lies in the appearance of the word "throne." The term appears five times in Psalm 89. Four times the word refers to the throne of David, which God promises to establish forever (vv. 4 [5], 29 [30], 36 [37], 44 [45]). The final reference is part of the complaint that God "hurled his throne to the ground." In each case, David's throne symbolizes his divinely appointed authority, which, earlier in Psalm 72, is for the explicit purpose of establishing justice. The one other occurrence of "throne" in Psalm 89 refers to the seat of God's power (v. 14 [15]). It states significantly that "righteousness and justice are the foundation of your throne." Those features of God's character that Psalm 72 wishes for the rule of the Davidic king are only attributed to God in Psalm 89.

In Book 4, which "responds" to the lament over the fallen monarchy, the throne of God is mentioned four times as well (Ps. 93:2; 94:20; 97:2; 103:19), with two of the occurrences dealing specifically with the ability and willingness of God to establish justice for the poor. Psalm 97:2 repeats the description of God's throne found in Psalm 89:29 [30], "righteousness and justice are the foundation of his throne." Psalm 94:20 links God's rule specifically to God's protection of the poor in a different way. The term occurs here in connection with those whose rule is characterized by wickedness and oppression of the poor.

The expression "wicked rulers" is a translation of two words that could be rendered "the throne of the wicked" (*kissē' hawwôt*). God's throne is characterized by righteousness and justice, in contrast to the wicked whose "thrones" are founded on violence against widows and orphans (vv. 4–7).[8]

With this emphasis on the justice of God's reign, Book 4 presents the emphatic claim that the Divine King offers protection for the righteous, something the human monarch was unable to do during the monarchical period of Israel's history. In this sense, therefore, Book 4 of the Psalter does seem to downplay the efficacy of the human king. Royal prerogative to defend the righteous and establish justice for the poor rests solely in God, at least in the present.

The Enduring Presence of and Praise for the King

Despite these signs that the righteous are encouraged to look exclusively to God, the Divine King, rather than to the human ruler for their protection, the Psalter never completely gives up on David as a sign of divine presence and justice. Indeed, one main weakness of Wilson's theory is the simple fact that royal psalms appear in the Psalter after Psalm 89, after monarchy was supposedly rejected in favor of God's exclusive rule (Ps. 101; 110; 132; 144). Particularly striking is the pairing of Psalms 144 and 145 near the end of the book. Psalm 144 is a royal, Davidic psalm and gives testimony to the human ruler's endowment with authority by God. Psalm 145 praises the Lord as king. These two psalms together suggest that divine and human rule continue to work together in the mind of the psalmist.[9]

The King as Victim of Exile

Perhaps more interesting, however, is the fact that the Psalms do not criticize the king for unfaithfulness or blame him for Judah's exile. Instead, he retains his privileged place in the destiny of the righteous, it seems. This fact is most evident when the Psalter's presentation of the king is compared with the very different presentation in the Deuteronomistic History (Joshua-Kings), a work that does point specifically to the king as the cause of exile. Indeed, the History declares concerning the Northern Kingdom (Israel) that, because of Jeroboam's sins,

> The LORD will strike Israel, as a reed is shaken in the water; he will root up Israel out of this good land that he gave to their ancestors, and scatter them beyond the Euphrates, because they have made their sacred poles, provoking the LORD to anger. He will give Israel up *because of the sins of Jeroboam,* which he sinned and which he caused Israel to commit." (1 Kings 14:15–16, emphasis added; cf. 2 Kings 17:7–23)

The History likewise pins the blame for Judah's exile on the recalcitrant Manasseh:

> *Because king Manasseh of Judah has committed these abominations,* has done things more wicked than all that the Amorites did, who were before him, and has caused Judah also to sin with his idols;

therefore thus says the LORD, the God of Israel, *I am bringing upon Jerusalem and Judah such evil that the ears of everyone who hears of it will tingle.* I will stretch over Jerusalem the measuring line for Samaria, and the plummet for the house of Ahab; I will wipe Jerusalem as one wipes a dish, wiping it and turning it upside down. (2 Kings 21:11-13, emphasis added)

The Psalter gives no hint of any such indictment of the king. That seems significant, especially since some of the royal psalms follow so closely on texts in the History as they describe God's promises to David. Psalms 2; 72; and 89 basically recapitulate the essential promises to David that God made through Nathan in 2 Samuel 7:1-17. In that text Nathan delivers to David an oracle in which God offers a grant of divine support summarized in God's pledge to "build a house,"–that is, a dynasty for him that will last forever. God pledges specifically, "Your house and your kingdom shall be made sure forever before me; your throne shall be established forever" (2 Sam. 7:16). David thus receives God's pledge that will apply to all his descendants who rule after him. Concerning each of the kings in his line, God assures, "I will be a father to him, and he shall be a son to me" (2 Sam. 7:14a); "I will make for you a great name, like the name of the great ones of the earth" (2 Sam. 7:9b); and "I will give you rest from all your enemies" (2 Sam. 7:11).

The royal psalms at the seams of Books 1-3 of the Psalter create a framework dominated by these promises. Psalm 2, for example, identifies the king as God's son (Ps. 2:7) and promises that his enemies will be dashed "in pieces like a potter's vessel" (Ps. 2:9). Psalm 72 is different in character in that it is cast as David's prayer for Solomon. Nevertheless, it contains two elements that are present in Nathan's oracle: the prayer includes a wish for the king's name to "endure forever" (v. 17) and for him to exercise worldwide dominion over his foes (vv. 8-9). Psalm 89, the final psalm in this sequence, contains the fullest expression of these features. This poem alludes to 2 Samuel 7:1-17, or perhaps to a source that influenced both texts, at numerous points. Verse 19 [20] ("Then you spoke in a vision to your faithful one") seems to have Nathan in mind.[10] The prophet is the "faithful one" who received God's message and delivered it to David (2 Sam. 7:17 specifically mentions the visionary experience of Samuel). The promise that God's steadfast love (*hesed*) would remain with David and his descendants is a key part of both texts. Psalm 89 and 2 Samuel 7:1-17 also share the notion that God would discipline his son, the Davidic king "with a rod" (*běšēbet*; 2 Sam. 7:14; Ps 89:32 [33]) and "with scourges" or "blows" or "floggings" (*bingāʿîm*; 2 Sam. 7:14 ; Ps 89:32 [33]), but his steadfast love would remain unconditionally (2 Sam. 7:15; Ps 89:33 [34]).

The psalmist could easily have interpreted exile as the "rod" and "scourges" with which God would deal with a disobedient monarch. But that is not the case. Psalm 89 does not indict the king for any wrongdoing, and does not call monarchy as an institution into question. To be sure, Psalms 72 and 89 both speak of the need for the king to be obedient for God's blessing (Ps. 72:12-14; 89:31-32 [32-33]).[11] Nevertheless, one is hard pressed to find any passage in Psalms 72 and 89, or any text in Books 1-3 that critiques the king. Psalm 78 is typical of the psalmist's address to God in light of Judah's suffering. The only sin the psalm calls to mind is the iniquity of Israel's ancestors:

> He established a decree in Jacob,
> and appointed a law in Israel,
> which he commanded our ancestors
> to teach to their children;
> that they next generation might know them,
> the children yet unborn,
> and rise up and tell them to their children,
> so that they should set their hope in God,
> and not forget the works of God,
> but keep his commandments;
> and that they should not be like their ancestors,
> a stubborn and rebellious generation,
> a generation whose heart was not steadfast,
> whose spirit was not faithful to God. (vv. 5-8)

As the psalm develops further, it recalls how God delivered Israel from bondage in Egypt, how God led them in the wilderness and brought them into Canaan, and yet the people were unfaithful. The one bright spot in this history comes at the end of Psalm 78 when, as the last chapter observed, the poem declares that God chose David to shepherd his sheep and, "With upright heart he tended them, / and guided them with skillful hand" (v. 72).

It is not certain why the Psalter does not indict the king for unfaithfulness. It is clear, however, that the Psalter does not identify the cause of exile so much as it deals with the question of how to believe in God's reign and in the promises made to David in light of that devastating event. As noted already, the Psalter treats the exiled people as the righteous who suffer before the wicked. Therefore, the question of Psalm 89 is essentially a question about the destiny of the righteous: "Lord, where is your steadfast love of old, / which by your faithfulness you swore to David?" (v. 49 [50]). Psalms 2–89, therefore, primarily raise questions about God's faithfulness in light of God's promises to David. If David (symbolic of monarchy in Judah) was not unfaithful, how should the promises to David be interpreted? In what ways should the hopes of the righteous be recast in light of the exile? The questions are really questions of theodicy.[12] How can the righteous know that, indeed, "the Lord reigns"?

Hope Again for God's Presence with the King: Psalm 101

The Psalter also expresses a quite positive expectation for the king and the future of kingship. Despite the fact that Book 4 of the Psalter responds to the loss of monarchy with the claim that "the Lord reigns," it offers no sign that monarchy was a mistake or that the faith of the righteous in the Davidic king was misplaced. Rather, the psalms in Book 4 suggest that the righteous' hope in a human ruler was recast as a future hope. The ongoing expectation and longing for a human king is particularly evident in Psalm 101.

In light of the content of Psalms 72 and 89, and the emphasis of Psalms 93–100 on the justice of God's reign, Psalm 101 is extremely important. Psalm 101 has often been overlooked in discussions of the theological message of Book 4. Indeed, the plethora of references to Moses and the mosaic era in Psalms 90–106 seem to have led some scholars to ignore this psalm and to deny the enduring place of the king in the hopes of God's people. But Psalm 101 is an important reminder that the king remains central to the concern for the destiny of the righteous.

Psalm 101 is largely a pledge by the king (cast by the superscription as David) to walk "the way that is blameless" (v. 2a). His promises of loyalty to God take the specific shape of defending the righteous and destroying the wicked. Because Psalm 101 has the character of a royal testimony, many scholars have concluded it was used originally (or at least some form of this psalm) in a coronation ritual or in a ceremony celebrating and reaffirming the king's reign.[13] That being the case, the placement of the psalm is rather puzzling.

The psalm's character as royal testimony is striking in light of the fact that God, the Divine King, has been presented in previous psalms as the one who is able to establish justice, and in light of the fact that the entire section in which the psalm is located is shaped by the circumstances of exile and loss of the monarchy. It is possible that the psalm appears in Book 4 as a statement of hope that God's reign will one day be worked out in the rule of a Davidic king. If the arrangement of psalms is taken seriously, the placement of the psalm alone might suggest that point. But one other feature of Psalm 101 perhaps indicates that this was precisely the message intended. Namely, verse 2aβ seems to be the king's plea to God to restore the vigor that allows him to defend the righteous. This line comes after the ruler's opening pledge to "sing of loyalty and justice" and after the declaration, "I will study the way that is blameless" (vv. 1–2aα). The words that follow seem to pose a question as to when God's favor will once again shine on the king. NRSV and JPS render the line, "When shall I attain it?" while NIV translates, "When will you come to me?"[14] In the translation in NRSV and JPS, the "it" in question is perhaps the "loyalty" and "justice" of which the king sings in verse 1, which in turn constitutes the "integrity" or "way that is blameless" that the king says he is studying in verse 2aα. But NIV may have the best translation. The king has just pledged to live in integrity. "Integrity" signals wholeness and completeness, which indicates that he reflects the character of God. The question that follows is, when will God restore God's favor that will permit the king to rule, to exercise that integrity in the form of justice for the poor? Moreover, the way the question is posed indicates the main concern is the concern the righteous have concerning God's presence: "When will you come to me?" As one of the righteous, the king desires to be near God. God's presence, in turn, empowers him to act on behalf of the righteous.

Given the location of Psalm 101 in Book 4, the king's question in verse 2 may be the most significant element of the psalm. As McCann rightly notes, "If it is not considered a later addition or emended somehow, it has the force of a plea for help that gives the rest of the psalm the character of a complaint."[15] Indeed, whether this line is a later addition or not, it casts the testimony of just rule as a hope for future rule. In the context of Book 4, Psalm 101 is a response to the downfall of the monarchy in the form of a plea that monarchy be restored. As McCann observes further, the juxtaposition of Psalms 101 and 102 give added weight to this view. Psalm 102 is another psalm of David and, thus, it presents the voice of the king once again. This psalm is the plea of "one afflicted," as the superscription indicates. Here David once again identifies with the poor and downcast (the word "afflicted" is the familiar ʿānî, a synonym for righteous). He complains about his own troubles, which would seem to mean mainly the destruction of the monarchy. He also prays for the restoration of Zion, the seat of the monarchy in Judah.[16] These two psalms together in Book 4 indicate that the righteous have not forgone their hope in the king. To the contrary, as they continue their faith in God's reign, they also continue to hope that divine rule will be incarnate in a king of Judah.

Conclusion

The present form of the royal psalms and the way they appear in the context of the Psalter indicates that kingship has undergone a significant reinterpretation. As chapter 6 showed, David is now identified with the nation. What was once worked out through the royal house is now fulfilled in the life of the whole people. That being the case, the identification of David with the nation effects a theologically significant transformation of both. The king is no longer one who exercises world dominion. He is a humble servant of the Lord who is characterized by trouble and suffering. The theme of the king's suffering at the hands of the nations is built into the structure of Books 1–3. Psalm 2 introduces this theme: "Why do the nations conspire…against the LORD and his anointed" (vv. 1–2). But the subject is expressed perhaps more pointedly and personally in Psalm 3. This psalm is set, according to the superscription, when David is driven out of Jerusalem by his son Absalom (2 Sam. 15). Here David appears for the first time in the Psalter. He is being persecuted and pursued by enemies. The psalm opens, "O LORD, how many are my foes! / Many are rising against me." The other psalms that "frame" Books 1–3 also express this theme. Psalm 41:5 notes that "My enemies wonder in malice / when I will die, and my name perish." Psalm 72 continues the same theme with a prayer that the king's name endure forever. Psalm 89 picks up the royal-messianic promises of the covenant only to question their validity: "Lord, where is your steadfast love of old, / which by your faithfulness you swore to David?" (v. 49 [50]) The psalm focuses on how the king has been humiliated: "Remember, O Lord, how your servant is taunted" (v. 50 [51]).

Cast as a suffering figure, David in the Psalms appears much like the one Second Isaiah identifies as the "servant of the Lord" (Isa. 42:1–4; 49:1–6; 50:4–11; 52:13–53:12). David is one who knows humiliation and shame, "a man of suffering and acquainted with infirmity" (Isa. 53:3). Kingship is transformed in the Psalter by its exclusive association with David and, in turn, by the characterization of David as God's servant who bears the shame of the people. The king in the Psalter is not one in whom the people find refuge so much as he is one who seeks refuge in God and models a life of dependence on the Lord for the people.

But the presence of David as an exemplary figure also points to a future leader, a "David" of the future who will lead in accord with the kingdom God brings. The hope is similar to that expressed in Ezekiel 37:24–28. The Ezekiel text presents a cluster of ideas that also appear in the Psalter in relation to the future David: the name David is given as the name of the ruler; he is referred to as the prince of the people and the servant of the Lord; through this one God will establish an everlasting covenant. Ezekiel's vision recalls the royal ideals of Deuteronomy 17:14–20.[17] In a similar way the Psalter remembers David and projects him onto the future as well.

The notion that the book of Psalms rejected kingship is difficult to maintain. After supposedly the king has been critiqued, the king appears in Books 4 and 5, albeit with other titles (most notably, "my lord" [*adonai*] in Ps. 110:1). Most importantly, three prominent psalms about the king appear in Books 4 and 5 and portray him still as God's representative, the one begotten by God at his coronation (Ps. 101; 132; and esp. 110). Furthermore, it would seem incongruous that the Psalter completely gave up on monarchy, since this book is the primary source for New Testament writers who present the significance of Jesus' work in royal terms. As J. J. M. Roberts points out, many of what have been taken to be central biblical themes owe their existence or their peculiar biblical shape to the imperial theology first developed in the David-Solomonic court and then transmitted and elaborated in the royal cult of the subsequent Judean court.[18]

In other words, the biblical tradition itself continued to maintain monarchy at least as a category for understanding faith long after the historical kings of Israel and Judah passed from the scene.[19] Even though the failure of monarchy surely influenced the shape of the Psalter, the king does not appear in the book as one to be despised or rejected. Rather, he is a suffering figure who represents the nation in its suffering. As the object of sympathy, the king is not blamed for exile, but rather is presented at one with the nation that experiences it.

For people of faith in all ages, Israel's struggle to understand how God continued to reign during and after the exile provides a model of faith. At its core, Israel's faith was not in a human king, but a divine king. Israel claimed "the Lord reigns" as its central tenet. The righteous believed they would find refuge under Yahweh's wings; God was their dwelling place, as God had been for all generations (Ps. 90:1). But for the righteous, divine security was made known in part through a human agent, the Davidic king. When forced to live without the monarch, the righteous' faith did not fail, though. It rested on the solid foundation of divine rule and divine justice, modulating only with respect to the present understanding of the agency through which that rule and justice would be expressed. The royal structure of faith and the belief in a human agent who brings God's justice for the righteous never disappeared. The persistence of that structure led the followers of Jesus to see in the Crucified One the "son of David," and to identify him as king. The church claims that the Divine Presence appeared in the person of Jesus, as if to answer the plea of the king in Ps 101: 2aβ ("When will you come to me?" NIV).

8

Mount Zion

City of God, Home of the Righteous

> *Out of Zion, the perfection of beauty,*
> *God shines forth.* (Ps. 50:2)

If the righteous' hope for God's justice is known mainly through the Lord's anointed, their desire to be "near God" is experienced mainly by means of the temple located on Mount Zion, where the king was enthroned. Zion is sometimes used as a synonym for Jerusalem (Ps. 128:5), but it more specifically refers to the hilltop in Jerusalem on which the temple was located (Ps. 84:4). As Judah's central worship site, Zion was the place God's people experienced God's nearness and, consequently, God's just reign. Their expressed desire to be near God–to be in Zion–is communicated as a desire to be in the temple or among worshipers there.

Worship on Zion gave the righteous a view of God's reign in the midst of the threats of the wicked that provided hope for living. Psalm 73 has already been explored as a psalm that gives testimony to the power of the worshiping community to create a reality that was different from the one regularly experienced. Observations about the fate of the righteous and the wicked dominate the psalm. Despite the opening confession that God is good to the upright, verses 2–12 call the affirmation into question. The problem is that the righteous, to whom supposedly "God is good" (v. 1), are at present plagued (vv. 5, 14). The wicked are not only not plagued (v. 5), they have all the outward signs of prosperity (the term in v. 3 is *šālôm*). They have health (v. 4) and wealth (v. 12). Moreover, although verse 10 is difficult, it seems to say that the wicked have the approval of many of

God's people.[1] Above all, the wicked are arrogant, living as though they could sustain themselves out of their own resources (vv. 6–9, 11). And still they prosper.

The psalmist wonders if devotion to God is in vain (v. 13) until entering "the sanctuary of God." There the psalmist perceives the "final destiny" (as NIV translates v. 17). The word for the location of the psalmist's revelation does not clearly refer to the temple. It is a plural term, "sanctuaries" (*miqdĕšim*). Nevertheless, the larger context suggests the Jerusalem temple. This is a place the psalmist can be "near God" and in which he or she professes the Lord as refuge (v. 28). The point is that the worship on the holy mountain gives the righteous a view of the world as it will be–indeed, as it is in God's plan and in God's future. In that the psalmist is assured of security.

This radical experience in the context of worship on Zion is not surprising in light of the importance of worship in general in the ancient world. For ancient people, who did not separate life into secular and religious realms, the cult had "life-creating, order-establishing, and meaning-giving power."[2] It mediated and ordered contact with God in a way that assured stability for living. For that reason the psalmist longs to be in the temple when at a distance (Ps. 42–43), and those who are privileged to abide in the temple precincts count themselves particularly blessed (Ps. 65:4 [5]).

This chapter explores the question of what exactly the righteous celebrated on Zion that gave them such a meaningful orientation to life. The discussion centers on psalms that celebrate God's reign on Zion. The chapter begins with Psalm 24, which is important for understanding the claim of God's sovereignty and the place the righteous have in relation to it. This psalm records a dramatic declaration of God's reign that was set in the temple. It also recognizes the righteous as sole participants in the celebration. The discussion then moves to particular aspects of God's reign that are hinted at or anticipated by Psalm 24, and to psalms that illustrate those aspects of divine rule.

An important note about the Psalms' presentation of Mount Zion: Much of what the Psalter says about Zion is only "true" to the believer. Zion is seen and experienced as described here only by those who believe God rules the world.

The King of Glory and the Call to Righteousness: Psalm 24

Psalm 24 was examined in chapter 2 as a psalm that describes the activity of the righteous: they "have clean hands and pure hearts" and "do not lift up their souls to what is false" (v. 4). In other words, the righteous promote the well-being of the community rather than simply looking out for themselves. As they do so, they participate in God's vision for the world. Chapter 2 also noted that the character of the righteous is closely tied to their praise of God. Now, this chapter examines in more detail the nature of that praise.

Psalm 24 has in its background a ceremony in which the Lord enters the holy city and occupies his throne ritually by means of the movement of the ark to its place in the temple.[3] The psalm is typically classified by form critics as an "entrance liturgy."[4] As chapter 2 discussed, Psalm 24 has at its center a set of questions and responses concerning who may ascend God's holy hill (vv. 3–6). The implication is that only the righteous may "seek the face of the God of Jacob" (v. 6). That is, the righteous alone can know God's favor and be "near God." Psalm 24 indicates that what the righteous experience on Zion specifically is an enactment of God's kingship. And, perhaps more importantly, they are permitted to "ascend the hill of the LORD" (v. 3a) because they acknowledge God's reign. Indeed, what essentially is celebrated on Zion is that "the Lord reigns."

Psalm 24:1–2 contain a general confession of the Lord's sovereignty over creation, which is central to his reign:

The earth is the Lord's and all that is in it
 the world, and those who live in it
for he has founded it on the seas,
 and established it on the rivers.

At first glance this profession of faith in God as creator may seem to have little to do with Zion. But the description of the Lord's creative work provides a prelude to the experience of God's sovereignty on the holy mountain. God's kingship is described primarily in terms of his ownership of the world as seen in the defeat of the chaotic waters. The seas and rivers symbolize the forces of chaos that threaten the order God has established (v. 2). On Zion, however, the Lord's ownership of the world and the stability and order of the cosmos God established on the watery chaos is made known. In the final four verses of the psalm, the Lord's kingship on Zion specifically is celebrated, thus bringing the praise of God as creator of the world to the specific identification of God as one who rules there (vv. 7–10).

Psalm 24 concludes with one of the most stirring proclamations of God's kingship in the Psalter. Verses 7–10 identify God as the "King of glory" and the "LORD of hosts." The latter title in particular is associated with the ark. The term "hosts" can also be translated "armies," and, indeed, the ark is often associated with warfare. But hosts/armies here probably does not refer to human military forces. Rather, the word denotes the heavenly forces at God's command, those around his heavenly throne who do his bidding (Ps. 29:1–2; 82:1; 89:6–7 [7–8]). The warfare that stands in the background of this psalm is God's defeat of chaos, which is implied in the opening verses of the psalm (vv. 1–2).

"King of glory" appears nowhere else in the Old Testament as a label for Israel's God. A similar label, "God of glory," however, does appear in Psalm 29:3 in a way that helps clarify the meaning of the expression in Psalm 24.

Psalm 29 calls worshipers to ascribe glory to God in a cultic shout (vv. 1–2, 9). The ascription is made because the Lord has shown himself a mighty warrior by his defeat of the chaotic waters (v. 3). Both titles for God in verses 7–10 identify the one enthroned on the cherubim, who rules in Zion, as the one who also reigns over the world in its entirety.

The actual entry of the ark into Zion and the temple is accompanied by a shout, "Lift up your heads, O gates! / and be lifted up, O ancient doors! / that the King of glory may come in" (v. 7). This and the following verses contain both a strong affirmation of faith in Yahweh and a polemical statement about the gods Yahweh is said to displace. As indicated above, "King of glory" refers to the one who created the world by the defeat of chaos.

In ancient Israel's environment, numerous gods were said to occupy this position. Marduk in Babylon, Baal in Canaan, or Chemosh in Moab could all bear such a title. But Psalm 24 says emphatically that such claims are false. Verse 10 sets the matter aright: "Who is this King of glory? / The LORD of hosts, / he is the King of glory." The psalm makes this claim also by subtle reference to the Canaanite Baal myth. At one point in the Baal epic the gods are dejected because of the power of Prince Sea (who represents chaos). They hang their heads in subjection to him. But Baal, who eventually defeats Prince Sea, encourages them, "Lift up your heads, O gods." Psalm 24:7 is likely an adaptation of this line.

Gates in ancient Israel had no moving parts that could "lift up." Rather, the psalm is using a secondary metaphor in which the worship leader speaks to the gates rather than the gods.[5] So, just as Baal returned victorious from battle to be proclaimed king in the Canaanite epic, Psalm 24:7–10 presents the entry of Yahweh into the temple to be declared king based on his defeat of the seas and rivers (v. 2). By borrowing from the language and form of Israel's neighbors' presentation of Baal, the psalmist makes the point again that Yahweh is the King of glory, and Baal is not.

After the opening words of praise in verses 1–2, and before the celebration of the entry of the ark in verses 7–10, appears a liturgy, or at least a passage influenced by a liturgy, that was probably used at the entry to the temple (vv. 3–6). The purpose of this section has to do with the holiness of Zion as the locus of God's rule. As Mays says: "What has been made holy is marked off from everything else by its identification with God. It must be kept separate from whatever is inimical to God and contradicts God."[6]

Verse 3 presents questions originally spoken by a priest or representative leader: "Who shall ascend the hill of the LORD? / And who shall stand in his holy place?" The answers given in verses 4–6, as chapter 2 has already pointed out, portray people of ideal faith, those who trust in God's rule, in line with the proper response demanded of those on the holy mountain. Those approved to ascend the holy hill are those who align themselves with God's will and submit themselves to God's reign; as a result they know the blessings of God's reign on Zion. They "shall never be moved" (15:5).

Psalm 24 is an example of the celebration of God's kingship on Zion and what that means to the righteous. On Zion God is declared creator, the one who masters chaos. He is also the one who is above all other gods. These claims would have been extremely important to the righteous who suffered under the threats of the wicked. To know that God still ruled over all other powers, despite present circumstances that could be taken to mean otherwise, must have given shape to life and faith.

Significantly, according to Psalm 24, only the righteous were permitted to share in this celebration of God's kingship on Zion. This perspective on the world, and on who rules the world, is their exclusive property. Hence, in a sense also, Zion "belongs" to the righteous. Only they are allowed to ascend the holy hill and gain access to the divine reign.

God "With Us": Psalm 46

Psalm 24 provides a good overview of what the righteous experienced in worship on Zion and why it was important. One aspect of the Zion celebration was God's victory over chaos in the ordering of the world. For people who had experienced defeat and exile, the belief in God as creator was closely tied to their belief in God as helper and defender. Isaiah 45:18–19 indicates that Israel could have interpreted the devastation of 587 B.C.E. as a sign that God had lost control of the world. But Israel was assured that God did not create a chaos. The Lord still reigns. In the Psalter Zion symbolizes the order within God's reign. This is seen particularly in Psalm 46.

Psalm 46 opens with a confession already identified with the righteous: "God is our refuge (*maḥsê*) and strength" (v. 1 [2]). In verses 7 (8) and 11 (12), a similar line appears to frame the entire psalm: "the God of Jacob is our refuge (*miśgāb*)." Verses 7 [8] and 11[12] include another expression that in Hebrew sounds quite similar: "the LORD of hosts is with us." "With us" (ʿ*immānû*) sounds like the word translated "our" in verse 1 (a word that literally reads, "for us"; Hebrew *lānû*).

The structure these three verses provide makes clear that the overarching message of Psalm 46 is the one already observed to be central to the concerns of the righteous: the righteous desire God's presence more than anything else. The expression "the LORD of hosts is with us; the God of Jacob is our refuge" sounds much like the name of the child the prophet Isaiah promised as a sign of God's presence: Immanuel, "God with us" (Isa. 7:14; ʿ*immānûʾel*). The psalm declares that this presence is known through the beauty and order of Mount Zion.

After the declaration of God's refuge in verse 1, the psalm confesses trust in God even in the midst of chaos' eruption into the order God established:

> Therefore, we will not fear, though the earth should change,
>   though the mountains shake in the heart of the sea;
> though its waters roar and foam,
>   though the mountains tremble with its tumult. (vv. 2–3 [3–4])

The translation, "though the earth should change…," may sound rather hypothetical and may suggest to some readers that the psalmist is here raising a far-fetched possibility that certainly will not come to pass. The Hebrew construction actually suggests a more real fear.[7] Verse 2 [3] is perhaps better rendered, "Therefore we will not fear at the earth's changing, / at the mountains shaking in the heart of the sea." This particular description of upheaval may have been influenced by earthquakes and other natural disasters, as some commentators have suggested.[8] Nevertheless, in the mind of people in the ancient Near East chaos was a persistent threat that transcended such events. God created the world mainly as an act of subduing chaos and the threat of the unruly waters never completely subsided.[9]

The sea that ancient Israelites believed to be beneath the inhabited territory was always an imagined danger. Even the mountains, thought to be most firmly anchored and secure, could be shaken if the waters of the "great deep" rebelled against the limits God established. Psalm 46:2–3 [3–4] has this threat of the reversal of creation in view, a view not unlike that the flood narrative in Genesis 6–9 describes.[10] The psalm declares that God will be "with us" even if the order of the world collapses.

Psalm 46 sets Mount Zion over against the chaotic instability of the earth below the mountain. Verse 5 [6] declares, "God is in the midst of the city; it shall not be moved." Zion is the symbol of God's creative work, of God's establishment of order at the beginning of time, and of God's continued maintenance of God's promise to keep the earth secure for humankind (Gen. 9:15). Anthropologists sometimes explain such an association of a mountain with the world's stability as belief in a "cosmic mountain."[11] Mircea Eliade explains the cosmic mountain as the center of the habitable world and as the axis between heaven and earth. As the center of the earth, the cosmic mountain was naturally the most secure place on earth, apart from which chaos was experienced.[12] This is precisely what Psalm 46:4–5 [5–6] is claiming about Zion. With chaos all around, God's mountain is the place of security, where the presence and order of the creator God may be known.

Psalm 46 also assumes that Zion, as center of the earth, was the location of Eden, the paradise of God. Ezekiel 28:13–14 makes this connection explicit. In an indictment of the king of Tyre (perhaps the patron deity of that city), God states that he was in the beginning in Eden (v. 13) and later in the same address he identifies his origins "on the holy mountain" (v. 14). No other text, and none of the Psalms make the connection this directly, but they portray Zion with features of the garden paradise that make the association almost unmistakable.

Jon Levenson argues that the creation account in Genesis 2:4b–25 has Zion, the cosmic mountain, in mind as the locus of Eden. He bases his thesis in part on the references to water that originates from Eden and goes forth to water the whole earth. This portrait of Eden as the source of the earth's water presumes that Eden is on a mountain. It is hard to imagine that the author of this text would consider any mountain other than Zion as the location. Moreover, the list of rivers that flow from Eden includes the name Gihon. Since this is the name of the sacred stream that supplied Mount Zion its water, it seems likely, again, that the author has Zion as his model as he writes of Eden.[13]

Although the Psalms do not identify Zion with Eden explicitly, the psalmic portrait of the holy mountain as a place of abundant water suggests that the two are equivalent. This imagery is prominent in Psalm 46: "There is a river whose streams make glad the city of God, / the holy habitation of the Most High" (v. 4 [5]). The river with its divisions is reminiscent of the river that divides in Eden: "A river flows out of Eden to water the garden, and from there it divides and becomes four branches" (Gen. 2:10). For the poet of Psalm 46, who lived with both the primordial dread of chaotic water and the reality of the scarcity of water necessary for life, Zion was a place where life-giving water flowed in abundance.

The river and streams of the city symbolized the blessings of God known to those who worshiped there. This image of Zion was a reminder to the righteous that God had created an orderly world. In such a world the wicked would perish as surely as God had subdued chaos in the beginning. For the author of Psalm 46, these features of Mount Zion gave reason to feel secure there, to be assured that "God is with us." For the righteous, it was a reminder that God still reigned and that the threats of the wicked (symbolized by chaos) could not prevail.

The Lord, above All Gods

One important dimension of Psalm 24's description of God's reign on Mount Zion is Yahweh's superiority to the deities of the nations. This claim appears in Psalm 24:7–10 in subtle ways. The message is more explicit in other psalms. This claim must have been particularly important for those who experienced exile. As a captive people, "the Lord reigns" was an essential claim. It carried the sense that God was superior to other deities and called them to account. This message is connected directly to the experience of the righteous on Zion.

Psalm 48 communicates this idea by describing Zion as being "in the far north" (Ps. 48:2 [3]). A better translation of this line is "on the summit of

Zaphon" (as JPS renders). The Hebrew term *ṣāpôn* does have the directional sense ("north") in some texts (Gen. 13:14), but that meaning seems to be secondary. As a geographical description of Zion, the expression "in the far north" makes little sense. Zion cannot be said to be in the north if plotted within any description of the land in the Old Testament.[14] But as a theological claim of Yahweh's rule, the reference makes perfect sense. Zaphon was the name of the mountain on which Baal exercised kingship in Canaanite mythology.[15] What the Canaanites claimed for Baal, Israel in this psalm claims for Yahweh. The Lord is "to be revered above all gods" (Ps 96:4; cf. 97:9). His city, therefore, is the place from which the world is governed. By saying that Mount Zion is on the "summit of Zaphon," the psalmist declares that the gods of Israel's neighbors are subordinated to the Lord.

Psalm 99 expresses the sovereignty of Yahweh as it identifies him as one both enthroned on the cherubim and reigning from Zion:

> The Lord is king; let the peoples tremble!
> He sits enthroned upon the cherubim; let the earth quake!
> The Lord is great in Zion;
>   he is exalted over all the peoples. (vv. 1–2)

From Zion the Lord, the one enthroned on the cherubim, rules over all people. This description assumes that the Lord is head of a divine council in which he exercises authority over all other divine beings from his dwelling place on Zion. To fill out the implications of Psalm 99's claims, two other psalms must be considered as well.

The idea that the Lord is "enthroned upon the cherubim" (Ps. 99:1) draws from the Canaanite depictions of El and Baal. Psalm 18 makes additional claims about Yahweh that further clarify how he should be conceived in relation to these other deities. Psalm 18:10 [11] depicts the Lord, like the Canaanite gods El and Baal, in close association with the cherubim ("He rode on a cherub"). A few verses later the psalm labels him the "Most High" (v. 13 [14]). This term (Hebrew *ʿelyôn*) appears in Canaanite literature as a description of El. It identifies him as the chief god of the pantheon, the father of the gods and the one who exercises administrative power over them. To call Yahweh "Most High," therefore, is to declare that Yahweh is the head of all the gods.

This point is expressed most clearly in Psalm 82. This psalm begins, "God has taken his place in the divine council; / in the midst of the gods he holds judgment" (v. 1). Like Canaanite mythology that depicts El as head of an assembly of deities, this opening verse of Psalm 82 portrays Yahweh as the head of the council. But make no mistake, neither this psalm nor any other psalm in the Psalter entertain the possibility that another deity might be elevated to the place of Yahweh (as Baal was in the Canaanite pantheon). Indeed, these other deities are like footmen, divine lackeys, if you will, for the Lord. The idea in Psalm 82 is much like that in Deuteronomy 32:7-9, which says that in the primordial age the Most High (Yahweh) "apportioned the nations...according to the number of the gods."[16] In other words, the Lord assigned each nation its patron deity. The Lord himself, however, had authority over each of these gods and their people. Psalm 82 calls the local gods to account for their failure to establish justice among their respective peoples:

> How long will you judge unjustly
>   and show partiality to the wicked?
> Give justice to the weak and the orphan;
>   maintain the right of the lowly and the destitute.
> Rescue the weak and the needy;
>   deliver them from the hand of the wicked. (vv. 2-4)

Because these deities have not exercised judgment, judgment comes upon them:

> I say, "You are gods,
>   children of the Most High, all of you;
> nevertheless, you shall die like mortals,
>   and fall like any prince." (vv. 6-7)

In the claim that the Lord reigns on Zion, therefore, other important claims about God's establishment of justice appear. God's rule over other deities means, in part, that they have no power over God's people. God ultimately calls them to account for not establishing justice. These ideas would have obviously been important for the righteous who sought justice in the face of the threats of the wicked.

"The Lord Has Chosen Zion": Zion and the Just Rule of God

The association of Zion with God's presence as king is often associated with the physical security of Zion against armies that would attack it. This idea appears in Psalm 48:1-3 (2-4), for example:

> Great is the Lord and greatly to be praised
>   in the city of our God.
> His holy mountain, beautiful in elevation,
>   is the joy of all the earth.
> Mount Zion, in the far north,
>   the city of the great King.
> Within its citadels God
>   has shown himself a sure defense.

These verses make several claims about Zion that derive directly from the notion that Zion is the locus of God's reign. Zion is the "city of the great King." The place is identified by God's presence as king. At least two other claims derive from this characterization of the city. First, because God rules in Zion as king he also protects Zion and makes it secure. It is a city "God establishes forever" (v. 8 [9]); therefore, it is impermeable to enemy attack as long as the Lord dwells there. The psalmist portrays Zion's security by describing the assembly of foreign kings (v. 4 [5]) who, "as soon as they saw it, they were astounded; / they were in panic, they took to flight" (v. 5 [6]).

More directly related to the needs of the righteous, Zion is presented as the exclusive property of God and, therefore, as a place humans cannot manipulate for their own political ends. Zion is secure in that sense against all enemies of God's justice.

The theological significance of Zion could be dismissed for many of the same reasons monarchy has been discounted. Zion was the locus of the monarchy's power and, thus, a part of the ideology of the Davidic king. As such, the Psalms' theological portrait of Zion could be read as little more than the propaganda of kings who were attempting to secure support for their reign. There is undoubtedly some truth in the idea that this city was controlled and its image shaped by and for the political benefit of Davidic kings.

The enduring portrait of Zion in the Psalms, however, suggests Zion's importance outstripped any manipulation of the place by human kings. The Psalms present Zion as a place controlled by God alone. God reigns on Zion and, consequently, Zion is a place where God's justice is known. Because of this identity as God's city, Zion is a place where the righteous are at home, but the wicked cannot enter. For the righteous it is a place of order and justice. Outside the gates of Zion they may be persecuted and oppressed, but inside they find shelter in God's presence. For that reason, the righteous long to be in Zion, to be "planted" there where they will be near God. In sum, Zion in the Psalms is a place where the destiny of the righteous becomes clear, where hope is manifest by an experience of God's reign. But the reason Zion provides such an experience must be clarified.

The most basic claim about Zion is that the Lord chose it as his dwelling place. Psalm 87:1–3 puts it this way:

> On the holy mountain stands the city he founded;
> the Lord loves the gates of Zion
> > more than all the dwellings of Jacob.
> Glorious things are spoken of you,
> > O city of God.

The claim that the Lord chose Zion as his dwelling place has two implications important for the discussion of why the righteous might seek Zion as a place of safety. First, Zion is important because it gives access to God's presence, known fully only in God's heavenly temple. (See Isa. 6, which describes a vision of the heavenly throne while in the earthly temple.) Zion is not secure in and of itself. Some texts seem to imply as much—that Zion is impermeable to any attack or threat simply because of its own qualities (Ps. 125:1)[17]—but God's choice is noted time and again as the reason for the centrality of Zion.

Other parts of the Old Testament communicate the same message, albeit in different terminology. The priestly tradition speaks of God's "glory" that rests on this place, but which God can remove at any time (Ezek. 10). Similarly, the Deuteronomist refers to Jerusalem as the place God chooses his "name" to dwell (Deut. 12:5). The "name" dwelt originally at Shiloh, but God changed the location because of the corruption of the original site (Jer. 26:6). In other words, Zion is important because God reveals himself there.

A second implication has to do with political claims of human rulers. As the Psalter describes Zion's unique place in God's economy, the notion that God chose Zion sets straight the nature of Zion and the place of those human political leaders who exercised authority over it. This point is important because it denies that the location has any stability apart from God. It is also important because it speaks against any claim by human rulers to have established Zion or rendered it secure. Only God's choice of Zion established it as the central place on earth. No human ruler chose or founded it.

This second point is extremely important because it presents a theological counter-claim to what could be understood as David's establishment of Zion. It is a rather certain historical fact, of course, that David captured Jerusalem, made it his capital, and refortified the city, as 2 Samuel 5:6–12 indicates. In these practical historical terms Zion was appropriately known as "the city of David." Moreover, as J. J. M. Roberts argues, the traditions about Zion probably took present form when David made Zion his capital.[18] Nevertheless, from the Psalms' point of view, God, not David, chose and established Zion. God, not David or a Davidic ruler, made it secure. Two psalms illustrate this point well. Psalm 78:67–70 presents God's choice of David and Zion in a theologically significant order:

> He rejected the tent of Joseph,
> > he did not choose the tribe of Ephraim;
> but he chose the tribe of Judah,
> > Mount Zion, which he loves.
> He built his sanctuary like the high heavens,
> > like the earth, which he has founded forever.
> He chose his servant David,
> > and took him from the sheepfolds.

Psalm 78 disregards the historical priority of David's reign in favor of a larger poetic and theological point. Verse 69 reports the building of the temple without reference to Solomon, David's son who constructed the sacred building. Instead it states that God "built the sanctuary." Perhaps more importantly, it suggests that God constructed the temple before David began to rule in Zion. In other words, in Psalm 78's presentation of these matters, God's choice of Zion, and even the reality of the temple that came after David, predates and takes precedence over David's rule on Zion. As Levenson observes, this sequence of events does not arise from a historical tradition different from that in Samuel and Kings. Rather, it appears "because to the psalmist, the essential meaning of the Temple lies in its foundation in primal times, *in illo tempore,* in other words, in its protological character."[19]

Psalm 132 deals with this sequence of events differently, but it makes the same point of Zion's priority. This work does highlight the fact that David was a driving force in making Zion the cultic center of the United Monarchy:

> O Lord, remember in David's favor
>   all the hardships he endured;
> how he swore to the Lord
>   and vowed to the Mighty One of Jacob,
> "I will not enter my house
>   or get into my bed;
> I will not give sleep to my eyes
>   or slumber to my eyelids,
> until I find a place for the Lord,
>   a dwelling place for the Mighty One of Jacob." (vv. 1–5)

The subsequent verses recount how David brought the ark to Jerusalem (vv. 6–10) and report God's promise to establish David's line forever (vv. 11–13). The reason for God's support of David and his descendants, however, is based on God's prior choice of Zion: "For the LORD has chosen Zion; / he has desired it for his habitation" (v. 13). Moreover, while this psalm expresses some reservation about the permanence of the Davidic line by stating the prerequisite, "If your sons keep my covenant / and my decrees that I shall teach them" (v. 12), God's choice of Zion is said to be eternal: "This is my resting place forever; / here I will reside, for I have desired it" (v. 14).

To be sure, it is possible to look behind this psalm and see the notion of God's choice of Zion as a tool David used to legitimate his selection of Jerusalem as capital when it had no previous sacral significance among the Israelites. If that explains the origin of the idea of God's preference for Zion, however, it is true that, as Roberts says, "Religious ideology often outlives the political realities it was in part created to justify."[20] Now the witness of the Psalter in Psalms 78:67–72 and 132 is that God's choice of Zion has priority over God's establishment of the Davidic monarchy. The Lord's dwelling on Zion is permanent and unconditional, in contrast to the

Davidic covenant, which has stipulations regarding the kings' covenant faithfulness. In other words, in the Psalms David not only did not establish Zion, his own establishment as king came after and was dependent on Zion, the place of God's reign.

Conclusion

For the righteous, Zion is the place God's reign is experienced and celebrated. It is the place God's righteousness has its way; and, therefore, the "way" of the righteous is upheld and rewarded. When the righteous are understood as Israel in exile, the claims of God's reign on Zion are particularly important. In the midst of what seems a chaotic world, in which godless kings deport God's people, there is hope that God still reigns.

The claims about Zion are really claims about who rules the world. The Psalms declare that the Lord reigns, and that reign is known most fully on Mount Zion. To many people of faith, particularly in North America, this attachment of God's kingship to a place may seem quite odd. When the location of God in Christ is considered, the concept should not seem strange at all. The Psalter's descriptions of Zion and the experience of the righteous there anticipate for Christians the experience of God in Christ. Moreover, the kingdom of God the New Testament describes is often associated closely with the same place the Psalms say is the locale of God's reign: Mount Zion. It is surely not coincidental that as John on Patmos envisions the new Jerusalem, it is a place where only the righteous have a place (Rev. 21:2–8, 27; 22:3–4).

9

Zion and the Longing of the Righteous

O that deliverance for Israel would come from Zion!
When the LORD *restores the fortunes of his people,*
Jacob will rejoice; Israel will be glad. (Ps. 14:7)

The previous chapter looked at the features of Mount Zion that made the holy mountain a place where the righteous sought God's presence. Mainly, Zion was such a place for the righteous because the worship of Zion's temple gave them an overwhelming assurance of God's reign and God's justice. God's control over the world was portrayed dramatically there. The cult of the Jerusalem temple offered a view of an alternative reality in which the righteous found protection and in which God's righteousness was really in control. For that reason the temple was for the righteous a place of orientation, of order and evidence of God's reign.

This chapter looks more closely at psalms in which the righteous express directly their desire to be on Mount Zion, to be on the holy mountain that symbolized God's control of the world, and to be among worshipers who ascribed to the ideals of God's justice.

The discussion below begins with Psalms 42–43 (which, again, are really one psalm). These psalms contain some of the most beautiful expressions of desire to be near God in all of scripture. The psalmist describes the longing for God's presence as a "thirst" for God. This desire grows out of the psalmist's distance from the holy mountain and its temple. These two psalms show well the Psalms' conception of Zion as a place of orientation to life and cosmic order. Some of the other psalms that will be discussed, such as 63; 57; and 142, seem to have their original setting in the worship of the temple or in cultic acts and institutions located there. These three psalms, however, have been recast as prayers by a righteous person who is now separated from the holy place.

The psalmist in these psalms is presented as being in some distant locale, closer to Sheol, closer to disorientation, to disorder, in a place where God's justice is not acknowledged.[1] In each case, the remote location that produces this longing is accompanied by the taunt of the enemy. This perhaps indicates that such psalms received their present shape when Mount Zion and its temple were inaccessible, or perhaps when the temple lay in ruins. Even then Zion did not cease to be a place of orientation. The chapter will attempt to come to terms with how Zion continued to serve its important function as a symbol for God's presence and God's reign in the exilic and post-exilic periods.

The chapter includes two psalms–52 and 92–that describe the righteous as one "planted" in the temple precincts. Psalms 52 and 92 extend the image of the righteous that opens the Psalter (Ps. 1:3). The righteous are not simply planted or grounded in God; they are near God by virtue of being in the temple. These two psalms show clearly that being in the temple was for the righteous a primary way of describing the life of faith and the main way to know God's presence and security.

Thirsting for God

Psalms 42–43

Psalms 42–43 express beautifully the righteous' longing to be near God in the temple on Zion. The psalm opens with a picturesque expression of this desire to be near God:

> As a deer longs for flowing streams,
>   so my soul longs for you, O God.
> My soul thirsts for God,
>   for the living God.
> When shall I come and behold
>   the face of God? (Ps. 42:1–2 [2–3])

The psalmist's "thirst" for God is expressed in verse 3 (4) in the context of enemies who taunt with the question, "Where is your God?" The question occurs again in verse 10 (11). As the psalm progresses, the psalmist expresses the longing for God two more times as "mourning" prompted by the oppression of the enemy (Ps. 42:9 [10]; 43:2). The righteous' faith is revealed in response to and in contrast with the wicked's faithless jabs. As observed in chapter 3, the interplay between enemy taunt ("Where is your God?") and the psalmist's confession of faith in God's deliverance in this psalm is similar to that in Psalm 3, in which David confesses assurance of God's salvation in response to the wicked's insistence, "There is no help for you in God" (Ps. 3:2 [3]). Psalms 42–43 express the same pattern of recognition of enemies and confession of faith.

Psalms 42–43 communicate the psalmist's longing to be near God in three strophes: Psalm 42:1–5 (2–6) and the first word of verse 6 (7]); 6–11 (7–12)]; and Psalm 43:1–5. Each section ends with the refrain, "Hope in God; for I shall again praise him, / my help and my God." Repetition of other elements provide additional structure (for example, "Where is your God," in 42:3 [4] and 10 [11]; "Why must I walk about mournfully" or similar language in 42:9 [10] and 43:2).[2]

The psalm has a movement that transcends these formal elements of structure. The psalmist travels, spiritually at least, from wilderness "exile" to the temple. The "journey" begins with the question, "When shall I come and behold the face of God?" (42:2 [3]) That is, the psalmist inquires as to when he can again enter the temple, the place where he can know God's presence ("behold the face of God"). The trip progresses then from the distant locale where "tears have been my food day and night" and the enemy goads, "Where is your God?" (42:3 [4]) to "the altar of God, / to God my exceeding joy" (43:4). There, among the worshiping community, the psalmist is able to offer praise (42:11 [12]; 43:5).[3] This psalm makes clear that the destiny of the righteous is among those who worship in the place where God's presence is known, in the temple on Mount Zion.

Psalm 63

Psalm 63 is similar to Psalms 42–43 in its expressions of longing to be near God. It shares with Psalm 42:2 (3) the expression, "my soul thirsts" (Ps 63:1 [2]), a phrase that appears only in these two psalms. Unlike Psalms 42–43, however, Psalm 63 seems to have its origin in a ceremony in the temple, or at least such a setting can be inferred.[4] The psalmist "looked upon you in the sanctuary, / beholding your power and glory" (v. 2 [3]), and "sings for joy" "in the shadow of your wings" (v. 7 [8]). These statements, along with the reference to meditating "in the watches of the night" (v. 6 [7]), have led some scholars to propose that Psalm 63 originated in a ceremony in which a worshiper took refuge from enemies in the temple. According to this view, the person prayed for safety while spending the night in the holy place.[5]

In present form, however, the psalm is a prayer by one who *remembers* God's presence in the temple while at a distance from it. The title of the psalm gives a setting for the righteous, David, "when he was in the Wilderness of Judah." This setting may point to David's time of fleeing from Saul (1 Sam. 23:14–15; 24:1) or from Absalom (2 Sam. 15:23, 28; 16:2). Regardless of the exact occasion imagined, it is striking that the title does not enhance the original temple setting, but casts the psalm as the words of David at some distance from the holy place.

The temple and God's presence is David's goal and desire, but the psalm in present form is a reflection on his longing for the God that he has experienced in the temple in the past. In this setting the enemies are particularly important. The psalm highlights David's precarious place in the face of an enemy. Indeed, the psalm's title, along with the references to "those who seek to destroy my life" in verses 9–10 (10–11) accent David's trouble that drove him to the wilderness. David seeks God and "thirsts for God" in response to and in the context of the enemy's threats. (For a similar expression of faith, see Ps. 61:2–4 [3–5]). The temple and its worship is a place of orientation, but David is disoriented because of the enemy. In this disoriented state he hides out. The enemy represents the forces of chaos in the wilderness, the place where God's presence and power are questioned.

Seeking God as Refuge in the Temple: Psalms 57 and 142

Chapter 1 observed that the righteous often express their trust in God in terms of "seeking refuge" in the Lord. Psalms 57 and 142 are examples of psalms in which the psalmist's seeking refuge in God takes the concrete form of finding safety in the temple. In both of these psalms, however, the desire to be near God in the holy place is cast as a longing the psalmist has while at a distance. In this way, Psalms 57 and 142 are similar to Psalms 42–43 and 63 discussed already.

In Psalm 57 the psalmist speaks of taking shelter under Yahweh's wings (v. 1 [2]); in both psalms the psalmist offers prayer for relief from enemies (57:4 [5], 6 [7]; 142:3b [4b], 6b–7 [7b–8]) that sounds as though the psalmist prayed these words while in the temple seeking protection from foes. Both psalms, however, are identified as psalms of David when he was "in the cave," far from Mount Zion and its worship. The note in both these superscriptions points to the stories in 1 Samuel 22–24. David fled from Saul and hid in the cave of Adullam (1 Sam. 22:1). From that hiding place David gathered around him a band of warriors. Later David hid in a cave at En-gedi (1 Sam. 24:3). In that hiding he encountered Saul, the enemy who plagued and pursued him. With this canonical setting for the profession of "seeking refuge in God" in view, Psalm 142 has interesting implications for understanding these psalms as confessions of the righteous. The psalm begins with a description of how the psalmist cries to the Lord (vv. 1–2 [2–3]). Insightfully, Calvin understands the Hebrew word *maskîl* in the title as a reference to David giving instruction in how to pray. (The root *śkl* can communicate the sense of "instruct"; see Neh. 9:20.)[6] Although this may not be the intention of the Hebrew label for this psalm, the work is couched as a kind of lesson in the art of prayer. In verses 1–2 (2–3) David "reports" on how he prays (the verbs can be understood as communicating typical action). Then the prayer itself begins in verse 3 (4); note the shift from third-person reference to God in verses 1–2 (2–3) ("to the Lord") to second-person referral in verses 3–7 (4–8) ("to *you,* O Lord"). In the prayer David states that he is utterly abandoned ("there is no one who takes notice of me"; v. 4 [5]) in the midst of enemies (v. 3 [4]), but God is his refuge (v. 5 [6]). In verses 6–7 (7–8) David shows how he is the typical and representative righteous person. He professes absolute helplessness before his enemies ("they are too strong for me"; v. 6b [7b]) and relies on God's salvation. Specifically he petitions God, "Bring me out of prison" (v. 7 [8]).

The editors who set the psalm in this particular event in David's life may have understood "prison" to refer to the cave where David is confined. It is easy to imagine, as some scholars have done, an actual imprisonment here.[7] Given the superscription, however, the prison must be taken as either the cave at En-gedi or as a metaphor for the complete vulnerability to enemy threats. Either way, what is primary is the persecution by enemies of this one who is innocent. The psalm ends with the interesting note that "the righteous will surround me, / for you will deal bountifully with me" (v. 7b [8b]).

David in the cave, with Saul pursuing and hemming him in, is the quintessential righteous one. When threatened by foes, he relies on God. Because he places himself in the hands of God, he is confident of his destiny. The righteous surround him because his vindication represents God's protection of them as well. These psalms may be informed by cultic rituals, but in present form and present literary context they express the longing of the righteous at a distance from the temple and its cult. The main issues for those who pray these two psalms are the threats of the wicked and the anxiety of awaiting God's deliverance.

"Planted" in the Temple: Psalms 52:8 (9) and 92:12–15 (13–16)

In light of the way Zion symbolized God's protective presence and the way the worship of the Jerusalem temple made God's presence accessible, it is no wonder the righteous longed to be in that place. One of the most evocative images of the righteous is as a tree planted in the temple precincts. This metaphor of the individual worshiper planted on Mount Zion has in its background the tradition of Israel being planted in the land of promise. Exodus 15:17 describes Israel's planting with language that suggests Zion is the garden in which the people are placed: "You brought them in and planted them on the mountain of your own possession, / the place, O LORD, that you made your abode, / the sanctuary, O LORD, that your hands have established."

Psalm 80 contains a similar description of how God placed Israel in the land. Although it makes no specific reference to Zion as the exact plot for Israel's planting, the Lord is described as the one "enthroned upon the cherubim" (v. 1 [2]) and "God of hosts" (v. 4 [5]), both designations that link him with the ark and the temple. As with Exodus 15:17, Psalm 80 describes God planting Israel after bringing them out of Egypt:

You brought a vine out of Egypt;
    you drove out the nations and planted it.
You cleared the ground for it;
    it took deep root and filled the land.
The mountains were covered with its shade,
the mighty cedars with its branches;
it sent out its branches to the sea,
    and its shoots to the River. (vv. 8–11 [9–12])

Just as the people were made secure by being planted, so also the righteous person is compared to a tree planted in the temple precincts. Two psalms present the righteous this way:

Psalm 52:8 (9):
But I am like a green olive tree
    in the house of God.
I trust in the steadfast love of God
    forever and ever.

Psalm 92:12–15 (13–16):
The righteous flourish like the palm tree,
    and grow like a cedar in Lebanon.
They are planted in the house of the Lord;
    they flourish in the courts of our God.
In old age they still produce fruit;
    they are always green and full of sap,
showing that the Lord is upright;
    he is my rock, and there is no unrighteousness in him.

The emphasis in both psalms is on being planted "in the house of God." Both psalms probably draw from the actual appearance of the temple on Zion and from images of other sacred places in the ancient Near East. First Kings 6 depicts Solomon's temple as one with carvings of such arboreal pictures at every turn: "He carved the walls of the house all around about with carved engravings of cherubim, palm trees, and open flowers in the inner and outer rooms" (v. 29; cf. vv. 18, 32, 35; 7:36).

Moreover, the text indicates that part of the temple and palace complex was the "House of the Forest of...Lebanon," which had cedar beams that approximated a verdant forest (1 Kings 7:2–12). All of this indicates that the temple mount was intended to depict a paradise. Indeed, as the last chapter noted, in the poetic imagination and in the experience of worshipers on Mount Zion, the place was not just *a* paradise, but the very location of the garden of God, *the* paradise from which the world was created (see above; Ezek. 28:13–14). It is not surprising, therefore, that Mount Zion and the temple precincts are depicted as places where trees grow in abundance. What does seem somewhat unique in the ancient Near East is the use of such trees as symbolic portrayals of the righteous who know the security of Zion.

The notion of planting the righteous on the holy mountain sets the image in Psalms 52 and 92 apart from other, more general, plant metaphors that signify human existence and stability. Indeed, the more general image is common in ancient Near Eastern literature and in the Old Testament. In one Sumerian tradition humankind's origins are depicted as humans sprouting from the earth: "When destinies had been established for all engendered things, when An had engendered the year of abundance when people had broken through the ground like plants…"[8]

Other extra-biblical texts portray stability and security with arboreal imagery. Perhaps the text that has the clearest analogy to biblical imagery is that the depiction of the wise person in the fourth chapter of the Egyptian work, the "Instruction of Amen-em-Opet":

> As for the heated man of the temple,
> > He is like a tree growing in the open.
> In the completion of a moment (comes) its loss of foliage,
> > And its end is reached in the shipyards;
> (Or) it is floated far from its place,
> > and the flame is its burial shroud.
> (But) the truly silent man holds himself apart.
> > He is like a tree growing in a garden.
> It flourishes and doubles its yield;
> > It (stands) before its lord.
> Its fruit is sweet; its shade is pleasant;
> > And its end is reached in the garden…[9]

It is easy to see the close relationship between this description of the wise person (the "silent man," a common description of the prudent person in Egyptian wisdom) and Jeremiah's depiction of "those who trust in the LORD" as "like a tree planted by water" (Jer. 17:7–8; cf. Ps. 1:3 to be discussed further in chapter 10). Note that these more general descriptions speak of the wise, righteous, or trustful person being like a tree that flourishes because it is planted in a garden, by a water source and thus is able to send out roots to a source of nourishment. In contrast, Psalms 52 and 92 do not speak of water at all. Rather, they emphasize the location in or near the temple. An abundance of water that would feed these trees is merely the by-product of the life-giving presence of God on the holy mountain.

The language and imagery of being planted on Mount Zion suggests a submission to the rule of God that is at the heart of the Psalter's piety and at the center of Zion theology as well. Psalm 52:8 (9) communicates this submission by tying trust in God to being "like a green olive tree / in the house of God." The one who confesses being planted in the temple contrasts with the one "who would not take / refuge in God" (v. 7 [8]). The psalmist's trust is the key to security, to being "like a green olive tree / in the house of God," while the boastful "mighty one" (v. 1 [2]) described earlier in the psalm will be uprooted "from the land of the living" (v. 5 [6]) because of a failure to rely on God and to align self with God's will.

Psalm 92:12–15 (13–16) speaks with a similar piety. As already seen in relation to Psalm 1:3, the Hebrew word *šātûl* is often translated "planted"; however, the term has the more specific nuance of "transplanted" (compare with the word *nātaʿ* that may denote planting as of a seed or a plant in an original location; Jer. 2:21). The Hebrew *šātûl* connotes a plant that begins from its seed in one location and then is moved to a more advantageous plot of ground by a caretaker, in this case by the Divine Gardener.[10]

For the psalmist, the benevolence of the true King, the creator and ruler of the universe, was known on Mount Zion. Therefore, it must have been quite natural to speak of and to desire being transplanted there, to be rooted near God. Although too much could be made of this terminology (and the term *nātaʿ* sometimes has similar theological implications; see Ps. 80:9–10 [10–11]), the word *šātûl* nevertheless must be read within this web of associations that were surely part of the psalmist's world.

For the righteous to be transplanted was a sign that they were part of God's rule over the cosmos and part of the order God intended for it. This indicates that the righteous have security as a result of their being made part of the garden of God. Trusting in God's rule, which is known in the paradise on Zion, they are made secure by the Divine Gardener who has supplied their every need.

The Spiritual Pilgrimage to Zion: Psalm 84 and the Shape of the Psalter

This chapter began by showing how the righteous desire to be on Zion and in its temple. This place provided a safe haven from the enemy because of God's presence and the experience of God's justice there. Zion had such importance because Yahweh chose it as the location of his presence, not because of any inherent quality of Zion itself. In other words, Mount Zion was significant because it gave access to the heavenly abode of God. That distinction is extremely important when considering how the righteous understood Zion's role during and after the exile. It seems clear that Zion did not cease to be important as the object of the righteous' longing. Psalms 42–43 and 63 testify to that fact. Since Zion was never understood as the actual dwelling place of God, but as a place that gave access to God's true temple, it was also possible that one's physical presence on Zion was not essential—not completely essential at least—to gain such access to the heavenly temple. Psalm 84 hints at this fact. This psalm portrays those on pilgrimage to Zion experiencing an abundance of water, which is a sign of God's blessing in the holy city. But for the pilgrims to Zion, the blessing is received on their journey, before reaching the place of worship itself:

> As they go through the valley of Baca,
> > they make it a place of springs;
> > > the early rain also covers it with pools.
> > They go from strength to strength;
> > > the God of gods will be seen in Zion (v. 6 [7]).

The identity of the "valley of Baca," and whether or not Baca is actually a place-name is debated. The similarity of the consonants of this word in Hebrew to those that signify weeping (*bkh*) leads some to conclude that "valley of Baca" would be better translated "valley of tears."[11] P. Kyle McCarter probably has the best solution. He argues that Baca refers to a "parched place" on a pilgrim's route to Jerusalem that is also referred to in 2 Samuel 5:23.[12] That understanding makes most sense in relation to the statement that those who travel through the valley "make it a place of springs." Indeed, the psalm suggests that the springs and water courses of Zion, signs of God's blessed presence on the holy mountain, are experienced by those who have put their trust in God and who prepare to be near God on Zion, even before they reach the temple mount (see Ps. 87:7). In the expectation of being on Zion, the psalmist glimpses Eden, the garden of God. The righteous may find their orientation to life while anticipating the sight of Zion.

This view of the righteous' experience of God's presence on Zion assumes a temple, though an experience of God's blessings and its life-orienting power occurs before they actually reach Zion. Was it possible to have such an experience apart from pilgrimage to the temple when the temple stood in ruins or the worshiper had no access to it? Much in the Psalter suggests it was.

In Psalm 84 those who make the dry valley a place of springs are those "in whose heart are the highways to Zion" (v. 5b [6b]). That is, the people described have the heart of a pilgrim. It would seem possible with such a heart to make spiritual pilgrimage to Zion. Erich Zenger suggests that the book of Psalms, and particularly Book 5 of the Psalter, facilitated such a spiritual pilgrimage.[13] He points out that the last part of the Psalter contains almost no direct references to cultic practices. At the same time, however, it offers hints that prayer and meditation have become acceptable alternatives. As Psalm 141:2 says, "Let my prayer be counted as incense before you, / and the lifting of my hands as an evening sacrifice." Moreover, the central part of Book 5 seems to be influenced by, while not mentioning specifically, the three great feasts of the Jewish calendar: Passover (Ps. 113–118), Shabuoth (which Christians call Pentecost; Ps. 119), and Booths (Ps. 120–136).

It seems that the Psalter itself is intended to give access to Zion, to help create in its readers the hearts of pilgrims.[14] If this idea is correct, it adds another dimension to the idea that the book of Psalms is supremely concerned with the destiny of the righteous. Indeed, one purpose of the collection of psalms may have been to give the righteous a means to "be near God" when Zion was not accessible.

Jesus Christ and the Temple "Not Made with Hands"

After the trauma of exile, the people of God never gave up the claim that such a tangible source of God's presence was needed. As the discussion of Psalm 84 and Book 5 of the Psalter just indicated, they did perceive ways to gain access to what the temple offered. The New Testament testifies to the particular way early Christians dealt with the need for God's presence in the temple: what the temple represented came to be embodied in the person of Jesus.

The relationship between Jesus and the temple appears in all four gospels in the account of Jesus cleansing the temple (Mt. 21:12-17; Mk. 11:15-17; Lk. 19:45-48; Jn. 2:13-22). The synoptic gospels may intend to portray in this scene a symbolic action by which Jesus indicted the worship practices of the temple, perhaps even calling into question the very system of animal sacrifice.[15] Thus, Jesus appears as a prophet like Jeremiah, whose own sermon against the injustices perpetrated in the temple produced a threat to his life (Jer. 7:1-15; 26:1-6).

Matthew 26:61 and Mark 14:58 also report false accusations to the effect that Jesus claimed he could restore the temple if it were destroyed.[16] This charge may refer to the idea that the temple would be rejuvenated in the messianic age (Ezek. 40-46; Tob. 13:10). The gospel of John, however, interprets this scene and Jesus' claim, "Destroy this temple, and in three days I will raise it up" (2:19) as a reference to the resurrection of Jesus. Jesus' boast is followed by the religious leaders' disbelief: "This temple has been under construction for forty-six years, and will you raise it up in three days?" (v. 20). John reveals that the leaders have misunderstood Jesus. The evangelist clarifies by noting, "But he was speaking of the temple of his body" (v. 21).[17]

This verse could have one of two meanings, of course. The "temple of his body" could refer to the physical body of Jesus as the true temple of God, or it could mean the community gathered around Jesus—the body of Christ—is the temple that is "raised up" (as perhaps Mk. 14:58 implies, a temple, "not made with hands"; see Eph. 1:23; Col. 1:18).[18] If the church is the temple intended here, the significance of the idea of Jesus as the "new temple" for the righteous is indeed close to the portrayal of Zion and its temple in the Psalms. It is the "place" where the true worshipers of God gather to proclaim God's rule. In the proclamation of that rule the righteous are assured that God will protect them from the wicked.[19]

The gospel of John seems to be making the more specific point that Jesus himself embodied God's presence just as the temple (and earlier the tabernacle) had done for Israel. The incarnation lends itself naturally to such an analogy since the Jerusalem temple was the physical locus of God's appearance to the righteous (Ps. 17:15; 27:4).[20] Jesus became the primary means by which the righteous are near God, as the temple once had given such access (Ps. 73:17, 28). This idea is supported perhaps most directly in Revelation 21. This chapter begins with a vision of a new Jerusalem (vv. 1–2) followed by the remarkable statement, "See the home of God is among mortals" (v. 3). The word translated "home" comes from the same root John uses to speak of the incarnation, "The Word became flesh and made his dwelling (*skn*) among us" (Jn. 1:14, NIV). In the Old Testament, and particularly in the Psalms, any statement that approximates this one—God's dwelling place being with humans—includes references to the temple. Indeed, the temple is God's "house" (Ps. 23:6; 27:4).

As Revelation 21 describes this new Jerusalem, it observes: "I saw no temple in the city, for its temple is the Lord God the Almighty and the Lamb" (v. 22). The point is that in the risen Christ the righteous are presented with the unmediated and unadulterated presence of God. This passage, of course, was written after the destruction of the temple in 70 C.E. The frailty of a humanly constructed worship place and its limited ability to mediate God's presence must have been abundantly apparent. In that setting John gives his vision of a temple not made with human hands (compare Mk. 14:58), a temple that is now a person, the resurrected Jesus (Jn. 2:21).[21]

10

Torah

The Ultimate Refuge

> *If your law had not been my delight,*
> *I would have perished in my misery.* (Ps. 119:92)

The last four chapters explored how the righteous experience God's protective presence on Mount Zion, and in the person of the Davidic king. The trauma of Jerusalem's destruction in 587 B.C.E. required the righteous to alter their faith in these signs of God's presence. God's promises to the king were reinterpreted as promises to the people as a whole, though Israel hoped for a David of the future. Zion continued to be a place of pilgrimage, a place the righteous could still "see God's face." But Zion's role for the righteous was altered as well. Prayer and "spiritual pilgrimage" became important alternatives to actually being in the temple (Ps. 141:1; cf. Ps. 120–134).

This chapter introduces one more sign of the "embodied hope" of the righteous: torah. As torah is discussed, it will become apparent that this chapter is really still about Zion in one important way. Namely, torah in the Psalms is described as a source of God's presence and protection for the righteous that is similar to that experienced on Mount Zion. Moreover, torah became a source of security for the righteous that fulfills the role once reserved for Mount Zion and its temple.

Torah became for the righteous a surrogate for Zion in its role as the connecting point between heaven and earth. After the final destruction of the temple in 70 C.E., the Jewish people began to think of torah as a replacement for the temple, as Judaism transformed into a "religion of the book" rather than a religion of ritual and sacrifice. This chapter will point out that the Psalter shows the first signs of such a shift in thinking, from temple to torah.

To make these points about torah, this chapter discusses three psalms that have torah as their central subject: Psalms 1, 19, and 119. Psalms 19 and 119 will be discussed for their overall features and message. The chapter will zero in on one verse of Psalm 1, verse 3, which describes the righteous, those who "meditate [on torah] day and night" (1:2b), as like "trees planted by streams of water." As the chapter will show, the description in Psalm 1:3 borrows vocabulary from other texts that describe the temple. The Psalter's opening psalm presents the righteous as secure and prosperous in the presence of God, as Psalms 52 and 92 portray the righteous. (See the discussion in chapter 9.) However, Psalm 1:3 presents the righteous' nearness to God as a result of devotion to and meditation on torah. This seems to mean that by the time the Psalter reached its present form, torah became for the righteous the ultimate sign of God's security. Before delving into this point, however, it is important to come to terms with some preliminary issues regarding torah.

What Is Torah?

When the psalmist declares that the righteous "on his law [torah]… meditate day and night" (Ps. 1:2), what exactly is the object of their meditation? The term *tôrâ* is often translated "law," but as shown already, this English word is very misleading and limits the understanding of torah in the Psalter. (See introduction.) Torah can indeed refer to a legal injunction (Ex. 12:49) or to a collection of laws (Deut. 4:8), but the word is used in the Psalter in a much more dynamic way. Hebrew tôrâ derives from a verb (*yārâ*) that means "to teach".[1] In Job 6:24, for instance, this verb appears in parallel with another word that means "understand" (*bîn*): "Teach me, and I will be silent; / make me understand how I have gone wrong." Torah essentially means "instruction." It is God's presentation of God's will for the world. Given this definition, "law" takes on a very important and positive connotation. The laws in the Old Testament were intended as "instruction" and, therefore, were signs of God's grace. They were not intended as stale legalistic tenets through which one could obtain righteousness. There is more to torah than just commandments.

Torah sometimes refers to instruction in the form of written texts–that is, scripture. Written torah in the Old Testament is associated mainly with Moses.[2]

Deuteronomy reports that Moses delivered speeches to Israel on the plains of Moab that would be instructive for Israel's life in the land. After promulgating the law to Israel, Moses commanded the people to erect stones after entering Canaan, and "write on them all the words of this law" (Deut. 27:3). Moses sets in place a ceremony for the renewal of the covenant. Moses himself, after giving his verbal instructions, "wrote down this law, and gave it to the priests, the sons of Levi, who carried the ark of the covenant of the LORD, and to all the elders of Israel" (Deut. 31:9). As the description of Moses' preservation of the torah comes to a close, Deuteronomy makes clear that torah in this case is a "book":[3]

> When Moses had finished writing down in a book the words of this law to the very end, Moses commanded the Levites who carried the ark of the covenant of the LORD, saying, "Take this book of the law and put it beside the ark of the covenant of the LORD your God; let it remain there as a witness against you" (Deut. 31:24–26).

This passage identifies torah as the written deposit of Moses' speeches now recorded in Deut 4:44–30:29.[4] Eventually torah became a term for all of the Pentateuch (Genesis through Deuteronomy), the five "books of Moses." It is *the* Torah, the first and most authoritative portion of the Jewish canon.[5]

As the Old Testament took shape, in time the whole corpus came to be understood as an extension of the Torah. Indeed, the Prophets (Joshua through Malachi) and the Writings (Psalms through Chronicles) are arranged and presented as works that depend on and expand the books of Moses. Joshua 1:7–8 opens the prophetic section of the canon with an injunction to keep the law of Moses always on the lips ("This book of the law shall not depart out of your mouth"; Josh. 1:8), and Malachi 4:4 (Hebrew versification, 3:22) concludes the Prophets with a similar imperative ("Remember the teaching of my servant Moses, the statutes and ordinances that I commanded him at Horeb for all Israel").

The Joshua text uses the language of Deuteronomy ("this book of the law") to identify torah as the written record of the speeches Moses made on the plains of Moab. Malachi's reference is more general, but nonetheless identifies the "teaching of Moses" with the record of what was revealed on Mount Horeb. The Psalter begins with references to torah as well (Ps. 1:2). As the first book of the third portion of the Jewish canon, the mention of torah in Psalm 1 identifies all that follows as divine instruction.[6] In other words, when Psalm 1:2 says of the righteous, "their delight is in the law of the Lord, / and on his law they meditate day and night," it offers the Psalms, along with the rest of scripture, as a source of God's teachings by which the "way of the righteous" (Ps 1:6) may be known. The Psalter is an expression of torah and an expansion of what one gains from reading and meditating on the books of Moses.

As Psalm 1 refers to torah, however, it seems to expand the notion of "instruction" to include more than just written texts. As already noted, Psalm 1 borrows language about torah from Joshua 1:7–8 in its declaration that the righteous "meditate day and night" on torah and, therefore, "in all they do, they prosper" (Ps. 1:3b). The psalm does not identify torah, however, as "this torah," a written document (as does Josh. 1:8), but more generally as "the law [torah] of the Lord." This may mean that torah includes more than written documents.

Psalm 119 makes the point more explicit. This psalm does encourage meditation on written texts, of course. It recalls many other biblical texts, thereby implicitly recognizing their authority and encouraging attention to their truths. For example, in verse 84 the psalmist cries, "When will you execute judgment on those who persecute me?" (NASB). The wording seems to be a paraphrase of Jeremiah 15:15.[7] Allusions to or paraphrases of passages from Jeremiah, Isaiah, Proverbs, and Job are common in the psalm.[8]

Nevertheless, in Psalm 119, torah does not seem to refer to written texts exclusively, perhaps not even in a majority of cases. This is evident in part by what is not present in the psalm. It does not mention Moses, Sinai, or even the term "book." Since Psalm 119 is arranged alphabetically, with each section beginning with a letter of the Hebrew alphabet, it would have been easy to work in such references in sections that begin with the letters *mem* (the first letter in the name Moses) or *samek* (the first letter in *seper*, "book"). The absence of such terms does not mean that the psalmist here does not associate torah with the Mosaic legislation at all, but it seems that such an association does not exhaust the meaning of the term. That torah implies more than an authoritative text in Psalm 119 is also clear from what the psalm does say directly. The psalmist throughout the poem prays for illumination to understand and observe the will of God:

> Teach me, O Lord, the way of your statutes,
> and I will observe it to the end.
> Give me understanding, that I may keep your law
> and observe it with my whole heart.
> Lead me in the path of your commandments,
> for I delight in it. (vv. 33–35)

Torah here seems to include something that is already known and something that continues to be revealed as well. As Jon Levenson says of the psalmist's commitment to torah in these verses, "On the one hand, he knows the Torah and has spent his life learning it. On the other, he prays to have it disclosed to him as if it is new."[9] Indeed, torah includes "received traditions," which are identified with wisdom handed down by teachers (vv. 99–100), but probably also with texts now known as part of the Old Testament. It also includes, however, truth about God revealed by nature (vv. 89–91) and "unmediated divine teaching" (vv. 26–29).[10]

In sum, torah in Psalm 119 and wherever the term appears in the Psalter is something dynamic. The term assumes normative written texts, but it is not limited to them. Torah also includes other expressions of the divine will and the divine vision for reality that illuminate the truth known already in texts considered scripture. Now the Psalms have a role as torah themselves. They both illuminate what was considered earlier as scripture (*the* Torah) and they provide words on which to meditate to experience the blessings of God.[11] The Psalms are part of the pluriform expression of divine instruction by which the righteous find a secure destiny, hope for their living.

Torah and the Shape of the Psalter

The importance of torah to the righteous in the Psalms is communicated in part by the significant location of psalms about torah in the Psalter. Three psalms that have torah as their central interest are important in the final form of the book: Psalms 1, 19, and 119. Although these three psalms are different in structure and content, they all three have devotion to the Lord's instruction as their organizing subject.

These psalms have typically been treated as leftovers in the Psalter since they are difficult to classify in the conventional form-critical categories. They reflect a late period in Israelite psalmody in which psalms were being composed for instruction. Each of the three shows an awareness of authoritative texts and each is written to encourage devotion to divine instruction. While these works do not have a clear place in the formal categories scholars use to classify psalms, however, they are among the most important psalms for understanding how the book of Psalms was conceived by its editors. As James L. Mays says, "This latest and smallest group of the psalms may provide the central clue to the way the psalms, individually and as a book, were read and understood at the time of their composition and inclusion."[12]

Psalm 1 deals with the problem of the destiny of the righteous. The psalm affirms that the righteous will be rewarded for their reliance on the Lord (v. 6). It claims the certain end of the wicked and their prosperity. Psalm 1 is paired editorially with Psalm 2. As noted in chapter 4, the second psalm is very different from Psalm 1 in subject matter. It treats the question of the nations' rebellion against the rule of God and the king God appointed to represent his rule on Mount Zion. Nevertheless, the two psalms share the general concern for faithfulness to God's will and hope for the vindication of those who depend on the Lord.

This pairing alters Psalm 1 and its message about the righteous in two important ways. First, the vindication of the righteous is placed in an eschatological context. At the time of the completion of the Psalter, Psalm 2's focus on the reign of God was understood in terms of the goal of history. It was not, as once thought, something rehearsed in the cult, but something closely akin to a prophetic visionary claim. Although Psalm 1 is shaped by the language of wisdom, its emphasis on the destiny of the righteous is "understood in terms of the coming kingdom of God."[13]

The second way the psalm's pairing with Psalm 2 alters the claims of Psalm 1 is that torah, the center of Psalm 1, has become closely associated with the king. The placement of these two psalms side-by-side alone would not suggest such an association, but there is more. Psalm 1 echoes the language of Joshua 1:7–8, a text that presents Joshua's main calling to observe the torah. This injunction to Joshua is really a royal concern. Indeed, Deuteronomy through Kings present the ideal notion that the Israelite monarch was to have the torah always before him and on his lips (Deut 17:14–20). The king was to model torah obedience.[14] The pairing of a psalm about the king (Ps. 2) with a psalm that draws from this Deuteronomic language naturally brings the two concerns together.

David is the exemplary Israelite, the model of righteousness, who shows what it means to have torah as his highest joy. Bringing king and righteous together transforms the understanding of each. David is the model of piety in a way he likely never was in historical reality. The righteous individual who appears in the wisdom literature appears again, and that person is affirmed in Psalm 1. But the person's destiny is bound up with that of Israel, represented by David, in a way that is not apparent in the wisdom books. Psalm 1's pairing with Psalm 2 and its use of Deuteronomic language and themes present the destiny of the righteous as a destiny determined by response to and reliance on God as known in the story of Israel's salvation from Egypt and formation as a nation in Canaan.[15]

The pairing of psalms about torah and kingship specifically occurs two other times in the book. Psalms 19 and 119 also appear alongside psalms that focus on God's reign. Psalms 18 and 19 both begin with the revelation of God's might through cosmic signs (18:8–16; 19:2–7), and both declare that the way and word of God are perfect (18:31; 19:8, 9). The pairing of Psalms 118 and 119 has an impact similar to that of Psalms 1 and 2. Psalm 118 tells of one who is rejected, though he is righteous (vv. 10–18, 20, 21–25). Psalm 119 is a prayer by one who constantly faces enemy threats, but who seeks solace and protection in torah. Together Psalms 118 and 119 put torah piety in an eschatological context. Hope for the coming kingdom, for God's reign, is a hope for realization of the truth that is proclaimed in the torah psalms.

These psalms give assurance that "The Lord watches over the way of the righteous, / but the way of the wicked will perish" (Ps. 1:6). Yet this destiny for the righteous is not the current reality. For now, the righteous suffer, and the wicked flourish. The righteous wait and hope for a different reality. In that waiting and hoping, torah is a primary source of comfort and a constant joy, in part because it verbalizes the reality that comes with the Lord's reign.[16]

The Protective Power of Torah

Torah, in whatever form it takes, is for the psalmist a source of protection and an expression of divinely supplied security, just as Mount Zion and the Davidic king are in certain psalms. According to Psalm 1, meditation on torah (v. 2) is directly connected with the righteous being secure, "like trees planted by streams of water" (v. 3). Psalm 19:11b (12b) declares "in keeping them (the divine precepts) there is great reward." The word for "reward" (ʿēqeb) used in this verse only occurs three times in the Old Testament. It points to consequences or results (see especially the term in Isa. 5:23: "who acquit the guilty 'as a reward for' a bribe," author's translation). As the term is used in this verse, it has a sense close to that used to speak of the future of the righteous: "destiny." Devotion to torah ensures a great destiny, a prosperous future. Hence, torah is portrayed as a mediator of divine blessings.

Torah as the Object of Trust: Psalm 119

The scholarly treatment of Psalm 119 has been preoccupied with the psalm's acrostic arrangement almost to the neglect of the psalm's theology.[17] Some scholarly treatments of Psalm 119 might give the impression that the psalm is completely devoid of theological significance. In reality, however, the psalm communicates the important idea that torah is all-encompassing; it underlies everything and applies to everything. Torah is a source of protection, of God's refuge, for anyone who meditates on it. This idea comes through in part in the structure of the psalm. It has twenty-two stanzas, corresponding to the twenty-two letters of the Hebrew alphabet. The lines in each eight-line stanza begin with the same letter of the alphabet, and the beginning letters progress from *aleph* (the first Hebrew letter) in the first stanza to *taw* (the last letter in the alphabet) in the last.

The psalm contains a host of synonyms for divine "law": *tôrâ* ("instruction"), *ʾēdâ* or *ʾēdût* ("decree"), *piqqud* ("order"), *miṣwâ* ("commandment"), *ʾimrâ* ("utterance"), *mišpat* ("law" or "judgment"), *ḥōq* ("ordinance"), and *dābār* ("word"). These eight terms appear also in Psalm 19:8–11, a fact that has led some to conclude Psalm 119 is merely an expansion of this shorter psalm. The fact that there are eight synonyms and eight lines in each stanza also led some to argue that each line of each stanza contains a different synonym.[18]

In reality, however, both of these theories are untenable. To make the latter theory work proponents must propose a series of emendations to the text of Psalm 119 (changes to the available Hebrew manuscript they believe reflects the original reading). A. Deissler has identified two additional synonyms: *ʾōraḥ* ("path") in verse 15 and *derek* ("way") in verses 3 and 37.[19] The neat structure some have tried to find in the psalm is simply not there. Despite that fact, however, the structure of the psalm is important theologically. The regular octads and the repetition of the synonyms, even if the theory of "one per poetic line" is forced, seems intended to create a meditative experience for the reader, an experience that is revelatory in some sense. Levenson suggests that the structure of the psalm functions as a mantra.[20] The message of the psalm cannot be received in a summary statement or in propositions. Rather, the message must be experienced through the constant reading and reflecting that the 176 verses require. Reading the whole psalm overwhelms one with torah!

A main idea that emerges from reading Psalm 119 is that meditation on torah brings security to the reader. The central feature of the righteous is their dependence on God. The language of trust, refuge, and hope forms the basis of their piety. (See chapter 1.) The righteous believe their destiny is secure or should be secure because they rely on the Lord. A few examples suffice to recall this connection between trust and security:

> Be merciful to me, O God, be merciful to me,
>   for in you my soul takes refuge. (Ps. 57:1 [2])

> Commit your way to the Lord;
>   trust in him, and he will act. (Ps. 37:5)

> In you, O Lord, I seek refuge;
>   do not let me ever be put to shame. (Ps 31:1 [2])

Psalm 119 uses language like that just mentioned, but it is not the Lord who is the direct object of trust. Rather, it is torah. The psalm has numerous sentences in which the psalmist declares trust/dependence on torah and then asks for protection or deliverance on that basis, just as in the first and third examples above:

> Let mercy come to me, that I may live;
>   for your law is my delight. (v. 77)

> May my heart be blameless in your statutes,
>   so that I may not be put to shame. (v. 80)

> I am yours; save me,
>   for I have sought your precepts. (v. 94)

Seeking, hoping, and trusting in torah in this psalm is the mark of devotion to God and the basis on which the psalmist prays for deliverance. Furthermore, this is the main issue that divides the righteous and the wicked:

> Their hearts are fat and gross,
>   but I delight in your law. (v. 70)

> Let the arrogant be put to shame,
>   because they have subverted me with guile;
>   as for me, I will meditate on your precepts. (v. 78)

> Salvation is far from the wicked,
>> for they do not seek your statutes. (v. 155)

Torah has become in this psalm the primary means by which the righteous express their dependence on God and through which God grants them reward. Verse 165 perhaps sums up the psalm's take on torah best: "Great peace (šālôm) have those who love your law; / nothing can make them stumble."

Adherence to torah has become the avenue through which the righteous secure their destiny. In other words, torah has become a surrogate for the Lord himself. Meditating on and trusting in torah has the same effect as seeking refuge in God. It assures them they will not be "put to shame" and that their end will be characterized by *šālôm*.

Torah as Source of Light and Life: Psalm 19

Previous chapters have observed that the righteous are most concerned about being in God's presence. Being "near God" (Ps. 73:28) is equivalent to being safe, prosperous, and blessed. Psalm 19 presents torah as a source of divine presence by portraying torah alongside images of paradise and an ordered creation. The psalm suggests that torah is the bearer of such order and gives access to the good in creation.

Psalm 19 has three main sections: verses 1–6 (2–7) describe how the glory of God is proclaimed by the elements of the universe. With voiceless expression the heavens, the firmament, and the divisions of time (day and night) shout God's greatness (vv. 1–4a [2–5a]). The sun is highlighted, however, as the special manifestation of God's greatness (vv. 4b–6 [5b–7]). The sun's circuit over the earth may represent the perfect justice of God. Indeed, the expression "nothing is hid from its heat" (v. 6b [7b]) may communicate the idea that God's justice sees all things and, eventually, will correct all things. This is precisely what the wicked deny.[21] But creation itself confirms it.

The second section of the psalm (vv. 7–10 [8–11]) highlights the benefits of torah. This portion of the poem has often been treated as separate from the first, with the two parts supposedly put together artificially.[22] It is certainly possible that the two sections did not originate from the same circle, but they have been placed together here to highlight an important feature of torah. Namely, torah has power like that of the sun. It enlightens (v. 8 [9]) and gives life anew (v. 7 [8]). Furthermore, the moral benefits of torah are described with language reminiscent of the sun's regularity ("perfect" in v. 7 [8]; "true" (or, better, "reliable") in v. 9 [10]).

The sun in its course through the sky in Psalm 19 is like the countenance of God in other texts. In this psalm, however, torah gives access to the power represented by the sun: justice and equity. The nearness of God is sometimes expressed as God shining his face upon the righteous (Num. 6:22–24). The righteous desire to "behold your face" (Ps. 17:15), which was perhaps experienced in the temple. (And the notion of seeing God's face may be related to seeing the sun at its rising in some cases.)[23] The psalms that focus on torah seem to indicate that torah provides such access to God's countenance. For example, Psalm 119:135 connects torah and the divine face: "Make your face shine upon your servant, / and teach me your statutes." The second part of the sentence ("teach me your statutes") is likely an explanation of the first ("make your face shine on your servant"). Psalm 19 seems to make the same connection by means of its structure.

Torah, Zion, and King

Previous chapters have shown that Zion and the king are closely related and are set in a particular relationship to each other. In the presentation of the two, Zion is given priority over the monarch. According to Psalms 78:68 and 132:13, God chose Zion as the divine dwelling place before God established David as king in Jerusalem. Psalm 78:69 even suggests the Lord constructed the temple before choosing David as the shepherd of Israel. With this order of presentation, the psalmist subordinates the monarch to the holy city, thereby ensuring that the Divine King is presented as the one who rules on Zion. The psalmist therefore directs the righteous to find their security in the Lord, the one who led them out of Egypt and ruled over them in the period before the monarchy. The king becomes a servant who suffers for and with Israel in exile. This relationship between the human king and the divine king is reinforced by the structure of the Psalter. Now the discussion turns to consider how torah is related to the king and to Zion.

Torah and King

The pairing of torah psalms with psalms about the king has the effect of bringing the king under the authority of torah. The one who will come will fulfill torah. Jamie Grant argues that this subordination of the monarch occurs by means of references to the law of kingship in Deuteronomy 17:14–20.[24] In that passage Moses instructs the Israelites concerning the establishment of monarchy: the king is to be one of their own people (v. 15); he is not to acquire great wealth (v. 16) or take many wives (v. 17), both of which are signs of royal abuse of power. Most importantly, the king is to have before him always a "copy of this law" (i.e., the Deuteronomic legislation in Deut. 4:44–30:29; see above, "What Is Torah?"). He is to "read in it all the days of his life" (v. 19), not "turning aside from the commandment, either to the right or to the left" (v. 20). According to Grant, the portrait of the righteous person as one who meditates on torah day and night in Psalm 1:2 is intended to call to mind this Deuteronomic law. It is far from certain that Psalm 1:2 was composed for such a purpose. As observed already, the description of torah in this verse is much more generalized than that in Joshua 1:7–8, from which the psalmist borrows. Nevertheless, Grant is certainly right that the pairing of torah and kingship psalms creates an image of the monarch as an idealized figure who represents a model of piety. He will depend on the Lord just as David did (1 Kings 2:1–4).

Torah and Zion: Psalm 1

One final feature of torah's protective capacity needs to be considered: by the time the Psalter reached its final form, torah was understood as a replacement for the temple. All the blessings of God that had once been experienced in the holy place were now attributed to the instruction of the Lord. Torah had become the ultimate refuge for the righteous. This idea is suggested by Psalm 1:3, which contains the image of the righteous already discussed:[25]

> They are like trees
>   planted by streams of water,
> which yield their fruit in its season,
>   and their leaves do not wither.

Understanding the purpose of the psalmist in describing the righteous this way requires us to understand a phenomenon in biblical writings somewhat foreign to modern ways of communicating. The biblical authors often cited or alluded to earlier texts, but they made slight changes to them to make a theological point for new circumstances. Michael Fishbane refers to this practice as "inner biblical exegesis" because the biblical authors are interpreting texts that are already authoritative for new situations.[26]

The use of previous texts is often subtle and unrecognizable to modern readers not accustomed to such methods. An example of the New Testament's use of this technique, however, may illustrate the point. Mark 6:30–44 reports the story of Jesus feeding the five thousand. The story opens by saying the crowds have followed Jesus into a "deserted" or barren place (*erēmon topov*, vv. 31, 32) to hear his teachings. It then says that Jesus looks upon them with compassion for "they were like sheep without a shepherd" (v. 34). The expression, "sheep without a shepherd" appears several places in the Old Testament, most notably Numbers 27:17, which reports Moses appointing Joshua to lead Israel after his death so the people would have proper guidance. The gospel writer perhaps wanted to portray Jesus in relation to Moses, and Jesus' disciples in the role of Joshua who came after Moses.[27]

Another comment gives an important nuance to Jesus' compassion and leadership. Jesus commands the people to sit down on "the green grass" (*tō chlōrō chortō*; v. 39). The reference to green grass is striking since the place has twice been described as barren. This reference, however, may intend to recall the words of Psalm 23:2 in the Greek version, usually translated "green pastures" in English translations (in Greek *topov xloēs*, "green place"). If Mark is indeed alluding to Psalm 23, then he presents

146 *The Destiny of the Righteous in the Psalms*

Jesus here as the good shepherd, similar to the Lord in Psalm 23. This should perhaps not be a surprise, since the gospel of John makes the same comparison explicitly (Jn. 10:1–18). What Mark does is only evident, however, if the reader is aware of the subtle references to other texts. The following discussion will suggest that the psalmist is making this type of argument in Psalm 1:3.

It may be helpful to imagine Psalm 1:3 as a collage of Old Testament words and images that work together to make the point that the one who meditates on the torah of the Lord is brought into the presence of God as if on Mount Zion. Consider how the pastiche may have taken shape. First and perhaps most obviously, Psalm 1:3 includes words from Jeremiah 17:8, a passage that describes those who trust in the Lord as secure and prosperous:

> They shall be like a tree planted by water,
>   sending out its roots by the stream.
> It shall not fear when heat comes,
>   and its leaves shall stay green;
> in the year of drought it is not anxious,
>   and it does not cease to bear fruit.[28]

Psalm 1:3 quotes the first part of this verse almost word-for-word: "they are like trees planted by water."[29] But Psalm 1:3 is different from Jeremiah 17:8 in at least three details. Each of these differences, in turn, helps the psalmist create a rather unique message—namely, that torah gives access to God's presence like Mount Zion.

Green Leaves and Constant Fruit

Psalm 1:3 includes two descriptions of the tree's leaves and fruit that indicate torah is being compared to Mount Zion. For example, instead of saying, as in Jeremiah 17:8, "its leaves shall stay green," Psalm 1:3 makes the point with a negative statement: "their leaves do not wither" (*ʿālēhû lōʾ yibbôl*). This combination of words occurs only one other place in the Old Testament: Ezekiel 47:12. Indeed, the Ezekiel text differs only in the fact that the term for "its leaves" (*ʿālēhû*) appears after the verb, not before it as in Psalm 1:3. The language shared between these two passages is so rare it is hard to deny the psalmist has borrowed it from Ezekiel (the verb here for "wither" is rarely used to communicate this idea, and among the texts that do, only Ezek. 47:12 is parallel to Ps. 1:3).[30] Ezekiel 47 appears near the end of the prophet's vision of a new temple that was meant to give hope to people in exile who were then temple-less. As Ezekiel describes the new place of worship, he uses images of paradise, similar to the descriptions noted in chapter 8. One of the images is of a stream that flows from the throne of God down to the Dead Sea, making everything in its path green and fertile. Along the river on the temple mount are trees about which Ezekiel says, "their leaves will not wither" (v. 12). Psalm 1:3's description of the trees (the righteous) whose "leaves do not wither" recall the trees planted by the stream that flows outside the temple in Ezekiel's vision.

Psalm 1:3 also seems to use the language of Ezekiel 47 in its description of the tree producing fruit. Jeremiah 17, of course, says that the tree it describes is fruitful. It uses a common verb to communicate this idea, Hebrew ʿāśâ ("to make").[31] Psalm 1:3 expresses the notion of "giving" fruit with another term that is much more unusual for this purpose, nātan ("to give" or "to yield").[32] The line reads, in a straight translation, "its fruit it gives in its season" (piryô yittēn bĕʿittô). No line in any other text can be adduced as a parallel to this one, as opposed to the way the reference to the leaves not withering seems to depend on Ezekiel 47:12. Another part of Ezekiel 47:12, however, is very similar. Ezekiel 47:12 says of the tree planted by the temple stream, "Its fruit shall not fail" or give out (lōʾ yittōm piryô). The verb yittōm is a form of the Hebrew root tmm meaning "to spend" or "wear out," but the consonants (yttm) differ in only one letter from the verb in Psalm 1:3 (yttn).[33] It seems more than coincidence that Psalm 1:3 does not follow the description of the tree in Jeremiah 17:8 in its details, but instead looks remarkably like Ezekiel 47:12.

The collage that began with Jeremiah's "like a tree planted by water" takes on a significantly different appearance by its combination with these lines from Ezekiel 47. Now the tree looks more and more like one of the trees planted by the stream in Ezekiel's vision, a stream that flows from the temple.

Planted by Streams *of Water*

One final element appears in the collage of the tree in Psalm 1:3. Psalm 1:3 includes the term "streams" (pĕlāgîm), a word not present in Jeremiah 17:8. If indeed Psalm 1:3 began with a quote from Jeremiah 17:8, the choice of this word is an interesting "departure" from that text. Jeremiah designates the water by which his tree is planted as "flowing" (yûbal, v. 8a). This description would certainly have fit the description of Psalm 1:3, if the psalmist simply desired to create a picture of stability by comparing the righteous to a tree planted in a place where its roots would be nourished. Moreover, if the psalmist had included Jeremiah's term, it would have created a clever wordplay with the word meaning "it withers" (yibbôl). Such creative plays on words are common in Hebrew poetry and were surely known to the artist who created Psalm 1. So, the appearance of the term "streams" would seem important for the psalmist's message about the destiny of the righteous.

The most obvious explanation for the psalmist's use of the word "streams" to describe the water by which the tree is planted is that this term is used in other texts to describe the water channels on the holy mountain, where the temple is located. The word *pĕlāgîm* ("streams") has this connotation in every text in which it refers to channels of water.[34] The two best examples are Psalms 46:4 (5) and 65:9 (10), both of which describe the abundant prosperity available on Mount Zion:

> There is a river whose streams (*pĕlāgâw*) make glad the city of God,
>   the holy habitation of the Most High. (Ps. 46:4 [5])

> You visit the earth and water it,
>   you greatly enrich it;
> the river (*peleg*) of God is full of water;
>   you provide the people with grain,
>   for so you have prepared it. (Ps. 65:9 [10])

In the first example the word in question clearly describes the courses of water that flow through the holy city. The water of these streams is contrasted with the chaotic sea beneath the mountain (46:2–3 [3–4]). The word is used similarly in Psalm 65:9 (10). The blessings of water that God gives are experienced on Mount Zion in the paradise-like temple. Here, too, the water in the "river of God" is presented as a counter-portrait of the chaotic waters that God tames (65:7 [8]).[35] The word has cosmic overtones and is therefore used here, as in Psalms 46:4 (5) and 65:9 (10) to portray the abundance of the paradise on Zion.[36]

With the term "streams," the collage in Psalm 1:3 is complete, and the righteous person has an unmistakable appearance. This person is "like a tree, planted," indeed, but planted by the waters that flow from the temple.

Torah as Heir to Zion

The psalmist essentially describes the righteous person in Psalm 1:3 similarly to the righteous in Psalms 52:10 (11) and 92:13–15 (14–16). In the previous chapter it was noted that the righteous are portrayed in Psalms 52 and 92 like trees planted in the temple. While Psalm 1 does not mention the temple explicitly, it uses language that evokes images of the temple for those attuned to biblical descriptions of Mount Zion and its place of worship. Psalm 1:3 is distinctive, however, in that it says the righteous are made secure—as though they dwell on the holy mountain (see chapter 9)—by meditating on torah. In other words, Psalm 1 seems to present the secure destiny of the righteous in a way similar to Psalms 52:10 (11) and 92:13–15 (14–16), but it suggests that torah, not the temple, is the direct source of that security. Torah has become the ultimate refuge for the righteous, and perhaps a source of security conceived as a replacement, or at least a surrogate, for the temple.

Generations later, the rabbis said this explicitly about torah. As they commented on Psalm 1:3, they interpreted in the way this verse has been interpreted here. That is, when they explained the meaning of being "planted by streams of water," they said that this reference is to Mount Zion or to the garden of Eden, which, as chapter 8 showed, are really the same. For example, *The Midrash on the Psalms* includes this comment on the meaning of Psalm 1:3: "The Holy One, blessed be he, lifted Abraham up and planted him in the Garden of Eden."[37]

So although Psalm 1:3 does not mention any specific location, the rabbis took the descriptions of "streams of water" and verdant trees as descriptions of the paradise from which the earth took shape. Perhaps even more important is a rabbinical explanation of Psalm 92:15 (16). It says that the righteous, being like an oak or a cedar in the house of God, still produces fruit in old age because he is devoted to torah.[38] Psalm 92:15 (16) does not mention torah, and yet the rabbis assumed the portrait of a secure state, like a tree planted in the temple, had in mind something that resulted from devotion to divine instruction. When the rabbis interpreted Psalm 1:3, they understood the "streams of water" by which the righteous are planted to refer to the garden of Eden, the place where the temple would eventually be built. When they explained Psalm 92:15 (16), they said the righteous person, who is like a tree planted in the temple, is so planted as a result of devotion to torah.

After the destruction of the second temple in 70 C.E., Judaism developed into a "religion of the book." With no earthly temple, torah became the primary access to the divine dwelling place in heaven. Through torah one could experience what worshipers once experienced on Mount Zion. Before 70 C.E., however, the roots of this relationship between torah and Zion seem to be present in Psalm 1. According to this psalm the righteous find a certain destiny because they make torah their constant delight. By meditating on torah constantly, the righteous experience and envision the reign of God. Thus, they are made secure, like a tree planted by the temple stream.

This shift from temple to torah is crucial for Christians as well as for Jews. Indeed, when the people of God recognized that the experience of the temple could be known by means of torah, it prepared the way for the church to understand the divine Word as a sign of God's presence. For Christians, of course, the Word would take on two forms. There would develop a written word, just as there would be in Judaism (torah). But the church would primarily find God's presence in the living Word, Jesus Christ. Appropriately, the church used the image of being planted to describe the life in Christ, just as Psalm 1 includes the image to portray the one obedient to torah: "As you therefore have received Christ Jesus the Lord, continue to live your lives in him, rooted and built up in him and established in faith, just as you were taught, abounding in thanksgiving" (Col. 2:6–7).

Conclusion

This book began by proposing that the Psalms' concern for the destiny of the righteous is a central organizing subject that provides a fruitful entrée into the Psalter as a whole. Indeed, it was argued that the concern for the righteous is crucially important for understanding the Psalter's many literary and theological dimensions.

The introduction pointed out that the sheer frequency of the vocabulary related to the righteous and their plight make this starting point appropriate. The term "righteous" (*ṣaddîq;* plural *ṣaddîqîm*) and related words such as "upright" (*yāšār*), "poor" (*'ānî*), "oppressed" (*dal*) and "needy" (*'ebyôn*) appear a combined 125 times in the Psalms, thus drawing frequent attention to the subject. Furthermore, the term "wicked" (*rāšā'*; plural *rěšā'îm*), which signifies those who oppress and persecute the righteous, appears so often (82 times in the Psalter) that the reader is constantly confronted with the concern for how life will turn out for the righteous.

The Psalms' intense interest in the righteous is even more extensive than this list of vocabulary reveals. Indeed, the prayers in the Psalter that call out to God for help are the prayers of those the Psalms call righteous. When this is recognized, it might well be concluded that the destiny of the righteous is the primary subject of the Psalms.

The introduction also pointed out that the concern for righteousness in the Psalms provides an important link between the faith of the Old Testament and central convictions of the Christian faith. The issue of righteousness and the concern for the future of the righteous appears in every part of the New Testament: in the teachings of Jesus (Mt. 25:31–46), in the gospel writers' descriptions of Jesus' ministry (Lk. 23:47), in the letters of Paul (Rom. 3:21–26; Gal. 3:6–9) and in other epistles (1 Pet. 4:18). Hence, a proper understanding of the righteous in the Psalms has potential to enhance understanding of how the testaments are related and to inform readers of the New Testament as to the foundations of New Testament faith.

The introduction noted that to understand the concern for the righteous in the Psalms and to discern how the Psalter informs the Christian faith, it is necessary to overcome the common misconception that the term "righteous" in this book refers to moral purity. To address this misunderstanding, this work showed that the term "righteous" in the Psalms (and in the Old Testament) is essentially a relational term, just as it is in the New Testament. Indeed, the Psalms identify righteousness mainly as an aspect of God's character in which humans may participate. (Hebrew has two terms for righteousness, one masculine, *ṣedeq,* and one feminine, *ṣědāqâ,* both of which are used for divine righteousness.) For example, Psalm 4 calls on

"God of my righteousness" (v. 1 [2], NASB), and Psalm 5 petitions God to "lead me, O Lord, in your righteousness" (v. 8 [9]). Therefore, the Psalter's understanding of righteousness is similar to that of Paul, who insists that humans can only be made righteous through the grace of God, who alone is perfectly righteous, and who revealed his righteousness in Jesus Christ (Rom. 3:21–26).

The main sign that the righteous are in right relationship to God is that they recognize that God is in control of the world, that "the Lord reigns." They place themselves under divine authority and look to God as the source of life and blessing. One way the righteous express their submission to God is by constantly meditating on the "law of the Lord" (Ps. 1:2). "Law" in this sense translates the word *tôrâ*, which means "instruction." To say that the righteous meditate on torah is to say the righteous constantly seek to understand what God is doing in the world and to align themselves with it. As people who meditate on this "instruction," the righteous are those who do not go their own way, but instead allow God to teach them.

The psalms also express the righteous' dependence on the Lord by saying the righteous person "seeks refuge" in God rather than in other sources of security (Ps. 2:12; 37:40). As a consequence of this stance before the Divine, the righteous do not rest in their own goodness. Instead, they readily confess their sins before God and seek God's mercy in response to their sinfulness (see Ps. 32). The righteous in the Psalms are also portrayed as those who respond to God in praise and joy and who call on God for help. Prayer and worship are the activities of the righteous because such activities grow out of an awareness of God as the source of all that is good. In other words, the righteous in the Psalms are very much the same as those Paul calls righteous, those who live by faith (Rom. 1:17). The righteous' right behavior, in turn, does not grow out of moral purity but is a result of right understanding of who controls the world.

After the introduction clarified these points, the book explored the concern for the destiny of the righteous in the Psalms in three main sections. Part I (chapters 1–3) expanded on three aspects of the character and destiny of the righteous that the introduction presented briefly. Chapter 1 looked at the righteous' relationship to God–their faith and dependence on God–by means of their prayers. It considered first the basic notion that the prayers of the righteous depict them as those who are aware of their helplessness and dependence on God. Psalm 131 provided a primary example. The one who prayed this psalm, with a "heart...not lifted up" and eyes "not raised too high" (v. 1) is a model of the righteous person who recognizes her or his need for God. Then the chapter looked more closely at prayers that express two particular kinds of need: prayers of confession and the so-called "psalms of vengeance." The former reveals the righteous' dependence on God for forgiveness of sins (Ps. 32), and the latter shows their dependence on God for protection from the wicked (Ps. 58). Reading these two types of psalms under the rubric of the destiny of the righteous provides an important theological perspective on the character of the righteous. Recognizing that the righteous are those who confess their sins to God (and the wicked are those who do not) makes clear that the label "righteous" does not represent a deluded or self-righteous claim. To the contrary, the righteous are those who do not think too highly of themselves. "Righteous" is never a self-designation in the Psalms. The label is always given to others and thus represents a divine perspective.

Similarly, the psalms that call to God to punish the wicked are not judgmental or vengeful. Rather, these psalms are spoken in recognition of both the overwhelming power of wickedness and the powerlessness of the righteous to act against it. When the righteous call God to judge the wicked, they are essentially asking for what Christians request when they pray, "thy kingdom come." Moreover, as the righteous appeal to God for help, they also give up their own inclinations to seek revenge and act violently in response to the wicked. With this in view, even the most difficult examples of the so-called psalms of vengeance (notably Ps. 137) can be understood in a positive light.

Chapter 2 considered the activity of the righteous that results from their relationship with God. It suggested praise is the primary "activity" of the righteous out of which all right action grows. Those who truly worship God are those who also act as though God is in control of the world (Ps. 15 and 24). This chapter then showed that the wicked are the opposite of the righteous. Indeed, the wicked are those who do not "take refuge" in God (Ps. 52:7 [9]), but who instead "rely on [their] own insight" (Prov. 3:5). As a result of their deluded reliance on self, the wicked take advantage of the righteous. Therefore, the righteous are often described as helpless before the wicked, who oppress and persecute them. (See especially Ps. 9–10). For this reason the righteous in the Psalms are constantly set over against the wicked, and God's righteousness is set over against wickedness; wickedness amounts to opposition to God's intentions to create šālôm.

The final chapter in Part I (chapter 3) took up the subject of the reward due the righteous, their destiny. It showed that the main feature of the righteous' destiny is simply "to be near God" (Ps. 73:28). That is, although the Psalms speak at times of material reward for the righteous (as in Ps. 37), the main outcome of their right relationship with God is the relationship itself. Psalm 23 provided an example of this point with its insistence that God's presence is all that is really needed (vv. 1 and 6). The Psalms' emphasis on the righteous prospering (Ps. 1:3) and the wicked perishing (Ps. 1:6) is not part of an artless retribution theology that focuses on material reward for obedience to God. Rather, the Psalms emphasize that the righteous' greatest "reward" is to be in God's presence. This is summed up in the psalmist's declaration, "One thing I asked of the LORD, / that will I seek after: / to live in the house of the LORD / all the days of my life" (Ps. 27:4). The righteous claim that the Lord is their "portion" or inheritance; thus, God is all they need (Ps. 73:26).

Part II (chapters 4–5) considered how the concern for the destiny of the righteous is seen in the shape of the Psalter. Chapter 4 showed, for example, that the concern for the destiny of the righteous is central to Psalms 1 and 2, which introduce the Psalter. In fact, although these two works are quite different in tone and content, they are united by an interest in the two ways one can choose in life: the way of the righteous and the way of the wicked (see the term *derek,* "way" in Ps. 1:6; 2:12). The final statement in Psalm 2 summarizes the character and destiny of the righteous: "Happy are all who take refuge in him" (v. 2:12d). This line enhances the connection between Psalms 1 and 2 and points forward to the many descriptions of the righteous as those who "take refuge" in the Lord in the rest of the Psalter. Hence, as Psalms 1 and 2 invite the reader into the book, they present the character of the righteous as an example to be followed and the problem of the destiny of the righteous as something to be solved.

The remainder of chapter 4 examined Books 1–3 of the Psalter (understood here as Ps. 3–89). This section gave particular attention to the role of David, the Lord's anointed, as the suffering one, as seen particularly in Psalm 3. The discussion showed that this psalm opens a larger section (Ps. 3–89) that moves to a point of supreme despair as Psalm 89 laments over the anointed's suffering. But it was also noted that this conclusion to Book 3 of the Psalter already contains signs of hope for the future. The promises to David are even here beginning to be transferred to God's servants, the chosen people. The ground is laid for David to be a future hope for the righteous. Chapter 5 then showed how the remainder of the Psalter deals with the suffering of the righteous people. The affirmation that "the Lord reigns" puts confidence in the future in God, not in the human king. But there remains hope that David will once again provide a sign of the divine presence.

Part III zeroed in on three important topics in the Psalms that represent the "embodied hope" of the righteous: the king, Mount Zion, and torah. Chapters 6 and 7 addressed the way the Davidic king served as defender of the righteous and the hope for God's establishment of justice (Ps. 2; 72; 101). One of the main concerns of these chapters was how the king was understood as a protector of the righteous after the Babylonian exile brought an end to monarchy in Israel. These chapters showed that David is the symbol for the suffering people, the righteous, and he is cast as a future hope, as one who will reappear in the future to defend God's servants (Ps. 89; 101).

Chapters 8 and 9 explored the Psalms' portrayal of Zion and particularly the righteous' longing to be on Zion and in its temple (Ps. 42–43; 63). The reason for such longing is that Zion is presented as the place God's reign is experienced and known and, therefore, the place where the righteous are most at home (Ps. 24).

Finally, chapter 10 considered the role of torah, God's "instruction" in the life of the righteous. Torah appears in Psalms 1; 19; and 119 as a source of protection for the righteous; torah is an expression of God's refuge; by meditation on torah the righteous find true security. Torah is also presented in the Psalms as the ultimate expression of protection for the righteous; indeed, torah serves as a substitute and replacement for Zion and is intended to provide direction for the activity of the king as well. The importance of torah to the righteous was seen particularly in Psalm 1:3, which declares that the righteous are "like trees planted by streams of water." This line depicts the righteous person as one who is secure and prosperous as a result of being planted near God. The proximity to the Lord is drawn with images used elsewhere to depict Mount Zion and its temple. In Psalm 1:3, however, torah, not the temple, makes the righteous secure (see v. 2).

These ten chapters consistently pointed out that the Psalter's presentation of the righteous serves as a foundation for the New Testament's understanding of the life and ministry of Jesus. Jesus is the righteous one who suffers (Lk. 23:47). He is like David who suffered at the hands of the wicked (Ps. 2 and 3). For the church, Jesus is the "embodied hope" of the righteous. He is the "new David" who is able to defend the righteous (Mt. 9:27; 20:30). He is the sign of God's presence, the locus of God's nearness to humans, as Zion had once been (Mk. 14:58). He is also the Divine Word who makes known God's intentions to the world, like torah (Jn. 1:1–18). This presentation of Jesus in relation to the righteous suggests that what the Psalter says about the righteous and their reliance on David, Zion, and torah might well be considered foundational to the church's conception of the Messiah. Jesus is both the hope for the future of the righteous, the one who provides evidence of God's kingdom and God's presence (Rev. 21:22), and one of the righteous as well. As with the righteous in the Psalms, Jesus, in his darkest hour, placed his trust in God with the cry, "Father, into your hands I commend my spirit" (Lk. 23:46; cf. Ps. 31:5 [6]).

Notes

Introduction

[1] As Patrick D. Miller notes concerning the righteous and the wicked, "how these two groups act, the way they go–whether one means their path of life or their ultimate fate–is very much the subject matter of the psalms;" see "The Beginning of the Psalter," in *The Shape and Shaping of the Psalter* (JSOTSup 159; ed. J. Clinton McCann; Sheffield: JSOT Press, 1993), 85.

[2] See the suggested use of psalms for particular pastoral situations in Perry H. Biddle Jr., *A Hospital Visitation Manual* (Grand Rapids, Mich.: Eerdmans, 1988); for a discussion of the ways the Psalms may be used in cases of grief and loss see Walter Brueggemann, "Psalms and the Life of Faith: A Suggested Typology of Function," *JSOT* 17 (1980): 3–22.

[3] Note for example that Luther found in the Psalms scripture's greatest witness to the doctrine of justification by faith alone; see James Samuel Preuss, *From Shadow to Promise: Old Testament Interpretation from Augustine to the Young Luther* (Cambridge, Mass.: Harvard University Press, 1969), 153–271.

[4] When he says that "not even one" person does what is right (v. 12), he is paraphrasing Ps. 143:2. He quotes numerous other psalms in the course of his argument; see the discussion of Douglas J. Moo, *The Epistle to the Romans* (NICNT; Grand Rapids, Mich.: William B. Eerdmans, 1996), 197–210.

[5] The verbal root *ṣdq* is used similarly in Old Aramaic texts to signify the loyalty of a king or high priest to his god; see the discussion in Klaus Koch, "*ṣdq*, to be communally faithful," *TLOT* 2:1047.

[6] See H. H. Schmid, "Creation, Righteousness, and Salvation: 'Creation Theology' as the Broad Horizon of Biblical Theology," in *Creation in the Old Testament* (ed. Bernhard W. Anderson; Issues in Religion and Theology 6; Philadelphia: Fortress Press, 1984), 102.

[7] James L. Mays, *The Lord Reigns: A Theological Handbook to the Psalms* (Louisville: Westminster John Knox Press, 1994), 32.

[8] William P. Brown draws the distinction between wisdom's attempts to form character and the Psalms' primary concern for action oriented to God's will (thus producing justice) in "Come, O Children...I Will Teach You the Fear of the Lord" (Psalm 34:12): Comparing Psalms and Proverbs," in *Seeking Out the Wisdom of the Ancients: Essays Offered to Honor Michael V. Fox on the Occasion of His Sixty-Fifth Birthday* (ed. R. L. Troxel, K. G. Friebel, and D. R. Magary; Winona Lake, Ind.: Eisenbrauns, 2005), 85–102 (see esp. 87–88).

[9] See the treatment of E. R. Achtemeier, "Righteousness in the Old Testament," *IDB* 4:80.

[10] Each of these terms can indicate a particular social or economic status as Deut. 15:4, 7, 11 indicates.

[11] Mays, *The Lord Reigns*, 33.

[12] Patrick D. Miller Jr., *Interpreting the Psalms* (Philadelphia: Fortress Press, 1986), 22–23.

[13] See the discussion of Joachim Becker, *Israel deutet seine Psalmen: Urform und Neuinterpretation in den Psalmen* (Stuttgarter Studien 18; Stuttgart: Verlag Katholisches Bibelwerk, 1967), 22–24 and esp. 41–68.

[14] Patrick D. Miller, *They Cried to the Lord: The Form and Theology of Biblical Prayer* (Minneapolis: Fortress Press, 1994), 239–40.

[15] *Sanhedrin* 106b identifies the wicked in this case to be those torah sages who did not practice what they taught. The classic example for them, interestingly, was Doeg the Edomite, who revealed to Saul David's whereabouts (the superscription of Ps. 52; 1 Sam. 21:1–8; 22:6–19).

[16] On the form and hermeneutical significance of the titles of these psalms see Brevard S. Childs, "Psalm Titles and Midrashic Exegesis," *Journal of Semitic Studies* 16 (1971): 137–50.

[17] Mays, *The Lord Reigns*, 123.

[18] Ibid., 96.

[19] Though as W.D. Davies and Dale C. Allison point out, the identification of Jesus as a "son of David" could be intended to associate Jesus with Solomon since Solomon was

remembered in Jewish tradition as a healer; see *A Critical and Exegetical Commentary on the Gospel According to Saint Matthew* (ICC 1; Edinburgh: T. & T. Clark, 1988), 156–57.

[20]See the discussion and the significant effort in this in Mays, *The Lord Reigns*. Compare Nancy L. deClaissé-Walford, *Introduction to the Psalms* (St. Louis: Chalice Press, 2004).

[21]See especially the seminal work of Gerald H. Wilson, *The Editing of the Hebrew Psalter* (SBLDS 76; Chico, Cal.: Scholars Press, 1985); see also deClaissé-Walford, *An Introduction to the Psalms;* the essays in J. Clinton McCann Jr., ed., *The Shape and Shaping of the Psalter;* James L. Mays, "The Place of the Torah-Psalms in the Psalter," *JBL* (1987): 1–12, reprinted in Mays, *The Lord Reigns*, 128–35; this recent work is summarized by David Howard, "The Psalms in Current Study," in *Interpreting the Psalms: Issues and Approaches* (ed. Philip S. Johnston and David G. Firth; Leicester, England: Apollos, 2005), 23–40; and by Patrick D. Miller Jr., "The Psalter as a Book of Theology," in *Psalms in Community: Jewish and Christian Textual, Liturgical, and Artistic Traditions* (SBL Symposium Series 25; ed. Harold W. Attridge and Margot E. Fassler; Atlanta: SBL, 2003), 87–98.

[22]This expression is used for example by Frank-Lothar Hossfeld and Erich Zenger, *Psalms 2: A Commentary on Psalms 51–100* (Hermeneia; trans. Linda M. Maloney; Minneapolis: Fortress Press, 2005), 5–6.

[23]See especially Wilson, *Editing*, 214–28.

[24]See Jerome F. D. Creach, *Yahweh as Refuge and the Editing of the Hebrew Psalter* (JSOTSup 217; Sheffield: Sheffield Academic Press, 1996), 74–77.

[25]Miller, "The Beginning of the Psalter," 85.

[26]On this point see the insightful argument of David P. Moessner, "*Two* Lords 'at the Right Hand'? The Psalms and an Intertextual Reading of Peter's Pentecost Speech (Acts 2:14–36)," in *Literary Studies in Luke-Acts: Essays in Honor of Joseph B. Tyson* (ed. Richard P. Thompson and Thomas E. Phillips; Macon, Ga.: Mercer University Press, 1998), 215–32.

[27]The expression "abiding theological witness" and its implication for understanding the Psalms as scripture is borrowed from Christopher R. Seitz, *Word Without End: The Old Testament as Abiding Theological Witness* (Grand Rapids, Mich.: Eerdmans, 1998); see esp. 3–12 and 61–74.

[28]In Mays, *The Lord Reigns*, 12–22.

[29]This thesis concerning the purpose of Pss. 90–106 is now widely accepted; it is expressed by Wilson, *Editing*, 214–28.

[30]Karl Barth, *Church Dogmatic IV: The Doctrine of Reconciliation* (Edinburgh: T. & T. Clark, 1980), 1:591–92.

[31]See the discussion in Davies and Allison, *Matthew*, 3:428; this interpretation of the passage is consistent with the saying in *t. Sanh.* 13.2: "there must be righteous men among the heathen who have a share in the world to come."

[32]Douglas R. A. Hare, *Matthew* (Interpretation: A Bible Commentary for Teaching and Preaching; Louisville: John Knox Press, 1993), 291.

[33]On the close relationship between the psalms of vengeance and liberation theology see especially Walter Brueggemann, *Israel's Praise: Doxology against Idolatry and Ideology* (Philadelphia: Fortress Press, 1988), 140–42.

[34]Walter Brueggemann, *The Message of the Psalms: A Theological Commentary* (Augsburg Old Testament Studies; Minneapolis: Augsburg Publishing House, 1984), 13.

[35]On the scapegoat mechanism in sacrificial systems see René Girard, *Violence and the Sacred* (trans. Patrick Gregory; Baltimore: The Johns Hopkins University Press, 1977); Girard discusses the implications of this idea for the Psalms in *The Scapegoat* (trans. Yvonne Freccero; Baltimore: The Johns Hopkins University Press, 1986), 104–9.

[36]On this issue see Gustavo Gutierrez, *The Power of the Poor in History: Selected Writings* (trans. Robert R. Barr; Maryknoll, N.Y.: Orbis Books, 1983).

[37]José Porfirio Miranda, *Communism in the Bible* (trans. Robert R. Barr; Maryknoll, N.Y.: Orbis Books, 1981), 44.

Chapter 1: Prayer and the Profile of the Righteous

[1]For an extensive discussion of possible settings that lie behind the prayers see Erhard S. Gerstenberger, *Psalm: Part 1, with an Introduction to Cultic Poetry* (FOTL; Grand Rapids, Mich.: Eerdmans, 1988); *Psalms: Part 2 and Lamentations* (FOTL; Grand Rapids, Mich.: Eerdmans, 2001); and Gerstenberger, *Der Bittende Mensch: Bittritual und Klagelied der Einzelnen im Alten Testament* (Wissenschaft Monographien zum Alten und Neuen Testament 51; Neukirchen-Vluyn: Neukirchener Verlag, 1980).

²Mays, *The Lord Reigns*, 27.

³Miller (*They Cried to the Lord*, 1) makes the point that theologians often speak of theology as an outgrowth of prayer.

⁴Ibid., 41.

⁵*The Ascetical Homilies of Saint Isaac the Syrian* (trans. Holy Transfiguration Monastery; Boston, Mass.: Holy Transfiguration Monastery, 1984), 67–68 (Homily 8). Language has been made more inclusive in the text. The original reads: "When a man knows he is in need of Divine help, he makes many prayers. And by as much as he multiplies them, his heart is humbled, for there is no man who will not be humbled when he is making supplication and entreaty."

⁶This evaluation of the length of Ps. 131 does not count Pss. 117 and 134 as prayers since they do not contain direct address to God.

⁷James L. Mays, *Psalms* (Interpretation; Louisville: Westminster John Knox Press, 1994), 408.

⁸Miller, *They Cried to the Lord*, 240–41.

⁹Klaus Seybold, *Introducing the Psalms* (trans. Graeme Dunphy; Edinburgh: T. & T. Clark, 1990), 149–50; Gottfried Quell proposes that vv. 1–3 were used when the woman made a thank-offering; see "Struktur und Sinn des Psalms 131," in *Das Ferne und Nahe Wort: Festschrift Leonard Rost* (ed. Fritz Maass; BZAW 105; Berlin: Töpelmann, 1967), 173–85.

¹⁰Miller, *They Cried to the Lord*, 240.

¹¹Ibid.

¹²It is worth noting that in Prov. 31:20 the matriarch exhibits compassion to the poor and thus sustains righteousness in the community: "She opens her hand to the poor, and reaches out her hands to the needy." See William P. Brown, *Character in Crisis: A Fresh Approach to the Wisdom Literature of the Old Testament* (Grand Rapids, Mich.: Wm. B. Eerdmans, 1996), 48–49.

¹³On the theological significance of the language discussed here see Seybold, *Introducing the Psalms*, 144–48.

¹⁴See Jerome F. D. Creach, *Yahweh as Refuge and the Editing of the Hebrew Psalter* (JSOTSup 217; Sheffield: JSOT Press, 1996), 22–49 for an overview of the various forms of these and related words.

¹⁵As A. V. G. Betts ("Tell el-Hibr: A Rock Shelter Occupation of the Fourth Millennium B.C.E. in the Jordanian Baydiya," *BASOR* 287 [August 1992]: 5) illustrates in an excavation east of the Dead Sea, these features of the landscape often provided natural defenses, strategic lookout points, and temporary shelter in times of war.

¹⁶On the language of seeing God's face see Mark S. Smith, "Seeing God in the Psalms: The Background to the Beatific Vision in the Hebrew Bible," *CBQ* 50 (198): 171–83.

¹⁷Saint Augustine, *Expositions on the Book of Psalms*, *NPNF* 8:192 (paragraph 10).

¹⁸One of the most promising proposals is that of Erhard Gerstenberger. On the basis of Babylonian texts and sociological models, he suggests that psalms like these were used in family healing ceremonies in which a ritual expert (perhaps a member of the extended family) helped the person back to health and full participation in the community. He bases this theory in part on biblical texts that show home-based ceremonies: Hezekiah calls on Isaiah to come to his home when he is sick (Isa. 38); David practices penitence at home with the "help" of Nathan (2 Sam. 12). See *Der bittende Mensch* (Neukirchen-Vluyn: Neukirchener Verlag, 1980), 167–69.

¹⁹J. Clinton McCann Jr., "Psalms," in *New Interpreter's Bible* (Nashville: Abingdon Press), 4:667.

²⁰See the study of Samuel E. Balentine, *The Hidden God: The Hiding of the Face of God in the Old Testament* (Oxford Theological Monographs; Oxford: Oxford University Press, 1983).

²¹Numerous exegetical stretches may be cited in this regard: for example, L. P. Trudinger (*JETS* 17 [1974]: 235–38) argues that Jesus' cry is actually a cry of victory since God has handed him over to be a sacrifice for sin; E. Best, *Temptation* lxiv–lxviii, suggests Jesus is aware he is bearing God's judgment for the sins of others (based on Mk. 10:38–39; 14:35–36); Jürgen Moltmann's extensive use of Ps. 22:1, though immensely helpful theologically should not be confused with historical analysis (which Moltmann, of course, acknowledges it is not); see *The Crucified God: The Cross of Christ as the Foundation and Criticism of Christian Theology* (New York: Harper & Row, 1974, esp. 150–53).

²²It is possible that the taunting "Aha!" of Mark 15:29 has another psalm in mind, but if so, it is surely a psalm that reflects the suffering of the righteous (perhaps Ps. 40:15 [16]//70:3 [4]).

[23] Erich Zenger, *A God of Vengeance? Understanding the Psalms of Divine Wrath* (trans. Linda M. Maloney; Louisville: Westminster John Knox Press, 1994), 32.

[24] For a full discussion see Marvin E. Tate, *Psalms 51–100* (WBC 20; Waco, Tex.: Word Books, 1990), 82–83.

[25] For example, Augustine used Ps. 58 in this way; see E. Hill, *Nine Sermons of Saint Augustine on the Psalms* (London: Longmans, Green & Co., 1958, 111), cited in Tate, *Psalms 51–100*, 89; and see the similar reading of this psalm by Dietrich Bonhoeffer, *Psalms: Prayer Book of the Bible* (trans. J. H. Burtness; Minneapolis: Augsburg, 1970), 21.

[26] Zenger, *A God of Vengeance?*, 48.

[27] Ibid., 50.

[28] Mitchell Dahood makes a credible argument that v. 10 does not express gloating either. He avers that the preposition *be* that is translated "in" (the blood of the wicked") should instead be rendered "of." If he is right, the verse is saying that the righteous will *not* have the blood of the wicked on their feet. See Dahood, *Psalms III: 101–150* (AB 17a; Garden City, N.Y.: Doubleday, 1970), 391–93.

[29] Girard, *The Scapegoat*, 108.

[30] See again Zenger, *A God of Vengeance?*, 63–86.

Chapter 2: Clean Hands and Pure Hearts

[1] See the discussion of Klaus Seybold, *Introducing the Psalms*, 171–73.

[2] *The Constitution of the Presbyterian Church (U.S.A.): Part I: Book of Confessions* (Louisville: Geneva Press, 1999): 7.001 and 7.111.

[3] As defined in *The Oxford American College Dictionary* (New York: G. P. Putnam's Sons, 2002), 1067.

[4] Mays, *The Lord Reigns*, 64–65.

[5] Walter Brueggemann, *Israel's Praise: Doxology against Idolatry and Ideology* (Philadelphia: Fortress Press, 1988), 74–76; the three points highlighted here are not offered by Brueggemann in the same way as presented here; rather, they are scattered through his discussion, as the page references below will show.

[6] Ibid., 86–87.

[7] Ibid., 136.

[8] Jan Bergman, Christoph Barth, and Helmer Ringgren, "גיל" in *Theological Dictionary of the Old Testament* (ed. G.J. Botterweck and H. Ringgren, trans. J.T. Willis, G.W. Bromiley, and D.E. Green; vol. 2; Grand Rapids, Mich.: Eerdmans, 1975), 470–71. The idea that the verb describes whirling comes from a connection of this verb to a similar Arabic term with that meaning; on the meaning "howl" see Hos. 10:5.

[9] See this term in Ps. 81:1 (2) in parallel with another term, $h\bar{a}r\hat{i}^{\,c}\hat{u}$ meaning "give a great shout" (1 Sam. 17:52).

[10] On the progression of lines in Hebrew poetry see Robert Alter, *The Art of Biblical Poetry* (New York: Basic Books, 1985), esp. 62–84.

[11] Robert Davidson, *The Vitality of Worship: A Commentary on the Book of Psalms* (Grand Rapids, Mich.: Eerdmans, 1998), 113.

[12] Hans-Joachim Kraus, *Psalms 1–59* (trans. Hilton C. Oswald; Minneapolis: Fortress Press, 1993), 375.

[13] Ps. 24 also has a larger interest in the nature and identity of Israel's God, as seen in the liturgy that celebrates God's kingship (vv. 1–2, 7–10). This portion of the psalm will be explored further in chapter 7.

[14] See Kraus, *Psalms 1–59*, 314 for a different perspective on this language; however, see C. A. Briggs (*The Book of Psalms* [ICC 1; Edinburgh: T. & T. Clark, 1903; repr. 1987], 215), who understands each term in v. 4 to refer to inner purity.

[15] See Mays, *Psalms*, 121.

[16] On the significance of the first commandment for internal purity see Patrick D. Miller, *The God You Have: Politics, Religion, and the First Commandment* (Facets; Minneapolis: Fortress Press, 2004), 45–60.

[17] Mays, *Psalms*, 84.

[18] On the concept of righteousness as world order see Schmid, "Creation, Righteousness, and Salvation," 107.

[19] Kraus, *Psalms 1–59*, 229.

[20] Ibid., 230–31.
[21] Richard D. Nelson, *Deuteronomy: A Commentary* (OTL; Louisville: Westminster John Knox Press, 2002), 321.
[22] Michael Welker, *Creation and Reality* (Minneapolis: Fortress Press, 1999), 80.
[23] C. van Leeuwen, "ršʿ to be impious/guilty," *TLOT* 3:1262–63.
[24] See the discussion in Tate, *Psalms 51–100*, 36–37.
[25] See the discussion in Hans-Joachim Kraus, *Psalms 60–150* (trans. Hilton C. Oswald; Minneapolis: Fortress Press, 1993), 338.
[26] See the discussion in Carol Meyers, "The Family in Early Israel," in Leo G. Perdue, Joseph Blenkinsopp, John J. Collins, and Carol Meyers, *Families in Ancient Israel* (Louisville: Westminster John Knox Press, 1997), 1–48, esp. 36–38.

Chapter 3: To Be Near God

[1] Mays, *Psalms*, 43.
[2] See for example Ps. 140:13: "the upright shall live in your presence."
[3] Mays, *Psalms*, 43–44. Samuel Terrien (*The Elusive Presence: The Heart of Biblical Theology* [San Francisco: Harper & Row, 1978]) argues that the theme of God's presence is a key to biblical theology; see 278–350 for a discussion of psalms that deal with the issue of divine presence.
[4] It is possible to translate the line, "My shepherd is the Lord," thus highlighting the fact that the psalmist could have chosen to be guided by someone or something other than the Lord. See the discussion of E. Pfeiffer, "Eine Inversion in Psalm xxiii 1b," *VT* 8/1: 219–20.
[5] Hermann Gunkel uses Ps. 23:1 to illustrate the nature of Hebrew poetry: "The Hebrew would say: 'The Lord is my shepherd. I shall not want.' The Greek would have expressed that the second sentence was a result of the first. The Hebrew omits a 'therefore.'" See *Introduction to Psalms: The Genres of the Religious Lyric of Israel* (trans. James D. Nogalski; Macon, Ga.: Mercer University Press, 1998), 1.
[6] J. Clinton McCann, Jr., *A Theological Introduction to the Book of Psalms* (Nashville: Abingdon Press, 1993), 128.
[7] Ron E. Tappy, "Psalm 23: Symbolism and Structure," *CBQ* 57/2 (1995): 266–68; the following discussion depends heavily upon Tappy's article.
[8] NRSV retains the wording, "I shall not want." NIV supplies an object: "I shall lack nothing." Similarly JPS renders, "I lack nothing."
[9] For example, in two texts from Rās ibn-Hāni this verbal root is used to speak of one-tenth of a jar of oil that is missing; see M. Heltzer, "Some Questions of Ugaritic Metrology and its Parallels in Judah, Phoenicia, Mesopotamia and Greece," *UF* (1989): 195–208.
[10] *UT* 49.II.14–19; see also *UT* 2060.9 for another example of the root meaning "missing;" these texts are discussed by Tappy, "Psalm 23," 266–68.
[11] Tappy, "Psalm 23," 255–80, esp. 268–69.
[12] Timothy M. Willis ("A Fresh Look at Psalm XXIII 3A," *VT* 37/1: 104–6) suggests v. 3a be translated, "He gathers me in" or "He herds me in." This rendering captures appropriately the sense of presence with the Lord that the verse seems to intend.
[13] On the importance of God's presence and the Lord's "rod and staff" that give evidence of that presence see John Goldinday, *Psalms*, vol. 1, Psalms 1–41 (Baker Commentary on the Old Testament; Grand Rapids, Mich.: Baker Academic, 2006), 351.
[14] See the identical expression in Ps. 27:4, where it clearly refers to the Jerusalem temple.
[15] Tappy, "Psalm 23," 274–75; on the structure of the "house of the father" in ancient Israel see L. E. Stager, "The Archaeology of the Family in Ancient Israel," *BASOR* 260 (1985): 1–35.
[16] G. Gerlman, "šlm to have enough," *TLOT* 3:1339.
[17] Mays, *Psalms*, 241.
[18] Both the Greek and Syriac versions have a singular term here, indicating most likely that they understood the expression to refer to the temple.
[19] Frank-Lothar Hossfeld and Erich Zenger, *Psalms 51–100*, 235–36.
[20] Diethelm Michel, "Ich aber bin immer bei dir: Von der Unsterblichkeit der Gottesbeziehung," in *Im Angesicht des Todes* (Pietas Liturgica 3; ed. Hansjakob Becker, Bernhard Einig, and Peter-Otto Ullrich; St. Ottilien: EOS, 1987), 648–49.

160   Notes to Pages 47–56

²¹W. D. Davies, *The Gospel and the Land* (Berkeley: University of California Press, 1974), 360–62.

²²Relying on evidence from Did. 3:7, which speaks of inheriting the earth in connection with the Messiah's return; and the emphasis on the kingdom of God in Matthew in relation to this promise (see Mt. 5:10, 20; 6:10, 33; 21:31). Davies, *The Gospel and the Land*, 361–62.

²³See the insightful discussion of this point by Walter Brueggemann, *The Land: Place as Gift, Promise, and Challenge in Biblical Faith* (OBT; 2d ed.; Minneapolis: Fortress Press, 2002), 157–72.

²⁴McCann, "Psalms," 828.

²⁵This is the opinion of Kraus, *Psalms 1–59*, 405; see Ps. 119:30.

²⁶This is the argument of Gerlman, "*šlm* to have enough," *TLOT* 3:1345; and Kraus, *Psalms 1–59*, 404. Note, however, that the argument that follows does not change substantially if their suggestion is adopted.

²⁷An exception is the expression "prince of peace" in Isa. 9:5, but that is a specifically royal title and bears little on our understanding of Ps. 37:37.

²⁸Miranda, *Communism in the Bible*, 42.

²⁹Tikva Frymer-Kensky, "The Planting of Man: A Study in Biblical Imagery," in *Love and Death in the Ancient Near East: Essays in Honor of Marvin H. Pope* (ed. John H. Marks and Robert M. Good; Guilford, Conn.: Four Quarters Publishing Co., 1987), 131.

³⁰William P. Brown, *Seeing the Psalms: A Theology of Metaphor* (Louisville: Westminster John Knox Press, 2002), 67.

Chapter 4: The Lord's Anointed and the Suffering of the Righteous

¹See Brevard S. Childs, *Introduction to the Old Testament as Scripture* (Philadelphia: Fortress Press, 1979), 513; and Miller, "The Psalter as a Book of Theology."

²Miller ("The Psalter as a Book of Theology," 90–92) gives a helpful summary of a portion of that movement.

³As the *Midrash Tehillim* says, "As Moses blessed Israel with the words, 'Blessed is the man' (Dt 33:29), so David blessed Israel with the words, 'Blessed is the man.'" See William G. Braude, *The Midrash on the Psalms* (Yale Judaica Series 13; New Haven: Yale University Press, 1998), 5.

⁴On the editorial features that divide the Psalter into these two sections see Gerald H. Wilson, "The Use of Royal Psalms at the 'Seams' of the Hebrew Psalter," *JSOT* 35 (1986): 85–94.

⁵On the movement from plea to praise, see Claus Westermann, *Praise and Lament in the Psalms* (Atlanta: John Knox Press, 1981) and *The Psalms: Structure, Content and Message* (Minneapolis: Augsburg, 1980); see also the application of Westermann's ideas by Walter Brueggemann, "The Costly Loss of Lament," *JSOT* 36 (1986): 57–71.

⁶See James L. Mays, "The Place of the Torah-Psalms"; Patrick D. Miller, "The Beginning of the Psalter," 84–92; *Interpreting the Psalms*, 1986), 81–88; Gerald Sheppard, *Wisdom as a Hermeneutical Construct* (Berlin; New York: W. deGruyter, 1980), 136–44; J. Reindl, "Weisheitliche Bearbeitung von Psalmen: Ein Beitrag zum Verständnis der Sammlung des Psalters," in *Congress Volume, Vienna 1980* (VTSup 32; ed. J. A. Emerton; Leiden: E. J. Brill, 1981), 333–56.

⁷Miller, "The Psalter as a Book of Theology," 90.

⁸On the role of untitled psalms in the Psalter see Gerald H. Wilson, "The Function of 'Untitled' Psalms in the Hebrew Psalter," *ZAW* 97/3 (1985): 404–13.

⁹See also the shared term "sit" (*yāšab*) in 1:1 and 2:4.

¹⁰On the significant role of this term in the Psalter see McCann, "Psalms," 666–67; and "The Shape of Book One of the Psalter and the Shape of Human Happiness," in *The Book of Psalms: Composition and Reception* (Supplements to Vetus Testamentum; ed. Peter W. Flint and Patrick D. Miller Jr.; Leiden: Brill, 2005), 340–48.

¹¹Mays, *Psalms*, 43.

¹²Mays, *The Lord Reigns*, 19.

¹³For a comparison of Jer. 17:5–8 with Ps. 1 see chapter 10 and the discussion in Creach, "Like a Tree Planted by the Temple Stream: Portrait of the Righteous in Psalm 1:3," *CBQ* 61 (1999): 34–46.

[14] Mays, *Psalms*, 42.

[15] Isaac the Syrian presents a helpful interpretation of Ps. 1:5; he proposes that "shall not stand in the judgment" means that the wicked will be separated from the righteous and from Christ; see *Ascetical Homilies*, 73 (Homily 9).

[16] C. A. Briggs and E. G. Briggs, *A Critical and Exegetical Commentary on the Book of Psalms* (ICC; Edinburgh: T. & T. Clark, 1987), 1:5.

[17] Gerald T. Sheppard (*The Future of the Bible: Beyond Liberalism and Literalism* [Toronto: United Church Publishing House, 1990], 67–68) thinks Ps. 2:12d was influenced by the similar line in Ps. 34:8 (9); for an argument concerning the addition of Ps. 2:12d to line Ps. 2 with Ps. 1, see Creach, *Yahweh as Refuge*, 74–75.

[18] Miller, "The Beginning of the Psalter," 88–89.

[19] Mays, *Psalms*, 49.

[20] See the argument of Richard D. Nelson ("Josiah in the Book of Joshua," *JBL* 100/4 [1981]: 531–40) that Joshua is described in such a way that his character anticipates Josiah, the ideal king who reformed Judah's worship according to the torah document found in the temple.

[21] On the role of untitled psalms in the Psalter see Wilson, "The Function of 'Untitled' Psalms."

[22] Pss. 10, 12, and 33 do not have titles. These works, however, seem intended to be read in each case with the psalm that precedes it. They fall under the Davidic identity because of that literary relationship. On this literary technique in the Qumran psalms scrolls see Wilson, *Editing*, 93-138.

[23] Mays, *The Lord Reigns*, 123.

[24] Ibid., 124.

[25] McCann, *A Theological Introduction to the Psalms*, 89.

[26] Mays, *The Lord Reigns*, 124.

[27] See the insightful comments by McCann, "The Shape of Book I of the Psalter and the Shape of Human Happiness."

[28] For a radically different interpretation of the psalm and its setting see Gerstenberger, *Psalms: Part I*, 174–77.

[29] See Kraus, *Psalms 1–59*, 423–24.

[30] G. Braulik, *Psalm 40 und der Gottesknecht* (Würzburg: Echter Verlag, 1975), 197–201.

[31] McCann, "The Book of Psalms," 844.

[32] This is true even though Book II does not begin with psalms attributed to David. Note also that Book II is part of a traditionally recognized editorial unit known as the Elohistic Psalter. It has long been recognized that Psalms 42–83 (Book II plus the collection of Asaph psalms at the beginning of Book III [Pss. 73–83]) contain the label ʾĕlōhîm ("God") for God more than four times as often as the personal name Yahweh ("LORD"). Moreover, Psalm 14 occurs with slight changes again as Psalm 53, and three of the lines of Psalm 14 that contain Yahweh, when reproduced in Psalm 53, have *elohim* instead. These data suggest to many scholars that Psalms 42–83 were once a separate collection and that the editors manipulated the appellations for God to create this unity. The theory is not without its flaws, not the least of which is an explanation of why an editor would have this editorial interest. Nevertheless, assuming that the theory is correct, there is much to suggest that when the Elohistic Psalter was incorporated into the present Psalter it was altered to create the current "book" structure we now know. It is important that the name Yahweh appears in higher frequency in the last three psalms in Book II (five times in Ps. 69; two times in Ps. 70; four times in Ps. 71; God appears ten times, three times, and ten times respectively). See the discussion in Peter C. Craigie, *Psalms 1–50* (WBC 19; Waco, Tex.: Word Books, 1983), 29–30.

[33] For this general point and many of the specific data that follows I am indebted to McCann, "Books I-III and the Editorial Purpose of the Psalter," in *The Shape and Shaping of the Psalter*, 93–107.

[34] Walter Brueggemann, "Bounded by Obedience and Praise: The Psalms as Canon," *JSOT* 50 (1991): 86.

[35] See for example the six columns represented in *The Hexaplar Psalter* (London: Samuel Bagster and Sons, 1843).

[36] For additional parallels see McCann, "Books I-III and the Editorial Purpose of the Psalter," 96.

[37] These psalms are also linked by common terms in their titles; they are identified with Heman (Ps. 88) and Ethan (Ps. 89), both Ezrahites, known otherwise in 1 Kings 4:31 and

1 Chron. 15:19. The significance of these figures in the titles of Pss. 88 and 89 is unclear, however.

Chapter 5: The Suffering Servants as the Lord's Anointed

[1] The enduring hope in and for the king has been downplayed in some recent study so as to give the impression that human rule has been completely rejected; as this chapter and chapter 6 will argue, the idea that monarchy has been abandoned altogether is untenable. The main proponent of the anti-monarchical view is Wilson, *Editing*; more recently Martin Leuenberger has argued that Books I-III of the Psalter are distinctly "messianic" while Books IV-V are "theocratic" in their emphasis on the kingdom of God; see *Konzeption des Königtums Gottes im Psalter: Untersuchungen zu Komposition und Redaktion der theokratischen Bücher IV-V im Psalter* (Theologischer Verlag Zürich 83; Zürich: Theologischer Verlag, 2004).

[2] Wilson, *Editing*, 214–15.

[3] Wilson implies that this is the case; see *Editing*, 227–28.

[4] Gerald T. Sheppard, "Theology and the Book of Psalms," *Int* 46/2 (1992): 150.

[5] Creach, *Yahweh as Refuge*, 94.

[6] See the similar statement in Ps. 144:3-4; 146:3-4.

[7] Bernard Gosse, "Le livre d'Isaïe et le Psautier. De 'mon elu' en Ps. 89,4, a 'mes serviteurs' et 'mes elus' en Isa 65,9," *ZAW* 115 (2003): 380.

[8] Just as Psalm 90 draws from the well-known intercession of Moses in Exodus 32, the last verse of Psalm 92 likewise alludes to Deuteronomy 32; Ps. 92:15 (16):
Showing that the Lord is upright ($y\bar{a}šar$);
He is my rock, and there is no unrighteousness ($'\bar{a}wel$) in him.
Deut 32:4:
The Rock, his work is perfect,
and all his ways are just.
A faithful God, there is no unrighteousness ($'\bar{a}wel$) (in him),
Just and upright ($y\bar{a}šar$) is he.
See Erich Zenger, "The God of Israel's Reign over the World (Psalms 90–106)," in *The Gott of Israel and the Nations: Studies in Isaiah and the Psalms* (ed. Norbert Lohfink and Erich Zenger; trans. Everett R. Kalin; Collegeville, Minn.: The Liturgical Press, 2000), 168.

[9] David M. Howard Jr. *The Structure of Psalms 93–100* (Biblical and Judaic Studies from the University of California, San Diego 5; Winona Lake, Ind.: Eisenbrauns, 1997), 168.

[10] For a detailed treatment of the unifying features of Psalms 93–100 see Howard, *The Structure of Psalms 93–100*, 166–83; and "Psalm 94 among the Kingship-of-Yhwh Psalms" *CBQ* 61/4 (1999): 667–85.

[11] Zenger, "The God of Israel's Reign," 170.

[12] Wilson, *Editing*, 215.

[13] Christoph Levin, "Der Büchereinteilung des Psalters," *VT* 54 (2004): 88–89.

[14] On the importance of Abraham in Book IV and in exilic and post-exilic literature see Creach, "The Shape of Book Four of the Psalter and the Shape of Second Isaiah," *JSOT* 80 (1998): 63–76.

[15] See the argument by Bernhard Gosse, "Le quatrieme livre du Psautier, Psaumes 90–106, comme reponse a l'echec de la royaute davidique," *Biblische Zeitschrift* 46/2 (2002): 246–52.

[16] Erich Zenger, "The Composition and Theology of the Fifth Book of Psalms, Psalms 107–45," *JSOT* 80 (1998), 88.

[17] McCann, "Psalms," 1121.

[18] Ibid., 1121–22.

Chapter 6: David: Defender of the Righteous

[1] Walter Brueggemann (*Theology of the Old Testament: Testimony, Dispute, Advocacy* [Minneapolis: Fortress Press, 1997], 567–704) speaks of Israel's "embodied testimony;" the discussion that follows is similar to his treatment of this subject; see also Samuel Terrien's important work *The Elusive Presence: The Heart of Biblical Theology* (New York: Harper and Row, 1978).

[2] Hermann Gunkel, "Königspsalmen," *Preussische Jahrbücher* 158 (1914): 42. Of course, Gunkel was not the first to identify this category of psalms. W. M. L. de Wette (*Commentar*

über Psalmen [Heidelberg: J. C. B. Mohr, 1811] was the first to use the designation; he spoke of royal psalms as works that had an historical king as its subject; his identification of Pss. 2, 45, 72, and 110 as royal challenged the predominate view that these works were eschatological poems about a future ruler.

[3]See the discussion in Sigmund Mowinckel, *The Psalms in Israel's Worship* (Basil and Blackwell, 1962), 1:12–13 and 46–50.

[4]For the full discussion, see Gunkel, *Introduction*, 99–120, esp. 102–3.

[5]J.J.M. Roberts, "The Religio-political Setting of Psalm 47," in *The Bible and the Ancient Near East* (Winona Lake, Ind.: Eisenbrauns, 2002), 271–72.

[6]Mowinckel, *Psalms in Israel's Worship*, 1:102–3.

[7]See the brief description of the occasion in Babylon and its contents in Jacob Klein, "AKITU," *ABD* 1:138–40.

[8]Scholars now recognize that the composition and use of the royal psalms are probably not as simple as Mowinckel thought. The royal psalms of Israel's neighbors consistently name the king in whose life the poem is set. This is not the case in the Psalter's royal psalms. One could attempt to explain this phenomenon by arguing that the royal psalms leave out the regal name for the psalms to be reused by other monarchs. The evidence from the comparative material, however, argues against the idea that the anonymity in these works is for the purpose of reuse. In a thorough investigation of this issue, Scott R. A. Starbuck shows that royal psalms in the ancient Near East were published, preserved, and "canonized" in association with particular kings to promote or memorialize the individual monarch. In other words, the very nature of the royal psalm works against the theory that they were reused. It seems more likely that the royal psalms, in present form, are not the exact liturgies of historical kings, as Mowinckel thought. They are later reflections on the institution of monarchy. Or, if they are the actual liturgies from the monarchical period, they were edited for a later purpose. That makes sense in light of the fact that the Psalter was shaped largely during and after the exile, when the monarchy ceased to exist in Judah. See the discussion in Scott R. A. Starbuck, *Court Oracles in the Psalms: The So-Called Royal Psalms in their Ancient Near Eastern Context* (SBLDS 172; Atlanta: Society of Biblical Literature, 1999), 27–39.

[9]Most notably Norman K. Gottwald, "The Participation of Free Agrarians in the Introduction of Monarchy to Ancient Israel: An Application of H. A. Landsberger's Framework for the Analysis of Peasant Movements," *Semeia* 37 (1986): 77–106; and supported tacitly in Brueggemann, *Theology*, 601.

[10]William P. Brown ("A Royal Performance: Critical Notes on Psalm 110:3aγb," *JBL* 117/1 [1998]: 93–96) makes a convincing argument that Ps. 110 also presents the king as God's son who, at his coronation goes forth from Zion to exercise divinely-granted authority.

[11]Mays, *The Lord Reigns*, 15.

[12]The term *yiśaq* is used here as in Prov. 31:25, which says of the capable wife that "she laughs at the time to come." The word has the sense of being undaunted and unconcerned.

[13]Richard J. Clifford, "Psalm 89: A Lament over the Davidic Ruler's Continued Failure," *HTR* 73 (1980): 40–41.

[14]A.S. Kapelrud, "Ugarit," *IDB* 4:724–32.

[15]So Walter Dietrich, "Gott als König: Zur Frage nach der theologischen und politischen Legitimät religiöser Begriffsbildung," *ZThK* 77/3 (1985): 255–59.

[16]James A. Sanders, *The Dead Sea Psalms Scroll* (Ithaca, N.Y.: Cornell University Press), 88 (column 28, lines 3–4).

[17]Ibid. See column 28, lines 10–11.

[18]See the discussion of 1 Sam. 16:14–22 and 2 Sam. 5 in P. Kyle McCarter Jr., *I Samuel: A New Translation with Introduction and Commentary* (AB 8; New York: Doubleday, 1980), 27–30.

[19]Mays, *Psalms*, 237.

[20]James L. Mays, *Amos: A Commentary* (Philadelphia: The Westminster Press, 1969), 108.

[21]Reading the preposition *bĕ* as part of the text instead of treating it as a scribal error as NRSV; see Hossfeld and Zenger, *Psalms 2*, 203.

[22]The translation typically given, and assumed here ("may he live"), is a correction based on the Greek version; Hebrew has "may they fear you," which is quite difficult in the context, though possible; the Hebrew could refer to the nations who fear the king, or to God, who is to be feared by the people; see Hossfeld and Zenger, *Psalms 2*, 203; Tate, *Psalms 51–100*, 220; and Mitchell Dahood (*Psalms 51–100*, 155), who propose a singular referring to the king's fear of God; the last opinion requires no greater difference in the consonants of the verb, and it certainly makes sense in context, but there is no textual support for it.

[23]This reading is supported by some modern commentators (Hossfeld and Zenger, *Psalms 2*, 203), but perhaps no one expressed the logic better than Calvin: "David, therefore, prayed that the king might be adorned with righteousness and judgment, that the just might flourish and the people prosper" (*Commentary on the Book of Psalms*, 3:108).

[24]Hossfeld and Zenger, *Psalms 2*, 216.

[25]John Calvin, *Commentary on the Book of Psalms,* 4:87.

[26]See the discussion of Mays, *Psalms*, 433.

[27]Ibid., 321.

Chapter 7: David: The Enduring Hope

[1]Expressed most fully in Wilson, *Editing*.

[2]See Wilson, *Editing*, 207–8 where he entertains this notion; but see Wilson's more extensive discussion of the issue in "The Use of Royal Psalms at the 'Seams' of the Hebrew Psalter," 85–94.

[3]Wilson, *Editing,* 227–28.

[4]Mays, *Psalms*, 101.

[5]Kraus, *Psalms 1–59*, 277–82.

[6]Mays, *Psalms*, 102; see Isa. 55:3 and Jer. 33:19–22, in which the covenant with David is reinterpreted as a covenant with the people or as a covenant that is conflated with the Abrahamic covenant.

[7]McCann, "Psalms," *NIB* 4:1037.

[8]Gosse, "Le quatrieme livre du Psautier, Psaumes 90–106," 244–45.

[9]See the argument of David Howard, along with his summary of similar opinions in "The Psalms and Current Study," 26–27.

[10]MT, however, has a plural form here, which may reflect the community orientation of the revelation and claims of the Davidic covenant at the time of the psalm's completion. Note also the plural form in v. 50 (Hebrew v. 51).

[11]Although Ps. 132:12 ("If your sons keep my covenant...their sons also, forevermore, shall sit on your throne") seems more conditional, the psalm ends with assurance that a "horn" will "sprout up for David" (v. 17).

[12]On the question in Ps. 89, see Walter Brueggemann, *David's Truth in Israel's Imagination and Memory* (2d ed.; Minneapolis: Fortress Press, 2002), 94.

[13]See the classic treatment of Mowinckel, *Psalms in Israel's Worship*, 1:65–68.

[14]Some argue that the text contains a scribal error and should be emended; they take the first word (*mātay*) as a mistaken form that should be identical to the term for "integrity" (*tāmim*) that precedes it; thus, they propose the reading, "Truth shall come to me;" see the explanation of this reading by Herman Gunkel, *Die Psalmen* (Göttingen: Vandenhoeck & Ruprecht, 1926), 434; but the emendation on which this reading rests is unnecessary since the words are logical as they appear in MT.

[15]McCann, "Psalms," 1081.

[16]Ibid.

[17]Joseph Blenkinsopp, *Ezekiel* (Interpretation: A Bible Commentary for Teaching and Preaching; Louisville: John Knox Press, 1990), 176–77.

[18]J.J.M. Roberts, "In Defense of Monarchy: The Contribution of Israelite Kingship to Biblical Theology," in *The Bible and the Ancient Near East*, 358.

[19]Ibid., 360.

Chapter 8: Mount Zion

[1]McCann, "The Book of Psalms," 969.

[2]F. Stolz, *Psalmen im nachkultischen Raum* (Theologische Studien 129; Zurich: Theologischer Verlag, 1983), 7.

[3]The term "enthroned" translates a Hebrew word that may also mean sit or dwell (root *ysb*); cherubim refer to the mythical creatures ancient Near Eastern people imagined guarded the thrones of kings or the entrances to temples. The notion that Yahweh is enthroned on the cherubim draws from a rich pool of language and imagery known widely in the ancient world; the expression is particularly close to the description of Baal as one who "rides on the clouds" (*rkb ʿrpt*), which appears in parallel to the naming of him as prince (*CTA* 2.4.8); also in Canaanite iconography El is portrayed sitting on a throne and flanked by cherubim; Psalm 18:10 (= 2 Sam. 22:11) combines this language and imagery by saying that Yahweh

"rode on a cherub"; the point is that Israel spoke of Yahweh "enthroned" and in association with the cherubim because these were common ways to talk about a deity as monarch; see Ben C. Ollenburger, *Zion, the City of the Great King* (JSOTSup; Sheffield: Sheffield Academic Press, 1987), 42.

⁴Gerstenberger, *Psalms, Part I*, 117-19.

⁵Frank Moore Cross, *Canaanite Myth and Hebrew Epic* (Cambridge: Harvard University Press, 1973), 97-98; J.J.M. Roberts, "The King of Glory," *The Bible and the Ancient Near East*, 104-9.

⁶Mays, *Psalms*, 24.

⁷As Mitchell Dahood points out, the combination of the verb "fear" and the preposition *bĕ* appears only in Jer. 51:46. There the preposition clearly introduces the object of fear. Since the preposition in Ps. 46:2 is attached to an infinitive, it should be taken similarly (see Dahood, *Psalms I:1-50*, 278; Dahood's suggestion that the phrase rendered "the earth changing" should be understood as "the jaws of the netherworld," however, is too hypothetical, based on very loose associations with Ugaritic texts). Even considering the range of uses of the preposition itself, irrespective of the associated verb, *be* would be best understood here as having an adversative sense ("in spite of"), resulting in the same translation offered above. See Ronald J. Williams, *Hebrew Syntax: An Outline* (2d ed.; Toronto: University of Toronto Press, 1976), par. 242.

⁸C.A. and E.G. Briggs, *A Critical and Exegetical Commentary on the Book of Psalms* (2 vols.; Edinburgh: T. & T. Clark, 1987 (first impression 1901), 1:394-95; Peter C. Craigie, *Psalms 1-50* (WBC 19; Waco, Tex.: Word Books, 1983), 344.

⁹See the seminal treatment of Jon D. Levenson, *Creation and the Persistence of Evil: The Jewish Drama of Divine Omnipotence* (San Francisco: Harper and Row, 1988).

¹⁰Note the description of the flood in Gen 7:11: ". . .on that day the fountains of the great deep burst forth, and the windows of the heavens were opened."

¹¹See the study of Richard J. Clifford, *The Cosmic Mountain in Canaan and the Old Testament* (Cambridge, Mass.; Harvard University Press, 1972); the discussion here is largely dependent on his work; for an example of the anthropological perspective, see. G. van der Leeuw, *Religion in Essence and Manifestation* (trans. J. E. Turner; London: Allen & Unwin, 1938), 55; he understands the cosmic mountain as a "primal and permanent element of the world: out of the waters of chaos arose the primeval hill from which rose all life."

¹²Mircea Eliade, *Images and Symbols* (trans. Philip Mairet; New York: Sheed & Ward, 1961), 27-56; *Cosmos and History: The Myth of the Eternal Return* (trans. W. R. Trask; New York: Pantheon, 1959), 1-48; *Patterns in Comparative Religion* (trans. Rosemary Sheed; New York: World, 1963), 367-87.

¹³Levenson, *Sinai and Zion: An Entry into the Jewish Bible* (Minneapolis: Winston Press, 1985),

¹⁴Gen. 15:18; Deut. 11:24; Josh. 1:4; note that in Josh. 15:1-12 the lines of Judah's territory are carefully drawn so as to exclude Jerusalem, probably in anticipation of David's capture of the city.

¹⁵Mays, *Psalms*, 189.

¹⁶The translation here is based on a Qumran manuscript (4QDeutʲ) and is supported by the Greek and Aramaic versions. MT actually reads, "according to the number of the Israelites." The Hebrew wording seems to reflect a later attempt to demythologize the passage.

¹⁷See John H. Hayes, "The Tradition of Zion's Inviolability," *JBL* 82 (1963): 419-26.

¹⁸J.J.M. Roberts, "The Davidic Origin of the Zion Tradition," in *The Bible and the Ancient Near East*, 313-30; the Jebusite origins of elements of the Zion tradition remain hypothetical; one possible example is 2 Sam. 5:6's statement of the Jebusites' confidence that the blind and lame could turn David back from his attack; this could well represent a tradition of Zion's inviolability.

¹⁹Levenson, *Sinai and Zion*, 106.

²⁰Roberts, "The Davidic Origin of the Zion Tradition," 329.

Chapter 9: Zion and the Longing of the Righteous

¹On the antithetical poles of temple and Sheol see the insightful work by Martin Ravndal Hauge, *Between Sheol and Temple: Motif Structure and Function in the I-Psalms* (JSOTSup 178; Sheffield: Sheffield Academic Press, 1995).

²See the treatment of Louis Alonso Schokel, "The Poetic Structure of Psalm 42–43," *JSOT* 1 (1976): 6–7.

³Robert Davidson, *The Vitality of Worship: A Commentary on the Book of Psalms* (Grand Rapids, Mich.: William B. Eerdmans, 1998), 143.

⁴To be sure, the term for "seek" (the Lord) is *šāmā'* and not the common cultic term *bāqaš*, which would indicate inquiring of the Lord through a prophet; nevertheless, the language that follows is distinctly cultic and evokes images of a temple ceremony.

⁵See the discussion of Tate, *Psalms 51–100*, 125–26; Tate's conclusion is similar to mine.

⁶Calvin, *Commentary on the Book of Psalms*, 5:244.

⁷Heinrich Schmidt, *Das Gebet der Angeklagten im Alten Testament* (BZAW 49; 1928), 9–10.

⁸Cited in "The Planting of Man: A Study in Biblical Imagery," in *Love and Death in the Ancient Near East: Essays in Honor of Marvin H. Pope* (ed. John H. Marks and Robert M. Good; Guilford, Conn.: Four Quarters Publishing Company, 1987), 130; for a discussion of the tradition see Thorkild Jacobsen, "Sumerian Mythology: a Review Article," *JNES* 5:135 and n. 4.

⁹This is the translation of J.A. Wilson in *ANET*, 422 (of section 4.6.1–12 of Amen-em-Opet).

¹⁰Lawrence Stager, "Jerusalem as Eden," *BAR* 26/3 (2000): 45; *ANEP*, 155; Brown, *Seeing the Psalms*, 67.

¹¹See the full discussion in Tate, *Psalms 51–100*, 353–54.

¹²P. Kyle McCarter, *II Samuel* (AB 9; Garden City, N.Y.: Doubleday, 1984), 155–56; he questions the identity of the place with balsam trees and points to a possible Arabic parallel that refers to dryness as the likely explanation for the term.

¹³Zenger, "Psalms 107–45," 100–101.

¹⁴See the argument of Matthias Millard, *Die Komposition des Psalters: Ein formgeschichtlicher Ansatz* (Tübingen: J.C.B. Mohr, 1994), 228–29.

¹⁵Though the specific practices being questioned are clear in the context; for possible alternatives see Raymond E. Brown, *The Gospel According to John* (AB 29; Garden City, N.Y.: Doubleday & Company, 1966), 121–22.

¹⁶The claim may have been an embarrassment to the early church since the temple was obviously not rebuilt; this may be the reason Luke does not include the accusations against Jesus; see Brown, *John*, 122; see Tg. Zech 6:12–13.

¹⁷The misunderstanding scene is a typical vehicle for communicating Jesus' true meaning in John; see R. Alan Culpepper, *Anatomy of the Fourth Gospel: A Study in Literary Design* (Philadelphia: Fortress Press, 1983).

¹⁸Brown, *John*, 124–25.

¹⁹Note also that certain Qumran texts speak of the faithful community as the holy place; see DVD, V, 28; 4QpPs 37:2, 16; 1 QS 8:5, 10; 1 QH 7:18.

²⁰See the discussion of John Calvin, *Institutes of the Christian Religion* (Library of Christian Classics 20; ed. John T. McNeill; trans. Ford Lewis Battles; Philadelphia: The Westminster Press, 1960), 2.14.4.

²¹G. R. Beasley-Murray, *The Book of Revelation* (NCBC; Grand Rapids, Mich.: Eerdmans, 1974), 326–27.

Chapter 10: Torah

¹See the full discussion in G. Liedke and C. Petersen, "*tôrâ* instruction," *TLOT* 3:1415–22.

²Note, however, that Ezekiel also gives torah. Ezekiel 40–48, set after the destruction of Jerusalem in 597 B.C.E., records a vision of a temple in Jerusalem, with exact measurements of the parameter and thickness of its walls, beginning with the outermost wall and working inward to the most holy chamber at the center. When the description of the temple is complete, a heavenly guide orders Ezekiel to write down these instructions (43:11) that he had earlier declared audibly (40:4). The written document is then referred to as "the law of the temple" (43:12), a scroll to be read among and observed by the exiled people of Judah. On the role of this written text among the exiled people see Steven S. Tuell, "Ezekiel 40–42 as Verbal Icon," *CBQ* 58/4 (1997): 649–64. It is certainly possible that Deut 34:10 ("Never since has there arisen a prophet in Israel like Moses, whom the Lord knew face to face") is meant to establish Moses' authority over Ezekiel. Whether this is the case or not, it is

striking that only these two figures have written torah associated with them and that the Deuteronomist felt the need to argue for Moses' supremacy over other prophets.

[3] The Hebrew term here (*seper*) refers more accurately to a scroll. Books, bound volumes with individual pages, were not common until after the Common Era.

[4] For the implications of these references, see S. Dean McBride Jr., "Polity of the Covenant People," *Interpretation* 41 (1987): 229–44.

[5] For the rabbis, here and everywhere the term appears in the Old Testament, torah can only be the Pentateuch, the books of Moses. See Jon D. Levenson, "The Sources of Torah: Psalm 119 and the Modes of Revelation in Second Temple Judaism," in *Ancient Israelite Religion: Essays in Honor of Frank Moore Cross, Jr.* (ed. Patrick D. Miller Jr., Paul D. Hanson, and S. Dean McBride Jr.; Philadelphia: Fortress Press, 1987), 559.

[6] Although there is no single canonical arrangement that has the Psalms first in the Writings, Luke 24:44 seems to suggest this view. The Erfurt Codices provide manuscript evidence for this place of the Psalms in the canon.

[7] Levenson, "Sources of Torah," 563.

[8] Alphonse Deissler, *Psalm 119 (118) und seine Theologie* (Münchener Theologische Studien 1/11; Munich: Karl Zink, 1955), 270–77.

[9] Levenson, "Sources of Torah," 565.

[10] Ibid., 570.

[11] See Childs, *Introduction to the Old Testament as Scripture*, 513.

[12] James L. Mays, "The Place of the Torah Psalms in the Psalter," *JBL* 106/1 (1987): 3–12; repr. in *The Lord Reigns*, 128–35.

[13] Mays, "The Place of the Torah Psalms," 8.

[14] See the discussion of Richard D. Nelson, "Josiah in the Book of Joshua," *JBL* 100/4 (1981): 531–40; and for the structure of the history around the theme of torah obedience see Rudolf Smend, "Das Gesetz und die Völker: Ein Beitrag zur deuteronomistischen Redactionsgeschichte," in *Problem biblischer Theologie* (ed. Hans Walter Wolff; Munich: Chr. Kaiser Verlag, 1971), 494–509.

[15] On the use of psalm pairs to create a larger theological point, see Walter Zimmerli, "Zwillingspsalmen," in *Studien zur altestamentlichen Theologie und Prophetie* (Theologische Bücherei, Altes Testament 51; Munich: Chr. Kaiser Verlag, 1974), 261–71; and see again Mays, "The Place of the Torah Psalms," 10.

[16] Mays, "The Place of the Torah Psalms," 11.

[17] But see the treatment of Deissler, *Psalm 119*.

[18] See the discussion in Levenson, "Sources of Torah," 561–62.

[19] Deissler, *Psalm 119*, 68–70.

[20] Levenson, "Sources of Torah," 566.

[21] Brown (*Seeing the Psalms*, 91) points out that Egyptian artwork during the fourteenth century B.C.E. (Amenhotep IV, ca. 1353–1336) depicts the rays of the sun each ending in a hand that drops ankh signs (symbols of life) onto the royal family.

[22] For example, Kraus (*Psalms 1–59*, 269) thinks these two sections originally had nothing to do with each other.

[23] See Smith, "Seeing God in the Psalms."

[24] Jamie A. Grant, *The King as Exemplar: The Function of Deuteronomy's Kingship Law in the Shaping of the Book of Psalms* (Academia Biblica 17; Atlanta and Leiden: SBL and Brill, 2004); this publication was not available to me at the time of writing; I relied on Grant's shorter treatment of the issue in "The Psalms and the King," in *Interpreting the Psalms: Issues and Approaches* (ed. Philip S. Johnston and David G. Firth; Leicester, England: Apollos, 2005), 101–18.

[25] The following argument follows my previous treatment of the issue in "Like a Tree Planted by the Temple Stream: The Portrait of the Righteous in Psalm 1:4," *CBQ* 61/1 (1999): 34–46.

[26] Michael Fishbane, *Biblical Interpretation in Ancient Israel* (Oxford: Clarendon Press, 985). He notes for example that the author of Job 7:17–18 uses Ps. 8:5–7, and the author Gen. 9:1–7 uses Gen. 1:26–29, in both cases altering the meaning of the earlier text by cing it in a new context. See 285–87 and 318–19.

[27] On the use of this terminology in Matthew see Dale C. Allison Jr., *The New Moses: A thean Typology* (Minneapolis: Fortress Press, 1993), 213–17.

[28] Both Ps. 1:3 and Jer. 17:8 are, in turn, similar to a passage from an Egyptian text n as the Instruction of Amen-em-Opet which probably predates them:

> As for the heated man of the temple,
> He is like a tree growing in the open.
> In the completion of a moment (comes) its loss of foliage,
> And its end is reached in the shipyards;
> (Or) it is floated far from its place,
> And the flame is its burial shroud.
> (But) the truly silent man holds himself apart.
> He is like a tree growing in a garden.
> It flourishes and doubles its yield;
> It (stands) before its lord.
> Its fruit is sweet; its shade is pleasant;
> And its end is reached in the garden.

From Amen-em-Opet 4.6.1–12. The translation is that of J. A. Wilson in *ANET*, 422.

[29] The comparison just offered would seem to argue against the possibility that Jer. 17:8 is borrowed from Ps. 1:3a as William L. Holladay has argued in *Jeremiah 1: A Commentary on the Book of the Prophet Jeremiah, Chapters 1–25* (Hermeneia; Philadelphia: Fortress Press, 1986), 489–90; see my argument on this point in "Like a Tree Planted by the Temple Stream," 37–39.

[30] Isa. 1:30; 34:4; 64:5; Jer. 8:13.

[31] See the term used in the same way in Gen. 1:11, 12; 2 Kings 19:30; Isa. 37:31; Jer. 12:2; 17:8; Ps. 107:37.

[32] This word connotes a tree's yielding fruit only in Ezek. 34:27 and Lev. 26:4 and 20, texts that speak simply of trees of the field. Zech. 8:12 uses the term in a similar way, but it refers to a vine, not to a tree.

[33] To be sure, the words do not have the same relationships in the two lines. In Ps. 1:3 "its fruit" is the object of the verb while in Ezek. 47:12 it is the subject. Nevertheless, in light of the almost certain reliance on Ezek. 47:12 in the case of Ps. 1:3's statement about the tree's leaves not withering, it seems more than accidental that this line about the tree's fruit is so close in appearance to another part of the Ezekiel text.

[34] In five other places a form of the same root describes the flowing of some substance, tears (Ps. 119:136; Lam. 3:48), oil (Job 29:6), or water (Prov. 5:16; 21:1).

[35] As Mitchell Dahood recognized long ago, the Hebrew word *peleg* is the word of choice, it seems, for texts that describe the holy mountain, its temple, and its source of water with mythic imagery; see *Psalms I* (AB 16; Garden City, N.Y.: Doubleday, 1966), 4

[36] Isa. 30:25 and 32:2, the other two occurrences of the term to denote water channels, also portray water with cosmic significance. See my treatment of these texts in "Like a Tree Planted by Streams of Water," 42–43.

[37] *The Midrash on the Psalms* (trans. W. G. Braude; 2 vols.; Yale Judaica Series 13; New Haven: Yale University Press, 1959): 2.13.

[38] *m. Qid.* 4:14 followed by *b. Qid.* 82b.